HISTORY OF CLARKE COUNTY

BY

JOHN SIMPSON GRAHAM

1923

Press of
BIRMINGHAM PRINTING COMPANY
Birmingham, Ala.

This volume was reproduced from
An 1923 edition located in the
Publisher's Private Library,
Greenville, South Carolina

All rights reserved. No part of this publication may be reproduced,
stored in a retrieval system, transmitted in any form,
posted on to the web in any form or by any means
without the prior written permission of the publisher.

Please direct all correspondence and orders to:

www.southernhistoricalpress.com
or
SOUTHERN HISTORICAL PRESS, Inc.
PO BOX 1267
375 West Broad Street
Greenville, SC   29601
southernhistoricalpress@gmail.com

Originally published: Birmingham, AL, 1923
Reprinted with New Material by:
Southern Historical Press, Inc.
New Material Copyright 1994 by
Southern Historical Press, Inc.
Greenville, SC
ISBN #0-89308-693-2
All rights Reserved.
Printed in the United States of America

CONTENTS

John Simpson Graham	2
Introduction	3
Court House	4
Clarke County, Alabama	5
Oil Well	11
Derrick	12
Salt Lands of Clarke	13
Ochre Mining	13
Views	16
White Sulphur Well	17
Choctaws in Clarke	18
Battle of Maubila	19
White Settlers in Clarke	25
Battle of Burnt Corn	27
Terrible Massacre at Fort Mims	34
In the War of 1812	52
Daring of Heaton	55
Isham Kimbell	58
The Griffins	60
Bashi Skirmish	61
Heroes of the Canoe Fight	69
Migration to Clarke	84
Indian Ball Game	86
Jackson in 1816	88
Home of Dr. David Taylor	91
Jackson Ferry	109
General Peace	110
Alabama Territory	111
Coffeeville	116
Suggsville	116
Alabama a State	118
Population of Clarke	119

Clarke County 1850-1860	144
Mule Traffic in Clarke	145
Tallahatta Springs	146
Civil War	149
War Records of Clarke County Veterans	150
Reconstruction	164
Americanism Triumphant	168
Oven Bluff	173
Jackson 1875	174
Lumber Mill	175
Lock No. 1 Scenes	177
Red Cross	179
World War Soldiers	180
Thomasville	187
Choctaw Enterprise	193
Jackson Spring	193
Historic Facts Concerning Jackson Spring and Old Line Road	194
Grove Hill	195
Court House	196
County High School	199
Rockville	200
Choctaw Bluff	201
Choctaw Corner	201
Allen	201
Gainestown	201
Whatley	202
Fulton	202
Dickinson	202
Walker Springs	202
Salitpa	203
Tallahatta Springs	204
Jackson Churches	204

Jackson in 1923	206
C. L. Warner Residence	207
Business Houses	210
Jackson Physicians	211
Drug Store	212
Town Officials	212
Ministers	212
School Buildings	213
Jackson's Schools	213
County Officers	218
History of Public Education in Alabama	221
Schools of Clarke County	239
King Institute	240
Representatives State Legislature	241
Senators	242
Probate Judge Since 1821	243
Doctors	244
Attorneys	245
Banks	246
Old Men of Clarke County	246
Voting Places	248
Criminal Court	248
High Water of 1874	249
Postoffices	250
Thomasville Newspapers	251
Newspapers of Grove Hill	252
The South Alabamian	253
Tolbert Spring	254
Autumn Time	254
A Footprint	255
Prohibition in Clarke	256
Women Vote	257
Watershed in Clarke	257

Protestants	257
Coma Garrett, Jr.	259
C. W. Boyles	259
Austico Busbee Taylor	260
John McDuffie	262
Jack R. Wilson	262
J. C. Stewart	263
Governor Murphy	265
Ben D. Turner	266
Benjamin Shields Barnes	268
In Memory of Dr. B. S. Barnes	269
Home of Dr. Nichols	271
Dr. Cobb Nichols	273
John W. Nichols	273
C. B. Jones	274
J. W. Tucker	275
Harwell G. Davis	276
John Austin Kimbrough, M.D.	278
G. A. Carleton	279
John Crawford Anderson	279
Dr. William McGowan	280
John Marshall Wilson	281
Isaac Grant	282
James Addison Newman	284
William Boroughs Newman	287
John A. Bolen, Sr.	288
David Chapman Matthews	291
Rev. John Stanley Frazier, D.D.	292
Rev. S. A. Adams	293
T. J. Bedsole	295
Isaac Pugh	296
Dr. Sidney S. Pugh	299
Jesse V. Boyles	300

Albert Sidney Johnson	300
David Taylor	301
Taylors of Jackson, Ala.	302
James A. Lankford	304
J. F. Gillis	305
Archibald Lonzo McLeod	305
Dr. Bryan Boroughs	307
A. M. Wing	309
John Simpson Graham	314
John P. Graham	317
Edward C. Graham	317
Rufus L. Graham	318
Dr. Thomas Rivers	322
Capt. Thomas I. Kimball	322
Dr. Gross Scruggs Chapman	323
Miss Alice Carter	326
Rev. T. H. Ball	326
Dr. L. O. Hicks	329
J. A. Savage	329
Deaths in the World War	330
Journey of Life	331
What the Author Stands For	333
Battle of Horseshoe Bend	334

INTRODUCTION

It is the purpose of the author of this book to write a history devoted almost exclusively to Clarke County and its people. No such history has ever been published. "Ball's History of Clarke County and Surroundings" contains much general history, necessitating much reading before reaching the pith of the story. However, there is much in Ball's History relating to early days of Clarke and its citizens. Mr. Ball was a scholar and an able writer. He had resided in the county many years before the Civil War and was familiar with the county and its citizens. We shall quote extensively from his valuable book. As to the conflicts between the whites and the Indians, occurring in Clarke County and along its borders, we shall quote largely from Pickett's History. Pickett is a fluent writer and perhaps accurate in his details.

The author of this book has been a citizen of Clarke County since 1875, and since that time much has transpired in the county under his personal observation. We have watched with pride and satisfaction the progress made in the county for the past forty-eight years.

This book will doubtless be read with much interest by the present generation living in Clarke, as well as by the generations to follow. If it should be preserved and handed down through the coming years, it may, in the far distant future, fall under the eye of some descendent of some Clarke countian and enable him or her to look to back through the avenue of time and get a mental picture of Clarke County in the nineteenth and twentieth centuries.

COURT HOUSE

CLARKE COUNTY, ALABAMA

Clarke County is situated between the Alabama and Tombigbee rivers, extending from the cut-off on the south, north to the north boundary line of the south third of Township 12, a distance of about 65 miles. The county has an area of about 1,200 square miles, or 768,000 square acres, and has a population of between 31,000 and 32,000. The county is not bounded on the east its entire length by the Alabama river, there being a small strip of territory on the west side of the Alabama river belonging to Monroe County. The county varies in width, owing to the meanderings of the two rivers, its greatest width being about 35 miles.

Clarke County was established in December, 1812, by an act of the legislature of the Mississippi territory. However, the county did not embrace as much territory then as it now does. It was carved out of Washington County, taking in all the territory of that county lying east of the Tombigbee river and west of the Choctaw County boundary line, and from the south boundary line of Township 5 to a line running from Choctaw corner to the Tombigbee river. Alabama was made a territory in November, 1817, when some more territory was added to Clarke County. Mississippi was admitted to the Union in the same year (1817). Alabama was admitted into the Union in December, 1819, and later on the boundary lines of Clarke County were established as they now stand.

What was here 1000 or even 500 years ago we are left to draw upon our imagination. We are reasonably sure, however, that there were here the same hills and valleys we now have; the same forests (though more dense than now); the same lakes and flowing streams; the same babbling brooks and bubbling springs; the same kind of wild games. Doubtless there were in large numbers, the bears, the wolf, panther, the wildcat, the catamount, the fox, the raccoon, the opossum, the otter, the mink, the squirrel, the deer, the turkey and other small game, for we now have all these things (in smaller numbers), except the panther and the wolf.

Clarke County is a rich agricultural section. In this county there are large sections of chocolate soil susceptible of the highest state of culture, with a great variety of growth. There are also large tracts of gray soil underlaid with clay subsoil, making it well adapted to almost any variety of farm or fruit growth. The county also contains large tracts of rich alluvial river and creek botton lands especially adapted to corn and forage crops. Thousands of acres of black lime hill lands are found in the county, furnishing soil conditions as well adapted to grape and fruit culture as are the great fruit sections of California.

The county is well adapted to the raising of all kinds of live stock, the climate being so mild that it is not absolutely essential to house at any season of the year. The velvet bean, which agricultural statistics show to be the cheapest and most valuable feed, will grow profusely on all soils with little cultivation and no fertilization. This bean is a southern plant and matures only in the extreme south. There are also a large number of native grasses on which cattle thrive.

Sheep raising could be made profitable in the county, there being several hundred thousand acres of cut-over land which would furnish fine grazing for sheep. However, in order to get the greatest profit out of the business, it would be advisable to have a large flock, large enough to justify the employ of a shepherd to look after them as David looked after his father's sheep in the olden times. Dogs are very destructive to sheep, and they would have to be protected from the ravage-prowling cur. We have no stock law in this county, and if the dogs could be gotten rid of there would be no drawback to sheep raising.

Crops can be grown here abundantly in every season of the year. Spring crops are cotton, corn, sugarcane, Irish potatoes, velvet beans, etc. Summer crops are sweet potatoes, peas, peanuts, Soudan grass, sorghum, etc. Fall crops are clover, hairy vetch alfalfa and all cover crops.

Trucking can be carried on the year round, there never being a time of the year that some of the different crops of this nature cannot be raised for the market. Soil and climate are adapted to any of the truck crops that can be raised in the temperate zone. Our principal truck crops are strawberries, cantelopes, watermelons, Bermuda onions, snap beans, cucumbers, cabbage, collards, sweet potatoes, Irish potatoes, English peas and sweet corn.

Peaches, pears, apples, Satsuma oranges, grapefruit, Japanese persimmons, plums, apricots, pomegranates, etc., are grown extensively and produce enormous crops.

The South is the home of the pecan tree. Paper-shell pecan nuts cannot be grown more successfully anywhere else in the world. These are the highest priced nuts in the world and the richest food value. No other nut touches it either in price or in quality. The demand is increasing every year and prices are advancing. An acre of bearing trees is worth $1,000. In fact, there are many groves that a thousand dollars an acre will not buy. This industry is now entirely at its formative stage and on a sound business basis, and thousands of dollars are being invested in it annually by some of the shrewdest business men and financiers of the country. This immediate section is peculiarly adapted to the growth of the nut.

The county offers many enterprises. Rabbit Creek has several water-power sites which would develop three to four hundred horsepower per site. Bassett Creek has an ideal factory site which would furnish at least four hundred horsepower. Rabbit Creek empties into Bassett Creek and Bassett Creek empties into the Tombigbee River a few miles below Jackson.

The Tombigbee River is one of the largest in the South and is navigable from Mobile to the coal fields of Alabama. The government has spent something like four million dollars on locks and other improvements for this stream, making it today the most important river in the United States, for through its seventeen locks now pass many large steamers and self-propelled barges plying between the coal fields and Mobile, the most logical port on the Gulf of Mexico and the natural gateway to the Panama Canal.

The lands along this stream are as fertile as any in America and produce crops in abundance. Thousands upon thousands of acres of these rich bottom lands yet lie virgin, uncleared and uncultivated, and can be bought for a small sum per acre. Once cleared and put into cultivation, the land becomes very valuable from two prominent and important facts: First, it produces from a half to one bale of cotton and forty to forty-five bushels of corn per acre, and other crops in equally as large proportions, without the use of commercial fertilizer, there never being any need for this costly item which has ruined many farmers. The value of these lands is not realized by their present owners, and today it can be bought for a meagre sum, but once the real worth becomes demonstrated there will be a fabulous price asked. Today is the time for the land seeker to buy.

Along the banks of this river and on lands that can be bought for a low price are some of the finest hardwood timbers that can be found in the whole country and the supply is almost inexhaustible.

The steamboats that ply the Tombigbee are not surpassed by the finest packets on the Mississippi. From a pleasure standpoint, one could want nothing better than a week's trip up the river on one of these palatial boats, viewing the magnificent scenery which is unsurpassed by even the famous Hudson.

The waters of the river are abounding in fish of all varieties, ranging from the shark to the smallest of the finny tribe.

For the sportsman this county is a paradise either for fishing or hunting. All the wild game known to the South abounds, such as bears, deer, turkeys, geese, ducks, quail, doves, squirrels, etc. Besides the river, there are a number of lakes and streams that furnish fishing. In these are found bass, trout, all kind of perch, and the larger fish for market purposes. There are a number of families around in the county who secure their livelihood from this source.

Besides the numerous things mentioned above, there is found in the county inexhaustible quantities of yellow ochre and china clays. A large ochre plant is established two and a half miles north of the depot of Jackson, which will receive particular mention later. There is also a quantity of Fuller's earth found in the county, many other valuable things which will receive attention later on.

The Southern Railroad passes through the county, crossing the Tombigbee River and entering Clarke County quite near the north boundary line of fractural Section 18, Township 6 North, Range 2 East, and running in a northeastward direction along the valley of Bassett Creek and passing out of the county a short distance north of Thomasville. On the completion of this road, the county took on new energy and has progressed rapidly since that time. This road was completed through the county in 1887. Nothing builds up a country like railroads. Having the Alabama River on the east and the Tombigbee on the west and a railroad passing through the county, the shipping facilities are as good as one would wish. There are hundreds of saw mills scattered throughout the county and lumber is being shipped from this county to all parts of the world. We will make particular mention of some of the more important saw mills of the county on other pages of this book.

OIL WELL

The Mutual Oil Company, a corporation, is drilling a well in Section 35, Township 8 North, Range 1 West, a mile and a half west of Salitpa postoffice, with the hope of finding oil. Geologists pronounce this the most flattering undeveloped oil field anywhere east of the Mississippi River. There are two separate and distinct anteclines in the county, one north of Jackson and one south of Jackson. The surface indications are said by geologists to be very flattering indeed. Many oil companies are holding leases on lands in this county. Several thousand acres of land have been leased by various oil companies since 1916. Had it not been for the World War, the field would doubtless have been thoroughly tested before now. The war, high prices of material and the discovery of much oil in Texas, all worked to block work in Clarke County. Geology is not an exact science; geologists can locate fields where oil has been, but they cannot determine its present location. For instance, they discover that in Clarke County, some time in the centuries gone by, there was an upheaval, ripping the county open from Section 21 (where it goes into the Tombigbee River), Township 5 North, Range 2 East, to the same river in Township 8 North, Range 1 West. This upheaval brought to the surface all formations of the earth below for a great depth, and from these formations geologists draw their conclusions.

DERRICK

SALT LANDS OF CLARKE

In March, 1819, the United States granted to the state of Alabama in trust for its people five sections of salt lands, two sections in Township 5 North, Range 2 East, and three sections in Township 7 North, Range 1 East. This county furnished much of the salt used in the South during the Civil War. Salt was made at three points in the county, designated as Lower Saltworks, Central Saltworks and Upper Saltworks. Central Saltworks was located in Section 34, Township 6 North, Range 2 East, the land being owned by a private individual. There were some salt springs on these lands, but these were not the only source from which salt water was obtained. Many overflowing wells were brought in and the supply of water is inexhaustible. These wells are still flowing and in silent tones seem to say: "Men may come and men may go; but we flow on forever."

THE SAMPLE-WILLIAMS CLAY AND COLOR COMPANY

The plant of the Sample-Williams Clay and Color Company is located in the northern end of the town, a distance of two and a half miles from the Southern Railway station, Tombigee river and tidewater. They are miners and shippers of yellow ochre and china clays, also manufacturers of all clay commodities, such as clap turpentine cups, hollow building blocks, brick, drain tile, flower pots, jugs, churns and all other clay novelties.

The ochre plant consists of a machinery building 30x30 feet, two stories high, boiler and engine room, four drying sheds, storeroom and warehouse, with a floor space of 9,645 square feet. The drying sheds contain racks for air-drying the ochre with a shelf space of 35,000 square feet. There is also a cooperage for making the barrels in which the manufactured product is shipped. The plant is equipped with a one hundred horse-power boiler, a fifty horse-power engine, two Worthington pumps, one disintegrator, one No. 22 Bauer Bros. attrition mill, one large fan for air floating, buckets and worm conveyors, necessary belting, and two tram railways and cars.

Underlying more than sixty acres of the company's holdings there is a bed of yellow ochre that ranges in thickness from four and a half to ten feet. The quality is so fine that it is unnecessary to wash it. In quality it is equalled by few American ochres and excelled only by the imported French.

This ochre is shipped to all parts of the United States, and is used extensively by the paint grinders, paper manufacturers, wholesale drug houses, wall-paper manufacturers, linoleum and oilcloth manufacturers.

The clay plant consists of one machinery building 30x60 feet, one engine-room, one single-story building 30x60 feet, equipped with racks and pallet boards for drying; one two-story building 21x100 feet, equipped also with racks and pallets for drying, the second story with lattice floor and potter's wheel for the manufacture of clay novelties; two twenty-two-foot down-draft "Y" tunnel kilns for burning its products; one standard brick shed, equipped with track and automatic lift cars. The machinery consists of one sixty horse-power engine, one Baird flower-pot machine, one pug mill, and one Bensing side-cutting table, with twelve-inch conveyer belt, and one J. C. Steele & Sons No. 4 brick machine, that has a capacity of thirty to fifty thousand brick per day. The machine is also equipped with dies for the manufacture of farm drain tile ranging in size from four inches up, and also the necessary dies for the manufacture of the famous hollow building block, a commodity that is just in its infancy in the South.

The shipping advantages of this factory are unexcelled, although situated some little distance from the river and railway. They have recently constructed a siding that allows them to have cars placed right at the factory doors.

They employ between forty and fifty men and have an expenditure each month of something like two thousand dollars.

The company owns outright ninety-three acres and mineral rights on sixty-four additional acres. The bed of clay underlies practically every acre, and ranges in thickness from twenty to thirty feet, making the supply absolutely inexhaustible.

The plant today is in its infancy, having been in operation for the past twelve months, and has made rapid strides during this time. While a new industry and young, it will be at some near future date one of, if not the largest, industries of the kind in the United States.

1 LAKE   2 CHOCTAW INN   3 SULPHUR WELL.

WHITE SULPHUR WELL

The White Sulphur Well lies just outside the corporate limits of the town, situated on the Southern Railway. This water is known far and wide for its medicinal qualities. There have been numberless cures of stomach and kidney troubles and rheumatism made by this water, many being cases which have baffled medical science. In connection with this well there is also an iron well noted for rebuilding the blood tissues of the body. The owners of these wells have constructed on the grounds a nice pavilion, bathrooms and swimming pool.

The Choctaw Inn, a modern and up-to-date hotel situated on a high hill overlooking the well, is kept open all seasons of the year for the comfort and pleasure of the countless numbers of visitors that come from all sections of the country—some seeking health, some pleasure.

This sulphur well was bored in 1862 in search of salt. The well proper is situated about 200 yards south of the Southern Railroad. It was inconvenient to reach and the surroundings disagreeable, so the owner conceived the idea of piping it up to the railroad. The Choctaw Inn is the old Savage Hotel, remodeled. A Mr. Savage, perhaps of Mobile, built a hotel there just after the Civil War and lived there for many years. The property has changed hands several times since 1875 and is now owned by T. B. Pace. Quite a number of people are entertained at the Choctaw Inn every summer.

It is strange that this neck of territory, lying here between two great rivers, so greatly blessed with natural advantages, so rich in soils, timber and minerals, should escape the eye and attention of man during all the ages since the formation of these hills and valleys, being uninhabited by man until about 400 years ago.

CHOCTAWS IN CLARKE

We have evidences that the Choctaw Indians inhabited this territory at least 400 years ago. According to history, there were several settlements in the county 383 years ago. There was a considerable town, called Maubila, located at either Croctaw Bluff or French's Landing, four miles above Gainstown. This town is said to have had eighty houses with the capacity of a thousand persons each, all facing on a large square of ground, with entrances at front and back by way of large gates. We do not know just how many inhabitants this town had, but it was capable of accommodating 80,000 people.

So far as we have been able to gather from history, the "pale faces" first set foot upon Clarke County soil in October, 1540, 383 years ago at this writing, when DeSoto and his men visited Maubila. According to the University Encyclopedia:

"Fernando DeSoto, Spanish discoverer, born in Jere do los Cavalleros in Estremadura about 1496 of a good but impoverished family, accompanied Pedraias Davilla to Darien in 1519; served on the expedition of Nicaragua in 1527, and afterward assisted Piazarro in the conquest of Peru; returning to Spain with a fortune of a 'hundred and four-score ducats.' Charles now gave him permission to conquer Florida at his own expense and appointed him governor of Cuba, and in 1538 he sailed from San Lucar with a richly equipped company—600 men, 24 ecclesiastics and 20 officers. The fleet anchored in the bay of Espiritu Santo (now Tampa Bay) in May, 1539; the ships were sent back to Cuba and the long search for gold was begun. For three years harassed by hostile Indians, lured onward by reports of wealth that lay beyond, the ever-decreasing company continued their march over a route that cannot now be verly clearly traced."

After DeSoto's visit to and at the battle of Maubila, he left Clarke County, going north, crossing the Tombigbee River perhaps up about Cotton Gin; went west to the Mississippi River, reaching that river in 1541. Worn out by disappointment, he died in 1542 and was given a watery grave in the Mississippi River. DeSoto was hunting for gold. He found no gold but lost his life. About one-half of his men died in the Mississippi Valley and the other half made their way into Mexico.

BATTLE OF MAUBILA

Account of the battle of Maubila is found in Pickett's history and reproduced below. According to Pickett's account, DeSoto arrived at Maubila October 18.

"DeSoto and Tuscaloosa were ushered into the great public square of Maubila with songs, music upon Indian flutes, and the graceful dancing of beautiful brown girls. They alighted from their chargers, and seated themselves under a 'canopy of state.' Remaining here a short time, the Chief requested that he should no longer be held as a hostage, nor required to follow the army any further. The Adelantado hesitated in reply, which brought Tuscaloosa immediately to his feet, who walked off with a lofty and independent bearing, and entered one of the houses. DeSoto had scarcely recovered from his surprise, when Jean Ortiz followed the Chief and announced that breakfast awaited him at the Governor's table. Tuscaloosa refused to return, and added, 'If your Chief knows what is best for him, he will immediately take his troops out of my territory.' In the meantime, Charamilla, one of the spies, informed the Governor that he had discovered over ten thousand men in the houses, the subjects of Tuscaloosa and other neighboring Chiefs; that other houses were filled with bows, arrows, stones and clubs; that the old women and children had been sent out of the town, and the Indians were at that moment debating the most suitable hour to capture the Spaniards. The General received this startling intelligence with the deepest solicitude. He secretly sent word to his men to be ready for an attack. Then, anxious to avert a rupture, by regaining possession of the person of the Chief, he approached him with smiles and kind words, but Tuscaloosa scornfully turned his back upon him, and was soon lost among the host of excited warriors. At that moment a principal Indian rushed out of the same house, and loudly denounced the Spaniards as robbers, thieves and assassins, who should no longer impose on their great Chief by depriving him of a liberty with which he was born, and his fathers before him. His insolence, and the motions which he made to shoot at a squad of Spaniards with a drawn bow, so incensed Baltasar de Gallegos that, with a powerful sweep of his sword, he split down his body and let out his bowels! Like bees in a swarm the savages now poured out upon the Spaniards. DeSoto placed himself at the head of his men, and fought face to face with the enemy, retreating slowly and passing the gate into the plain. His cavalry had rushed to rescue their horses, tied outside the walls, some of which the Indians came upon in time to kill. Still receding to get out of the reach of the enemy, DeSoto at length paused at a considerable distance upon the plain. The Mobilians seized the Indian slaves, packed upon their backs the effects of the expedition, which had now arrived and lay scattered about, drove the poor devils within the walls, knocked off their irons, placed bows in their hands and arrayed them in battle against their former masters. In the first sally, DeSoto had five men killed and many wounded, himself among the latter number. Having captured the baggage, the victors covered the ground in advance of the gate, and rent the air with exulting shouts. At that moment the Governor headed his cavalry, and followed by his footmen, charged them back into the town. The Indians rushed to the portholes and towers and shot upon the invaders clouds of arrows, compelling them again to retire from the walls. A small party of Spaniards were left in a perilous situation. Three cross-bow men, an armed friendly Indian, five of DeSoto's guard, some servants and two priests, not having time to join the others when first attacked in the square, took refuge in the house set apart for their commander. The savages sought an entrance at the door, but the unhappy inmates bravely defended it, killing many of the assailants. Others clambered upon the roof to open the covering, but were as successfully repulsed. Separated from their friends by a thick wall, and in the midst of thousands of enemies panting to lap their blood, their destruction appeared inevitable. During the long struggle for existence, the holy fathers engaged in earnest prayer for their deliverance, while the others fought with a desperation which rose with the occasion.

Seeing the Spaniards again retreat, the Indians rushed through the gates, and dropping down from the walls, engaged fiercely with the soldiers, seizing their sweeping swords and piercing lances! Three long hours were consumed in the terrible conflict first one side giving way and then the other. Occasionally DeSoto was strengthened by small squads of horsemen who arrived, and without orders, charged into the midst of the bloody melee. The Governor was everywhere present in the fight, and his vigorous arm hewed down the lustiest warriors. That sword, which had often been dyed in the blood of Peruvians, was now crimsoned with the gore of a still braver race. The invincible Baltasar de Gallegos, who struck the first blow, followed it up, and was only equaled by the commander in the profuse outpouring of savage blood. Far on the borders of the exciting scene rode his brother, Fray Juan, a Dominican friar, who constantly beckoned him to quit the engagement on foot, and take the horse which he bestrode, in order to fight the better. But Baltasar, gloating on blood, heeded him not; when presently an Indian arrow, which made a slight wound upon the back of the worthy father, caused him to retire to a less dangerous distance. Indeed, during the whole battle the priests kept the plain, watched the awful carnage with intense anxiety, and often fell upon their knees, imploring Almighty God to give victory to the Spaniards.

At length the matchless daring of DeSoto and his troops forced the Indians to take a permanent position within Maubila, closing after them its ponderous gates. The sun began to lower towards the tops of the loftiest trees, when Moscoso and the last of the army arrived. He had strangely loitered by the way, allowing the soldiers to scatter in the woods and hunt at their leisure. His advanced guard heard at a distance the alarm of drums and the clangor of trumpets. With beating hearts they passed back the word along the scattered lines, from one to the other, and soon the hindmost rushed to the support of their exhausted and crimson-stained comrades. Joined by all his force, DeSoto formed the best armed into four divisions of foot. Provided with bucklers for defense, and battle-axes to demolish the walls, they made a simultaneous charge, at the firing of an arquebuse. Upon the first onset, they were assailed with showers of arrows and dreadful missles. Repeated blows against the gates forced them open. The avenues were filled with eager soldiers, rushing into the square. Others, impatient to get in, battered the stucco from the walls and aided each other to climb over the skeleton works. A horrible and unparalleled carnage ensued. The horsemen remained on the outside to overtake those who might attempt to escape. The Indians fought in the streets, in the square, from the tops of the houses and walls. The ground was covered with their dead, but not one of the living entreated for quarters. The Spaniards were protected with bucklers and coats of mail, while the poor Indians were only covered with the thin shield which the Great Spirit gave them at the dawn of their existence. The troops entered the town in time to save the two priests and their companions, who had so long held out against such fearful odds. The battle, which now waxed hotter and more sanguinary than ever, cannot be as graphically described as the heroic deeds on either side so justly deserve. Often the Indians drove the troops out of the town, and as often they returned with increased desperation. Near the wall lay a large pool of delicious water, fed by many springs. It was now discolored with blood. Here soldiers fell down to slake the intense thirst created by heat and wounds, and those who were able rose again, and once more pitched into a combat characterized by the most revolting destruction of human life. For some time the young females had joined in the fight, and they now contended side by side with the foremost warriors, sharing in the indiscriminate slaughter. Heated with excitement, smarting with his wounds, and provoked at the unsubdued fierceness of the natives, DeSoto rushed out alone by the gate, threw himself into the saddle, and charged into the town. Calling, with a loud voice, upon "Our Lady and Santiago," he forced his charger over hundreds of fighting men and women, followed by the brave Nuno Tobar. While opening lanes through the savage ranks and sprinkling his tracks with blood, he rose on one occasion to cast his lance into a gigantic warrior. At that instant a powerful arrow went deep into the bottom of his thigh. Unable to extract it, or to sit in his saddle, he continued to fight to the end of the battle, standing in his stirrups. Everywhere that mighty son of Spain now gorged upon Alabama blood! His fearless bounds filled the boldest soldiers with renewed courage. At length the houses were set on fire, and the wind blew the smoke and flames in all directions, adding horror to the scene. The flames ascended in mighty volumes! The sun went down, hiding himself from the awful sight! Maubila was in ruins, and her inhabitants destroyed!"

After DeSoto and his men left this county we heard no more of the white man in these parts until about 260 years later.

WHITE SETTLERS IN CLARKE

In the year 1800 the white people began to settle in this county, and by 1813 there were quite a number of settlers along the west side of the county. In 1813 the Indians became very troublesome and the whites became alarmed and began the erection of forts at various points in the county. According to Ball's history of Clarke County, they were located as follows:

Fort Madison was situated in the northeast corner of Section 1 in Township 6, Range 3 East, four and a half miles south and about one mile and a half west of the village of Suggsville on the dividing ridge. It covered about one acre of ground. A trench was dug around the outside limits three feet in depth and into this the bodies of pine trees were inserted side by side cut about 15 feet in length. A continuous wall of pines some 12 feet in height therefore surrounded the enclosure. Within were the tents and cabins of the neighboring settlers. Colonel Carson's company occupied Fort Glass.

Fort Singuefield was built in the same manner, but was smaller than Fort Madison. It was located in Section 13, Township 8, Range 3 East.

Fort White was a short distance northeast of Grove Hill.

Carney's Fort was on the Tombigbee at Gullet's Bluff, a few miles below Jackson.

McGrew Fort was nearly north of Old St. Stephens in the corner of Section 1, Township 7, Range 1 West.

Landrum's Fort was on Section 18, Township 8, Range 2 East, now in Good Springs' Beat.

Mott's Fort was in the same neighborhood.

Turner's Fort was near the residence of Abner Turner.

Easley's Fort was on the Tombigbee River in Section 11, Township 11, Range 1 West.

Powell's Fort was near Oven Bluff.

Fort Glass was south of Suggsville.

Lavier's Fort may have been south of Suggsville.

These forts were perhaps built in the year of 1913 in the same year that occurred the battles of Burnt Corn, Fort Mims, Fort Sinquefield, Bashi Skirmish and the Canoe Fight.

The battles of Burnt Corn and Fort Mims did not occur in Clarke County, but they are so closely connected with the county, and Clarke countians being in both of these battles we deem it appropriate to make mention of them.

A full account of all these battles is found in Pickett's

History and reproduced below. All these battles occurred in 1813, July, August, September, October and November, respectively.

BATTLE OF BURNT CORN—ARRIVAL OF GEN. CLAIBORNE'S ARMY

"Peter McQueen, at the head of the Tallase warriors; High-Head Jim, with the Autaugas; and Josiah Francis, with the Alabamas, numbering in all three hundred and fifty, departed for Pensacola with many packhorses. On their way they beat and drove off all the Indians who not take the war talk. The brutal McQueen beat an unoffending white trader within an inch of his life, and carried the wife of Curnells, the government interpreter, a prisoner to Pensacola. The village of Hatchechubba was reduced to ashes.

"The inhabitants of the Tombigby and the Tensaw had constantly petitioned the governor for an army to repel the Creeks, whose attacks they hourly expected. But General Flournoy, who had succeeded Wilkinson in command, refused to send any of the regular or volunteer troops. The British fleet was seen off the coast, from which supplies, arms, ammunition and Indian emissaries were sent to Pensacola and other Spanish ports in Florida. Everything foreboded the extermination of the Americans in Alabama, who were the most isolated and defenceless people imaginable. Determined, however, to protect themselves to the best of their means and abilities, they first sent spies to Pensacola to watch the movements of the Indians there under McQueen, who returned with the report that the British agents were distributing to them ample munitions of war. Colonel James Caller ordered out the militia, some of whom soon rallied to his standard in the character of minute volunteers. He marched across the Tombigby, passed through the town of Jackson, and by the new fort upon the eastern line of Clarke, and from thence to Sisemore's Ferry, upon the Alabama, where, on the western bank, he bivouacked for the night. The object of the expedition was to attack the Indians as they were returning from Pensacola. The next morning Caller began the crossing of the river to the east side, which was effected by swimming the horses by the side of the canoes. It occupied much of the early part of the day. When all were over the march was resumed in a southeastern direction to the cow-pens of David Tait, where a halt was made. Here Caller was reinforced by a company from Tensaw Lake and Little River, under the command of Dixon Bailey, a half-breed Creek, a native of the town of Auttose, who had been educated at Philadelphia under the provisions of the treaty of New York of 1790. Bailey was a man of fine appearance, unimpeachable integrity, and a strong mind. His courage and energy were not surpassed by those of any other man. The whole expedition under Caller now consisted of one hundred and eighty men, in small companies. Two of these were from St. Stephens, one of which was commanded by Captain Bailey Heard, and the other by Captain Benjamin Smoot and Lieutenant Patrick May. A company, from the county of Washington, was commanded by Captain David Cartwright. In passing through Clarke County, Caller had been reinforced by a company under Captain Samuel Dale and Lieutenant Girard W. Creagh. Some men had also joined him, commanded by William McGrew, Robert Caller, and William Bradberry. The troops of the little party were mounted upon good frontier horses, and provided with rifles and shotguns of various sizes and descriptions. Leaving the cow-pens Caller marched until he reached the wolf-trail, where he bivouacked for the last night. The main route to Pensacola was now before them.

"In the morning, the command was reorganized by the election of Zachariah Philips, McFarlin, Wood, and Jourdan, to the rank of major, and William McGrew, lieutenant-colonel. This unusual number of field officers was made to satisfy military aspirations. While on the march, the spy company returned rapidly, about 11 o'clock in the forenoon, and reported that McQueen's party were encamped a few miles in advance, and were engaged in cooking and eating. A consultation of officers terminated in the decision to attack the Indians by surprise. The command was thrown into three divisions — Captain Smoot in front of the right, Captain Bailey in front of the centre, and Captain Dale in front of the left. The Indians occupied a peninsula of low pine barren, formed by the windings of Burnt Corn Creek. Some gently rising heights overlooked this tongue of land, down which Caller charged upon them. Although taken by surprise, the Indians repelled the assault for a few minutes, and then gave way, retreating to the creek. A portion of the Americans bravely pursued them to the water, while others remained behind, engaged in the less laudable enterprise of capturing the Indian pack-horses. Caller acted with bravery, but, unfortunately, ordered a retreat to the high lands, where he intended to take a strong position. Seeing those in advance retreating from the swamp, about one hundred of the command, who had been occupied, as we have stated, in securing Indian effects, now precipitately fled, in great confusion and terror, but, in the midst of their dismay, held on to the plunder, driving the horses before them. Colonel Caller, Captain Bailey, and other officers, endeavored to rally them in vain. The Indians rushed forth from the swamp, with exulting yells, and attacked about eighty Americans, who remained at the foot of the hill. A severe fight ensued, and the whites, now commanded by Captains Dale, Bailey and Smoot, fought with laudable courage, exposed to a galling fire, in open woods, while McQueen and his warriors were protected by thick reeds. The latter, however, discharged their pieces very unskillfully. Captain Dale received a large ball in the breast, which, glancing around a rib, came out at his back. He continued to fight as long as the battle lasted. At length, abandoned by two-thirds of the command, while the enemy had the advantage of position, the Americans resolved to retreat, which they did in great disorder. Many had lost their horses, for they had dismounted when the attack was made, and now ran in all directions to secure them or get up behind others. Many actually ran off on foot. After all these had left the field three young men were found still fighting by themselves on one side of the peninsula, and keeping at bay some savages who were concealed in the cane. They were Lieutenant Patrick May, of North Carolina, now of Greene County, Alabama, a descendant of a brave revolutionary family; a private named Ambrose Miles and Lieutenant Girard W. Creagh, of South Carolina. A warrior presented his tall form. May and the savage discharged their guns at each other. The indian fell dead in the cane; his fire, however, had shattered the lieutenant's piece near the lock. Resolving also to retreat, these intrepid young men made a rush for their horses, when Creagh, brought to the ground by the effects of a wound which he received in the hip, cried out, 'Save me, lieutenant, or I am gone!' May instantly raised him up, bore him off on his back and placed him in the saddle, while Miles held the bridle reins. A rapid retreat saved their lives. Reaching the top of the hill they saw Lieutenant Bradberry, a young lawyer of North Carolina, bleeding with his wounds, and endeavoring to rally some of his men. The Indians, reaching the body of poor Ballad, took off his scalp in full view, which so incensed his friend Glass that he advanced and fired the last gun upon them.

"The retreat was continued all night in the most irregular manner, and the train was lined, from one end to the other, with small squads, and sometimes one man by himself. The wounded traveled slowly, and often stopped to rest. It was afterward ascertained that only two Americans were killed and fifteen wounded. Such was the battle of Burnt Corn, the first that was fought in the long and bloody Creek War. The Indians retraced their steps to Pensacola for more military supplies. Their number of killed is unknown. Caller's command never got together again, but mustered themselves out of service, returning to their homes by various routes, after many amusing adventures. Colonel Caller and Major Wood became lost, and wandered on foot in the forest, causing great uneasiness to their friends. When General Claiborne arrived in the country he wrote to Bailey, Tate and McNac, respectable half-breeds, urging them to hunt for these unfortunate men. They were afterward found, starved almost to death and bereft of their senses. They had been missing fifteen days.*

"General Ferdinand Leigh Claiborne, the brother of the ex-Governor of the Mississippi Territory, was born in Sussex County, Virginia, of a family distinguished in that commonwealth from the time of Charles I. On the 21st November, 1793, in his twentieth year, he was appointed an ensign in Wayne's army on the Northwestern frontier. He was in the great battle in which that able commander soon after defeated the Indians, and for his good conduct, was promoted to a lieutenancy. At the close of the war he was stationed at Richmond and Norfolk, in the recruiting service, and subsequently was ordered to Pittsburg, Forts Washington, Greenville and Detroit, where he remained with the rank of captain and acting adjutant-general until 1805, when he resigned and removed to Natchez. He was soon afterward a member of the Territorial Legislature, and presided over its deliberations. We have already seen how active he was in arresting Aaron Burr, upon the Mississippi river, at the head of infantry and cavalry. On the

---

*Conversations with Dr. Thomas G. Holmes, of Baldwin County, Alabama, the late Colonel Girard W. Creagh, of Clarke, and General Patrick May, of Greene, who were in the Burnt Corn expedition.

8th March, 1813, Colonel Claiborne was appointed brigadier-general of volunteers, and was ordered by General Wilkinson to take command of the post of Baton Rouge. In the latter part of July he was ordered by General Flournoy to march with his whole command to Fort Stonnart, and instructed to direct his principal attention to "the defence of Mobile."

"On the 30th July, General Claiborne reached Mount Vernon, near the Mobile river, with the rear guard of his army, consisting of seven hundred men, whom he had chiefly sustained by supplies raised by mortgages upon his own estate.* The quartermaster at Baton Rouge had only provided him with the small sum of two hundred dollars. He obtained, from the most reliable characters upon the eastern frontier, accurate information in regard to the threatened invasion of the Indians, an account of the unfortunate result of the Burnt Corn expedition, and a written opinion of Judge Toulmin, respecting the critical condition of the country generally. It was found that alarm pervaded the populace. Rumors of the advance of the Indians were rife, and were believed. In Clarke County — in the fork of the rivers — a chain of rude defenses had hastily been constructed by the citizens, and were filled to overflowing with white people and negroes. One of these was at Gullett's Bluff, upon the Tombigby, another at Easley's Station, and the others at the residences of Sinquefield, Glass, White and Lavier. They were all called forts.

---

*Upon the conclusion of the Creek War General Claiborne returned to Soldier's Retreat, his home, near Natchez, shattered in constitution, from the exposure and hardships of the campaigns, and died suddenly at the close of 1815. The vouchers for the liberal expenditures which he made were lost and his property was sold.

Two block-houses were also in a state of completion at St. Stephens.

"The first step taken by Claiborne was the distribution of his troops, so as to afford the greatest protection to the inhabitants. He despatched Colonel Carson, with two hundred men, to the Fork, who arrived at Fort Glass without accident. A fed hundred yards from that rude structure he began the construction of Fort Madison. He sent Captain Scott to St. Stephens with a company, which immediately occupied the old Spanish block-house. He employed Major Hinds, with the mounted dragoons, in scouring the country, while he distributed some of the militia of Washington County for the defence of the stockade. Captain Dent was despatched to Oaktupa, where he assumed the command of a fort with two block-houses within a mile of the Choctaw line."*†

TERRIBLE MASSACRE AT FORT MIMS.

"In the meantime, the wealthy half-bloods about Little river had dropped down the Alabama, in their boats, and had secreted themselves in the swamp about Lake Tensaw. Uniting with the whites, they soon began the construction of a fort around the residence of Samuel Mims, a wealthy Indian countryman, to whom we have often alluded, and

---

*MS. papers of General F. L. Claiborne.
†It will be noted that numbers of Clarke Countians were in this battle, prominent among them being Sam Dale, one of the heroes of the Canoe Fight ,and G. W. Creagh, whose descendants, a few at least, still reside in this county.
The Indians were somewhat successful in this battle, and were thus led to be more aggressive than they had previously been. In the month following they made an attack on Fort Mims. Account of that terrible conflict is given below by Pickett.

who, originally, was one of the pack-horsemen of the Honorable George Galphin.

"Being about to relate a horrible affair, in which people of all ages and both sexes were subjected to savage butchery, a particular description of the place where it occurred is deemed necessary. Mims lived within four hundred yards of the Boat Yard, upon Lake Tensaw, a mile east of the Alabama river, and two miles below the Cut-Off. His house was a large frame building of one story, with spacious shed-rooms. Around it pickets were driven, between which fence-rails were placed. Five hundred port-holes were made, three and a half feet only from the ground. The stockading enclosed an acre of ground, in a square form, and was entered by two ponderous but rude gates, one on the east and the other on the west. Within the enclosure, besides the main building, were various outhouses, rows of bee-gums, together with cabins and board shelters, recently erected by the settlers, wherever a vacant spot appeared. At the southwest corner a block-house was begun, but never finished. This defence was situated on a very slight elevation. A large potato field lay adjoining on the south, in which were a row of negro houses. Woods intervened between the picketing and the lake, while in a northern direction cane swamps, which grew denser as they approached the river, were hard by. On the east the flat lands continued for several miles, interspersed with cane marshes and some ravines. It was altogether a most ill-chosen place for a fort, as it ultimately proved.*

"No sooner was Fort Mims partially finished than the

---

*Claiborne's MS. papers.

citizens poured in, with their provisions and effects. Colonel Carson, who had reached Mount Vernon in advance of Claiborne, sent over Lieutenant Osborne, with sixteen men. Afterward Claiborne despatched one hundred and seventy-five more volunteers to Fort Mims under the command of Major Daniel Beasley, with Captains Jack, Batchelor and Middleton. He found seventy militia upon duty, commanded, for the present, by Dunn and Plummer, two inexperienced officers. Permitting them to elect their officers, the brave Captain Bailey was unanimously chosen for the post of captain, and —— Crawford for ensign. The next day General Claiborne, arriving at Fort Mims and inspecting the works, addressed a general order of instruction to Beasley, charging him 'to strengthen the picketing, build two more block-houses, respect the enemy, to send out scouts frequently, and allow the suffering people provisions, whether whites or friendly Indians.' Returning to his headquarters, at Mount Vernon, he, for the moment, directed his attention to other portions of the frontiers.† In the meantime, Major Beasley had extended the picketing on the east side sixty feet deep, forming a separate apartment for the accommodation of the officers and their baggage. He greatly weakened his command by sending small detachments to Forts Madison, Easley, Pierce, and Joshua Kennedy's saw-mill, where citizens had collected, and asked for assistance.‡ At this mill the government had a large contract for lumber to put Fort Charlotte, of Mobile, in repair, and build a fort at Mobile Point, and it was deemed neces-

---

*Conversations with Dr. Thomas G. Holmes, of Baldwin.
†Claiborne's MS. papers.
‡Conversations with Dr. Thomas G. Holmes.

sary to strengthen it with troops to prevent the Indians from burning it down.*

"The whole population of Fort Mims, consisting of whites, Indians, soldiers, officers and negroes, now amounted to five hundred and fifty-three souls. Crowded together in an Alabama swamp, in the month of August, much sickness prevailed.† In the meantime, Crawford was dismissed from the post of ensign for having deserted from the regular army, and Peter Randon, a half-breed, was appointed in his place. Beasley kept up a correspondence with Claiborne, several times acquainting him with alarms, which turned out to be false.‡

"The Creeks, whom we left returning to Pensacola from the battle ground of Burnt Corn, were again liberally supplied with arms and ammunition. Making their way back to the Tallapoosa without molestation, active preparations were made by them for immediate war. Warriors from the towns of Hoithlewale, Fooshatche, Cooloome, Ecunhutke, Souvanoga, Mooklausa, Alabama, Oakchoieooche, Pockuschatche, Ochebofa, Puckuntallahassee, Wewocoe and Woccocoie marched in a southern direction, while others, from Tallase, Auttose and Ocfuske, formed a front of observation toward Coweta to conceal the movement.§

"Associated with McQueen and Francis was William Weatherford, the son of Charles Weatherford, a Georgian, who had lived almost a life-time in the Creek Nation. His

---
†Conversations with Dr. Thomas G. Holmes.
‡Claiborne's MS. papers.
§Indian Affairs, vol. 1, p. 858. The Spaniards and the British agents charged McQueen's party to "fight the Americans. If they prove too hard for you, send your women and children to Pensacola, and we will send them to Havana; and if you should be completed to fly yourselves, and the Americans should prove too hard for both of us, there are vessels enough to take up all off together."—Ibid.

mother, Sehoy, was the half-sister of General McGillivray, and a native of Hickory Ground. William was uneducated, but was a man of great native intellect, fine form and commanding person. His bearing was gentlemanly and dignified, and was coupled with an intelligent expression, which led strangers to suppose that they were in the presence of no ordinary man. His eyes were large, dark, brilliant and flashing. He was one of 'nature's noblemen'— a man of strict honor and unsurpassed courage. He was now with the large Indian army, conducting them down to attack the Tensaw settlers, among whom were his brother and several sisters, and also his half-brother, David Tait.* How unhappily were these people divided! His sister, Hannah McNac, with all her sons, belonged to the war party, while the husband was a true friend of the Americans, and had fled to them for protection. Weatherford led his army to the plantation of Zachariah McGirth, a little below the present Claiborne, where, capturing several negroes, among whom was an intelligent fellow named Joe, from whom they learned the condition of Fort Mims, and the proper time to attack it, he halted for several days to deliberate. One of the negroes escaped, and conveyed intelligence to the fort of the approach of the Indians. Major Beasley had continued to send out scouts daily, who were unable to discover traces of the enemy. The inmates had become inactive, free from alarm, and abandoned themselves to fun and frolic. The negro runner from McGirth's plantation now aroused them for a time, and Fort Mims was

---

*David Tait was the son of Colonel Tait, a British officer, who was stationed at the Hickory Ground, upon the Coosa, in 1778, as we have seen.

further strengthened. But the Indians not appearing the negro was pronounced to be a liar, and the activity of the garrison again abated. At length two young negro men were sent out to mind some beef cattle that grazed upon the luxuriant grass within a few miles of the fort. Suddenly they came rushing through the gate out of breath, and reported that they had counted twenty-four painted warriors. Captain Middleton, with a detachment of horse, was immediately despatched with the negroes to the place, but being unable to discover the least sign of the enemy, returned about sunset, when one of the negroes, belonging to John Randon, was tied up and severely flogged for alarming the garrison with what Major Beasley deemed a sheer fabrication. Fletcher, the owner of the other, refused to permit him to be punished, because he believed his statement, which so incensed the major that he ordered him, with his large family, to depart from the fort by 10 o'clock the next day. The next morning Randon's negro was again sent out to attend the cattle, but seeing a large body of Indians, fled to Fort Pierce, being afraid to communicate the intelligence to those who had whipped him. In the meantime Fletcher's negro, by the reluctant consent of his master, was tied up and the lash about to be applied to his back; the officers were preparing to dine; the soldiers were reposing on the ground; some of the settlers were playing cards; the girls and young men were dancing, while a hundred thoughtless and happy children sported from door to door, and from tent to tent.

"At that awful moment one thousand Creek warriors, extended flat upon the ground in a thick ravine, four hundred yards from the eastern gate, thirsted for American blood. No eyes saw them but those of the chirping and innocent birds in the limbs above them. The mid-day sun sometimes flashed through the thick foliage and glanced upon their yellow skins, but quickly withdrew, as if afraid longer to contemplate the murderous horde. There lay the prophets, covered with feathers, with black faces, resembling those monsters which partake of both beast and bird. Beside them lay curious medicine bags and rods of magic. The whole ravine was covered with painted and naked savages, completely armed.

"The hour of 12 o'clock arrived, and the drum beat the officers and the soldiers of the garrison to dinner. Then, by one simultaneous bound, the ravine was relieved of its savage burden, and soon the field resounded with the rapid tread of the bloody warriors. The sand had washed against the eastern gate, which now lay open. Major Beasley rushed, sword in hand, and essayed in vain to shut it. The Indians felled him to the earth with their clubs and tomahawks, and, rushing over his body into the additional part of the fort, left him a chance to crawl behind the gate, where he shortly after expired. To the last he called upon the men to make a resolute resistance. The eastern part of the picketing was soon full of Indians, headed by five prophets, whom the Americans immediately shot down, while engaged in dancing and incantations. This greatly abated the ardor of the enemy, many of whom retreated through the gate for the moment. They had been assured that American bullets would split upon the sacred persons of the prophets, and pass off harmless. The unhappy inmates of

Fort Mims now made all efforts to defend the place, but their attempts were confused and ineffective. The assailants, from the old line of picketing, in the additional part of the fort, and from the outside stockading, commenced a general fire upon the Americans. Soldiers, negroes, women and children fell. Captain Middleton, in charge of the eastern section, was soon despatched, together with all his men. Captain Jack, on the south wing, with a company of riflemen, defended his position with great bravery. Lieutenant Randon fought from the guard-house, on the west, while Captain Dixon Bailey repulsed the enemy, to the best of his ability, on the northern line of pickets, against which much the largest number of Indians operated. The number of savages was so great that they apparently covered the whole field, and they now rent the air with their exulting shouts. Many of the younger prophets surrounded the main building, which was full of women and children, and danced around it, distorting their faces, and sending up the most unearthly screams. The pickets and houses afforded the Americans some protection, where the young men, the aged, and even the boys, fought with desperation. Captain Bailey was the man to whom the eyes of all the settlers were turned at this critical moment. He maintained his position, and was the only officer who gained the port-holes before they were occupied by the enemy. His repeated discharges made lanes through the savage ranks. Fresh numbers renewed their efforts against him, and often an Indian and an American would plant their guns across the same port-hole to shoot at each other. Bailey encouraged the whole population in the fort to fight, assuring them that Indians seldom fought long at one time, and, by holding out for a little while longer, many would be saved. Failing in his entreaties to prevail upon several to rush through the enemy to Fort Pierce, only two miles distant, there procure reinforcements, and attack the assailants in the rear, he resolved to go himself, and began to climb over the pickets for that purpose; but his neighbors, who loved him dearly, pulled him back.

"About three o'clock, the Indians, becoming tired of the contest, plundered the additional part of the fort, and began to carry off the effects to the house of Mrs. O'Neil, which lay three hundred yards distant, on the road to the ferry. Weatherford overtook them, on a fine black horse, and brought them back to the scene of action, after having impressed them by an animated address. About this time, Dr. Osborne, the surgeon, was shot through the body, and carried into Patrick's loom-house, where he expired in great agony. The women now animated the men to defend them by assisting in loading the guns and bringing water from the well. The most prominent among these was Mrs. Daniel Bailey, who, provoked at the cowardice of Sergeant Mathews, severely punctured him with a bayonet as he lay trembling against the wall. Many instances of unriveled courage could be enumerated, if our space permitted it. One of Jack's soldiers retreated to the half-finished blockhouse, after his commander and all his brothers-in-arms had fallen, and from that point discharged his gun at intervals, until he had killed over a dozen warriors. James and Daniel Bailey, the brothers of the gallant captain, with other men, ascended to the roof of Mims' dwelling, knocked off some shingles for port-holes, where they conttinued to shoot the lusty warriors on the outside of the picketing.

But the superior force of the assailants enabled them constantly to bring fresh warriors into the action. They now set fire to the main building, and many of the out-houses. The shrieks of the women and children went up to high heaven.

"To Patrick's loom-house had been attached some extra picketing, forming what was improperly termed a bastion. Hither Captain Bailey, and those of his command who survived, entered and continued to pour upon the savages a most deadly fire. Many citizens attempted to reach that spot, now the only one of the least security. The venerable David Mims, attempting to pass to the bastion, received a large ball in the neck; the blood gushed out; he exclaimed: 'Oh, God, I am a dead man!' and fell upon his face. A cruel warrior cut around his head and waved his hoary scalp exultingly in the air. Some poor Spaniards, who had deserted from the Pensacola garrison, kneeled around the well and crossed themselves, and, while interceding with the Most High, were despatched with tomahawks. 'To the bastion! To the bastion!' was now the fearful cry of the survivors. Soon it was full to overflowing. The weak, wounded and feeble were pressed to death and trodden under foot. The spot presented the appearance of one immense mass of human beings, herded together too close to defend themselves, and, like beeves in the slaughter-pen of the butcher, a prey to those who fired upon them. The large building had fallen, carrying with it the scorched bodies of the Baileys and others on the roof, and the large number of women and children in the lower story. The flames began to reach the people in the bastion. Dr. Thomas G. Holmes, an assistant surgeon in the garrison, seized an axe, cut some pickets in two, but did not take them down, suffering them to remain until a suitable opportunity offered to escape. The brave Dixon Bailey now cried aloud that all was lost, that his family were to be butchered, and begged all to make their escape, if possible. His negro man, Tom (still living, at Sisemore's plantation) took up his favorite son, who was thirteen years of age, but feeble with the fever, and bore him through the pickets, which Holmes now threw down, and gained the woods in safety. But, strange to say, the infatuated negro presently brought back the poor boy to a squad of hostiles, who dashed out his brains with war-clubs. Little Ralph cried out, 'Father, father, save me!' Of his Heavenly Father the poor little heathen had probably never heard.

"In front of the northern line of picketing was a fence, fifty yards distant, in every lock of which many warriors had placed themselves, to cut off all retreat; besides which, others stationed themselves at various points to shoot those who should run. Dr. Holmes, Captain Bailey, and a negro woman named Hester, the property of Benjamin Steadham, were the first to escape through the aperture. Holmes, receiving in his flight several balls through his clothes, but no wounds, strangely made his way over the fence, gained the swamp, and concealed himself in a clay hole, formed by the prostration of an immense tree. Bailey reached the swamp, but, being badly wounded, died by the side of a cypress stump. Hester received a severe wound in the breast, but reached a canoe in the lake, paddled to Fort Stoddart that night, and was the first to give intelligence to General Claiborne of the horrible affair.

"Returning again to the fatal spot, every house was

seen to be in flames. The bastion was broken down, the helpless inmates were butchered in the quickest manner, and blood and brains bespattered the whole earth. The children were seized by the legs and killed by beating their heads against the stockading. The women were scalped, and those who were pregnant were opened, while they were alive, and the embryo infants let out of the womb. Weatherford had, some time previous, left the horrid scene. He had implored the warriors to spare the women and children, and reproached them for their barbarity; but his own life was threatened for interposing, many clubs were raised over his head, and he was forced to retire. In after years he never thought of that bloody occasion without the most painful emotions. He had raised the storm, but he could not control it.

"The British agents at Pensacola had offered a reward of five dollars for every American scalp. The Indians jerked the skin from the whole head, and, collecting all the effects which the fire had not consumed, retired to the east one mile from the ruins, to spend the night, where they smoked their pipes and trimmed and dried their scalps. The battle had lasted from twelve to five o'clock.

"Of the large number in the fort, all were killed or burned up except a few half-bloods, who were made prisoners; some negroes, reserved for slaves; and the following persons, who made their escape and lived: Dr. Thomas G. Holmes; Hester, a negro woman; Socca, a friendly Indian; Peter Randon, lieutenant of Citizens' company; Josiah Fletcher; Sergeant Mathews, the coward; Martin Rigdon; Samuel Smith, a half-breed; —— Mourrice, Joseph Perry, Mississippi volunteers; Jesse Steadham; Edward Steadham; John Hoven; —— Jones, and Lieutenant W. R. Chambliss, of the Mississippi volunteers.

"Dr. Holmes lay concealed in the clay-hole until nine o'clock at night. The gin-house in the Boat Yard had been fired, and the conflagration threw a light over the surrounding country in addition to that still afforded by the ruins of Fort Mims. Hence, he was forced to resume his position until twelve o'clock, when the flames died away. Remembering that he had never learned to swim, he abandoned the idea which he first entertained, of crossing the Alabama and making his way to Mount Vernon. He therefore bent his course toward the high lands. He frequently came upon small Indian fires, around which the bloody warriors lay in profound sleep. Bewildered and shocked in every direction in which he turned by unwelcome and fearful sights like these, he at length, after a great deal of winding and turning, fell back into the river swamp, hid in a clump of thick cane, and there subsisted upon water, mutton-reed and roots. All this time he was in the immediate neighborhood of the scene of the tragical events we have described, and heard distinctly the Indians killing the stock of the citizens. When silence ensued, after the fifth day, he made his way to the Race-Track, and from thence to Pine-Log Creek, where he spent the night. Reaching Buford's Island the next day, and seeing the tracks of people and horses, he determined to fall in with them, although they should prove to be hostile Indians, so desperate had he become from starvation. At the Tensaw Lake, Holmes found the horses tied, and, rejoicing to find that they belonged to his friends, fired off his gun. John Buford and his party, supposing the discharge proceeded from the war party, fled up into a bayou in a boat, where they remained two days. The disappointed Holmes went to the abandoned house of Buford, where he fortunately obtained some poultry, which he devoured without cooking. Three days afterward he was discovered by Captain Buford and conveyed to Mount Vernon, where the other fourteen who had escaped had arrived and reported him among the slain.

"Martin Rigdon, Samuel Smith, Joseph Perry, —— Mourrice and Jesse Steadham escaped through the picketing together. The latter was shot through the thigh early in the action, and Mourrice in the shoulder. Leaping the fence in front of the bastion, over the heads of the squatting Indians, they reached the swamp, where they remained three days, when, finding an old canoe below the Boat Yard, they made their escape to Mount Vernon. Edward Steadham, who was wounded in the hand while flying from the bastion, entered the swamp, swam the Alabama above the Cut-Off, and arrived at Mount Vernon four days after the massacre. All the others who escaped so miraculously made their way with success through the Indian ranks, and had many similar adventures, reaching the American headquarters at the most imminent peril. Lieutenant Chambliss had received two severe wounds in the fort, and in running across the field received another. Reaching the woods, he crept into a log-heap. At night a party of warriors set fire to it, for the purpose of smoking their pipes, and when the heat was becoming intolerable, and he would soon have been forced to discover himself, they fortunately were called off to another camp-fire. He left that place immediately, wandered about, and for a long time was supposed to be dead. He made his way, however, to Mount Vernon, and from thence went to Soldier's Retreat, the residence of General Claiborne, near Natchez, where Dr. John Coxe, an eminent surgeon, extracted two arrow-heads and a ball from his body.*

The day after the fall of Fort Mims the Indians began to bury their dead, by laying their bodies between the potato-rows and drawing dirt and vines over them; but, from the great number of the dead, it was abandoned. Many were also wounded, who were put in canoes and conveyed up the river. Others wounded started home on foot, and died at Burnt Corn Spring. Most of those who were unhurt remained in the neighborhood to kill and plunder, while another party went to Pensacola with the scalps suspended upon poles.†

"Zachariah McGirth was the son of James McGirth, who was, as we have seen, an unprincipled but brave man, and a captain of a company of tories during the Revolutionary War, called the 'Florida Rangers,' forming a part of a battalion commanded by his brother, Colonel Daniel McGirth. When the war terminated Captain James McGirth fled to the Creek Nation, with his children, among whom was Zachariah. The latter married a half-breed Creek woman, named Vicey Curnells, had become wealthy, and was now an inmate of Fort Mims with his wife and eight children. About ten o'clock on the day of the massacre McGirth entered a boat with two of his negroes, and

---

*Claiborne's MS. papers.
†I am indebted to Dr. Thomas G. Holmes, of Baldwin County, Alabama, for the prominent facts in the foregoing narrative of the fall of Fort Mims. He made notes of the horrible affair a few years after the massacre took place, while the facts were fresh in his memory. I also conversed with Jesse Steadham, of Baldwin, and Lieutenant Peter Randon, the latter of whom I found in New Orleans, who also escaped.

went out of Lake Tensaw into the Alabama, with the view of ascending that river to his plantation, which was situated below Claiborne, for some provisions. Reaching the Cut-Off he heard a heavy discharge of guns at Fort Mims With pain and anxiety he continued to listen to the firing, and running his boat a mile down the river, in a small bayou, resolved to remain there, being firmly impressed with the belief that the Indians had attacked the fort. Late in the evening the firing ceased, and presently he saw clouds of black smoke rise above the forest trees, which was succeeded by flames. The unhappy McGirth now well knew that all was lost, and that in all probability his family had perished in the flames. Being a bold man, like his father, he resolved to go through the swamp with his negroes to the fatal spot. When he came within a quarter of a mile of the fort he placed the negroes in a concealed place, and approached alone. All was gloomy and horrible. Dogs in great numbers ran all over the woods, terrified beyond measure. Seeing that the savages had left the ruins, he returned for his negroes, and a little after twilight cautiously advanced. McGirth stood aghast at the horrible spectacle. Bodies lay in piles, in the sleep of death, bleeding, scalped, mutilated. His eyes everywhere fell upon forms half burned up, but still crackling and frying upon the glowing coals. In vain did he and his faithful slaves seek for the bodies of his family. Pile after pile was turned over, but no discovery could be made, for the features of but few could be recognized. He turned his back upon the bloody place, crossed the swamp to his boat, and paddled down the Alabama with a sad and heavy heart.

"McGirth, now alone in the world, became a desperate

man, ready to brave the greatest dangers for the sake of revenge. During the Creek War he was often employed in riding expresses from the Tombigby to Georgia, when no one else could be found daring enough to go through the heart of the enemy's country. After a long service amid such dangers, a friend accosted him one day in Mobile, and told him some people desired to see him at the wharf. Repairing there, he saw — common sight in those days — some wretched Indians, who had been captured. He was asked if he knew them. Hestitating, his wife and seven children advanced and embraced him. A torrent of joy and profound astonishment overwhelmed him. He trembled like a leaf, and was, for some minutes, speechless.

"Many years before the dreadful massacre at Fort Mims, a little hungry Indian boy, named Sanota, an orphan, houseless and friendless — stopped at the house of Vicey McGirth. She fed and clothed him, and he grew to athletic manhood. He joined the war party, and formed one of the expeditions against Fort Mims. Like the other warriors, he was engaged in hewing and hacking the females to pieces, toward the close of the massacre, when he suddenly came upon Mrs. McGirth and his foster-sisters. Pity and gratitude taking possession of his heart, he thrust them in a corner, and nobly made his broad savage breast a rampart for their protection. The next day he carried them off on horses, toward the Coosa, under the pretence that he had reserved them from death for his slaves. Arriving at his home, he sheltered them, hunted for them, and protected them from Indian brutality. One day he told his adopted mother that he was going to fight Jackson at the Horse-Shoe, and that, if he should be killed, she must endeavor to reach her friends below. Sure enough, the noble Sanota soon lay among the slain at Cholocco Litebixee. Mrs. McGirth, now being without a protector, and in a hostile region, started off on foot, with her children, for Fort Claiborne. After much suffering, they reached their deserted farm, below Claiborne, where Major Blue, at the head of a company of horse, discovered these miserable objects, and carried them to Mobile, where the interview just related took place with the astonished husband, who imagined that he had some months before surveyed their half-burnt bodies upon the field of Fort Mims. His son was the only member of his family who had perished on that memorable occasion.*

"General Claiborne despatched Major Joseph P. Kennedy, with a strong detachment, to Fort Mims, from his headquarters at Mount Vernon, for the purpose of interring the dead. Upon arriving there, Kennedy found the air darkened with buzzards, and hundreds of dogs, which had run wild, gnawing upon the human carcasses. The troops, with heavy hearts, succeeded in interring many bodies in two large pits, which they dug. 'Indians, negroes, white men, women and children lay in one promiscuous ruin. All were scalped, and females, of every age, were butchered in a manner which neither decency nor language will permit me to describe. The main building was burned to ashes, which were filled with bones. The plains and the woods around were covered with dead bodies. All the houses were consumed by fire, except the block-house, and a part of the pickets. The soldiers and officers, with one

---

*Conversations with Colonel Robert James, of Clarke County, Alabama, who often heard McGirth relate these particulars. McGirth, in 1834, made the same statements to me.

voice, called on Divine Providence to revenge the death of our murdered friends.'†

"In drawing our account of this sanguinary affair to a conclusion, it is proper to observe that General Claiborne was in no way to blame for the unfortunate result. He corresponded with Beasley, heard from him almost every day, and in his despatches constantly urged him to be prepared to meet the enemy."

IN THE WAR OF 1812

John Hoven, son of Benjamin Hoven, was born in South Carolina in 1794, and at the age of eighteen served as a soldier in the War of 1812. Benjamin Hoven moved to what is now Baldwin County in the early days of the nineteenth century. He and his family, including his son John, were in Fort Mims at its downfall.

History is silent, so far as we know, as to what happened to the Hoven family on that day of bloodshed and death, but tradition says that Benjamin Hoven and all of his family, except John and, perhaps, a daughter, perished there on that memorable day in August, 1813.

The following story was handed down from John Hoven to his son, William Hoven, and from William Hoven to his son, W. Henly Hoven, who lives near this place, and from him to the writer:

On the day of that sanguinary conflict between the Indians and the occupants of Fort Mims, John Hoven and four other men, who had been in the thickest of the fight

---

†Major Kennedy's MS. report to General Claiborne.

for hours, seeing that further resistance was without hope, and meant sure death, procured an ax and cut a hole through the back wall of the fort and made their escape. The fort was built by standing timbers on end in the ground, and all the men had to do was to cut away one or two of these timbers. These five men made their escape through this hole, as others did, as we shall see. A young woman who, according to Mr. Hoven's memory of the story, was a sister of his grandfather, John Hoven, made her escape through the opening in the wall, and when she reached the outside of the fort, she spied an officer's horse with saddle and bridle on, and she straightway proceeded to catch the horse, mount him, and make good her escape. She sat in the saddle while the noble horse swam the Alabama and Tombigbee rivers and landed her safe and sound at Old St Stephens. Another woman passed out through this hole in the wall, was shot in one of her legs, and she backed up against the wall of the fort, and in a few minutes her husband came out, and seeing his wife standing there, told her to follow him. She informed him that she was wounded and could not walk. The brave and true husband said, "Then, I will stand and we will die together."

It was late in the evening when John Hoven and the other four men made their escape. They at once proceeded to the river, perhaps below the Cut-Off, and, arriving at its bank, made ready to plunge in, when one of the five halted and began to cry and bemoan his predicament, saying he could not swim, and imploring the other men not to leave him. One of the men ripped out a big knife and told the disconsolate one to shut up his mouth and get into the water, else he would murder him. The man, preferring a watery grave to death by cold steel, plunged into the river and was the first man to land on the west bank of the river. When the men got out on the bank they heard Indians talking, so they put back for the east bank, and when they reached the east bank again they saw an Indian standing on the bluff with a gun, so they slipped back into the river and swam back. They swam the river seven times, the last time, discovering a dense canebrake, they proceeded to it and spent the night there. Next morning, feeling themselves fairly safe, they began to wend their way to Mobile. They were four days reaching Mobile. One of the men had all of his clothes torn from him, leaving nothing but a shirt collar on his neck. One of the men happened to have two shirts on; he pulled one of them off and gave it to the man, who put it on, and went into the city thus thinly clad.

Shortly after this John Hoven came to Clarke County, married, and settled some miles north of Jackson, and lived there, as an unpretentious farmer, until his death a short while before the Civil War. He was twice married. William Hoven was his son by his first wife, and King Hoven was his son by his second wife. William Hoven died more than thirty years ago. King Hoven is now living about three miles northwest of Jackson. John Hoven's second wife drew a pension on account of his service in the War of 1812. In the eighties she drew her first pension, getting at the same time a back pension amounting to more than a thousand dollars. She continued to draw a pension quarterly until her death, which occurred a few years later. Mrs. William Murray, who died a few months ago at the age of eighty years, was a daughter of John Hoven.

The victory of the Indians over the whites at Fort Mims stimulated them, and they soon began to give trouble to the whites in Clarke County, as the massacre at Fort Sinquefield evidences. A full account of this massacre is found in Pickett's History, and in order that the reader may get an intelligent idea of this conflict, we reproduce the account below:

DARING OF HEATON — BLOODY SCENES — GAINES AND THE CHOCTAWS

"While the larger body of Creeks were destroying the people at Fort Mims, Francis, the prophet, at the head of a hundred warriors, was spreading his depredations in the fork of the Alabama and Tombigby. Abner James and Ransom Kemball, with their large families, being inmates of Fort Sinquefield, and becoming dissatisfied at remaining among so many people, repaired to the house of Kemball, situated two miles from the fort. Here they were living when Francis suddenly surrounded the house, about three o'clock in the evening.

Abner James, his son Thomas, then fourteen years of age, and his daughter Mary, escaped, and fled to the fort. Isham

Kemball, then sixteen years of age, also safely reached Fort Sinquefield, and is now the clerk of the Circuit Court of Clarke County. All the others were despatched with war-clubs and scalped. After killing the stock and robbing the house the Indians retired to the swamps. In the early part of the night a slight rain commenced, which, it is believed, revived Sarah Merrill, the married daughter of James, whom the Indians had supposed to be dead. She felt among the bodies, which lay thick around her, and found her little boy, twelve months old, who also fortunately was alive. Some warm milk from her breast revived him more and more. Taking him in her arms, she with difficulty got upon her feet, and slowly walked toward the fort. Arriving within half a mile of that place, her bleeding wounds weakening her at every step, forced her to place the babe by the side of a log, while she went on and communicated his hiding place to the anxious garrison. Some generous men boldly sallied out, found the boy, and brought him to the fort. They are both now alive. The young woman was severely beaten with large clubs, and the scalp of the entire top of her head was taken off. The savages slung the little fellow against the side of the house, and cut around his head, but his hair being too short they did not pull off his scalp.

Hearing of the murders, Colonel Carson despatched from Fort Montgomery Lieutenant Bailey with seven dragoons, and three men employed as spies, to bury the dead and ascertain if the Indians were numerous. Twelve bodies were conveyed to Fort Sinquefield in an ox-cart, and thrown into a pit dug fifty yards from the gate. About the time that the funeral ceremonies were closing, and while nearly the whole garrison were engaged therein, Francis suddenly rushed with a hundred warriors down a hill toward them. The men snatched up the children, and every one of them reached the gate in time, except about ten women at the spring, who were engaged in washing. The Indians, failing to cut off the retreat of the main party, perceived with delight the helpless condition of these females, and rushed in that direction to secure them. Just at that moment Isaac Heaton, who had been out cow-hunting, riding up, with his long whip and large pack of dogs, gave a tremendous crack, and, encouraging his canine army, charged upon the Indians. Such was the fury of the dogs that the Creeks were forced to halt and fight them, which enabled Heaton to cover the retreat of the women until they arrived safely in the fort. His horse fell under him from the wound of an Indian gun, but rose again, and followed into the fort his heroic master, who had received no other injury than the riddling of his coat with rifle-balls. Only one poor woman — a Mrs. Philips, who was in an advanced state of pregnancy — was overtaken and scalped.

Heaton deserves to be remembered for this achievement — an eminent exemplification of bravery and presence of mind. The Indians now attacked the little stockade, but a brave resistance repelled them, with the loss of eleven warriors. Then, securing the dragoon horses, which had been tethered outside the walls, the savages rapidly retired. The Americans, having lost only one of their number, besides the unfortunate Mrs. Philips, the next day evacuated Sinquefield's fort, and marched to Fort Madison for better security, where the inmates of Forts Glass and Lavier had also flocked, swelling the population to over one thousand souls, including the command of Colonel Carson of two hundred and twenty men.

ISHAM KIMBELL

Mr. Isham Kimbell, who died in Jackson in 1881, was born in South Carolina March 31st, 1797. He was an active man when the author came to Jackson in 1875. He came to this county in the early part of the nineteenth century and was at Fort Sinquefield, or near Fort Sinquefield, at the time of the massacre of the Ransom Kimbell family and others, as has already been mentioned in these pages. He was then sixteen years of age.

We reproduce from Ball's History the following sketch:
"Isham Kimbell, with whose name the reader of these pages has become somewhat familiar, was born in North Carolina, March 31st, 1797. His father's family removed to South Carolina, and, probably in 1807, removed to the Tombigbee settlement, on the west side of the river, near McGrew's reserve. In the fall of 1812 they removed to a plantation on Bassett's Creek, not far from the home of Sinquefield. The tragedy enacted there in 1813 has already been related. His father died at Fort Madison. I. Kimbell, then a youth of sixteen, left thus alone in the world, received the care of his father's friend, Robert R. Harwell, and was placed as a clerk in a store at Pine Level, now Jackson. A brother living at Augusta, Georgia, then sent for him, with whom he remained until 1819. Returning then to Jackson, he was married in 1821 to Miss Martha T. Carney, daughter of Josiah Carney, from North Carolina. In the year 1833 he became clerk of the Circuit Court of

Clarke County. He held that office for twenty successive years, and finally resigned in 1849. He was also post-master and Registrar in Chancery. During his official life he resided near Grove Hill. He has been for many years past an inhabitant of Jackson. Commencing with nothing, he accumulated property amount in value to forty thousand dollars. He has a large family of sons and daughters. He is now nearly eighty-one years old."

"Mrs. Martha T. Kimbell, wife of Isham Kimbell, Esq., was the daughter of John and Sarah Carney, was born in North Carolina in 1797, December 26th, and came with her parents to the river settlement about 1812. She died at Jackson, June 2d, 1853. She was a member of the Methodist Church. It is said for her that "she appeared to have a humble, obedient confidence in the Scriptures that did not admit doubt." "Her faith seemed implicit." She was a "devoted wife, parent, Christian, and friend." The day before her death she gave impressive admonitions to her husband, her children, her friends, and her servants."

Mr. Kimbell had two sons and five daughters. His sons were John and Thomas I. Kimbell. One daughter married John C. Chapman, one married E. M. Portis, one married A. S. Smoot. His two youngest daughters, Miss Mary and Miss Carrie, never married. All have passed away. Mr. Kimbell has eight grandchildren living, namely: J. M. Chapman, Mrs. J. C. Rivers, of Mobile; Mr. H. B. Marsh, of the state of Texas; Mrs. C. W. Boyles, Mrs. Albert Prim, of Jackson; Mrs. O. H. P. Wright, of Selma; Dr. Isham Kimbell and Morris Kimbell, of Pascagoula, Miss. Major John Kimbell had several children, one of whom is now living, his name being Willie. Mr. Isham

Kimbell has numerous great-grandchildren and great-great-grandchildren living in this and other states.

THE GRIFFINS

The Griffins who were killed in the Bashi skirmish have many relatives still living in this county. In response to a written inquiry as to these brave pioneers, W. H. Griffin, of Campelle, says as follows:

"The two Griffins who were killed in the Bashi skirmish were brothers, and one of them was my grandfather's father. He was killed when my grandfather was a baby. It was three miles this side of Wood's Bluff, on the Bigbee river. The last time they were seen the Indians had killed one of them and the other was on his knees shooting at them, and that was the last ever seen or heard of them. My grandfather was William Griffin. He married a Miss Drinkard and had three children, two boys and one girl. My father was the oldest, and his name was Ivy Thomas Griffin. The next was a sister, who married twice. She had one child by her first marriage, who married Door White, of Thomasville, and she had two sons by her last marriage — J. W. Reid, of Campelle, and J. T. Reid, of Opine. The third child was John Griffin, who lived nearly all his life near Bashi and Choctaw Corner. He married a Miss Dunning, of Dixon's Mills, and they had a large family. My father married a Miss Holland, and they had seventeen children. Most of them are dead. Our oldest brother, T. W. Griffin, died in Thomasville about three years ago. There are four brothers living—William Griffin,

J. G. Griffin, F. F. Griffin and A. B. Griffin, and one sister, Mrs. J. B. White, of Aliceville, Ala."

The next conflict that occurred between the whites and the Indians took place in the northern part of the county, near Bashi, called the "Bashi Skirmish," which we also take from Pickett's History, and is as follows:

BASHI SKIRMISH

"Returning again to the seat of war, in the fork of the Tombigbee and Alabama, it will be seen that Colonel William McGrew advanced in pursuit of a party of the enemy, with twenty-five mounted militia. Coming upon them at Tallahatta, or Bashi Creek, a spirited action ensued. Colonel McGrew was killed, together with three of his company — the two Griffins and Edmund Miles — which put the remainder of the Americans to flight.

"General Flournoy, who had restricted the operations of Claiborne to those of a defensive character, now ordered the latter to advance with his army, for the purpose of defending the citizens while employed in gathering their crops; to drive the enemy from the frontiers, to follow them up to their contiguous towns, and to 'kill, burn and destroy all their negroes, horses, cattle, and other property that cannot conveniently be brought to the depots.' General Flournoy admitted, in the same order, that such usage was contrary to that of civilized nations, but stated that the conduct of Great Britain and the acts of her Indian allies fully justified it. On the same day that these instructions were received, Claiborne, at the head of Major Hind's Mississippi dragoons, a part of the twelve months' volunteers, and some companies of militia, marched from St. Stephens, crossed the Tombigby, and proceeded, by an indirect route, to the northern boundary, where Colonel McGrew had fallen. He found the body of that officer, and those of the privates, and interred them with military honors. On the march small bodies of the enemy hovered around, but could not be brought into action. A picket of infantry was attacked from an ambuscade, and three of them wounded; but before Major Hinds, who was a little in the rear, could come up the assailants leaped down a precipice, and escaped the pursuit of Captain Foster's detachment. Remaining two days at Fort Easley, upon Baker's Bluff, Claiborne scoured the whole country with detachments. In these expeditions he had five of his men severely wounded, among whom was Captain William Bradberry, who had acted so bravely at Burnt Corn. He was carried back to St. Stephens, and there died in great agony. Failing to bring the Indians to action, being convinced that they were in very inconsiderable force, and becoming destitute of subsistence, Claiborne marched to 'Pine Levels,' in the neighborhood of some good farms, a mile east of the Tombigby. He also sent a despatch to Flournoy, requesting him to suffer all the disposable force to march immediately to the Creek country.*

"The Indians were everywhere committing depredations, in small parties, and occasionally some of the settlers were killed. Tandy Walker, Benjamin Foster, and Evans, a colored man, had been despatched by the citizens of Fort Madison across the Alabama, in an easterly direction, as spies. Approaching the late battle ground at Burnt Corn they came upon a small camp of the enemy, upon whom they fired from a concealed position. The Indians fled with great precipitancy, while the spies seized some horses, plundered the camp, and retreated to Sisemore's Ferry. Here, late at night, while reposing in the cane, guns were fired upon them, and Evans was instantly killed. Walker escaped with a wound in the side and a broken arm, but the next day crossed the Alabama upon a cane raft and reached Fort Madison."

After the Bashi Skirmish, which occurred in October, 1818, the citizens of Clarke County determined that they would drive the Indians from the county, and in November occurred the "Canoe Fight," which Pickett reports as follows:

"Captain Samuel Dale, having now sufficiently recovered from his wounds, obtained the consent of Colonel Carson, who had returned to Fort Madison, to drive these small parties of the enemy from the frontiers. Dale was joined by a detachment of thirty of Captain Jones' Mississippi volunteers, under Lieutenant Montgomery, and forty Clarke County militia. Girard W. Creagh, the same who was attached to his company at Burnt Corn, was his lieutenant

---
*Claiborne's MS. papers.

upon this occasion. This expedition marched in a northern direction, visiting the abandoned plantations, and frequently discovering old traces of Indians. Dale returned to the fort, and the next day marched southeastwardly toward Brazier's Landing, now French's, where an Indian negro, named Caesar, who was in company, had two canoes concealed in the cane. In these they crossed the Alabama at the close of the day, and bivouacked on the eastern bank. They were thinly clad, and the frost was severe. When the sun first made its appearance over the tall canes Captain Dale put his command in motion and marched up the eastern bank, after having placed the canoes in charge of Jeremiah Austill, with six men, with orders to keep the boats parallel with those who marched on foot. Arriving opposite the farm of the late Dixon Bailey, who had heroically fallen at Fort Mims, as we have seen, Dale entered the boats, went over to the place, and discovered fresh signs of the mysterious foe, with whose habits he was so well acquainted. No sooner had he returned to his command on the eastern side than Austill discovered a canoe, occupied by Indians, descending the river, whom he immediately approached. They tacked about, paddled up the river, and disappeared in the thick cane near the mouth of Randon's Creek. A few minutes only elapsed before a heavy firing ensued, up the creek, where the expedition had encountered some savages on horseback — Captain Dale's rifle, which unhorsed one of these Indians, having given the alarm. The yell was raised, and they made an attempt to charge; but the hot fire of the Americans compelled them to make a precipitate retreat, with one of their number killed and several severely wounded.

"In the meantime, Austill had reached Randon's plantation, with the canoes, a quarter of an hour in advance of the main party.* When they came up Dale ordered them to cross to the western side, as it was found impracticable to continue the route on the eastern, on account of the cane and thick vines. While the company of Captain Jones or Lieutenant Montgomery was being ferried over, Captain Dale, Jere Austill, Lieutenant Creagh, James Smith, John Elliott, a half-breed, Brady and six others occupied a position in a small field, between a sand bluff and the river, where, kindling a fire, they began to boil some beef and roast a few potatoes for their morning repast. When all the command had passed the river except these men, and immediately after the negro, Caesar, had returned, with the smaller canoe, the men from the western side gave the alarm that the Indians were rapidly descending upon those who occupied the little field. They sprang from their hasty meal, retreated to the river side, and were partially screened from the enemy's fire by a small bank. While in this perilous situation, hemmed in by the Indians and the river, their attention was directed to a large flat-bottomed canoe, containing eleven warriors. Naked, and painted in a variety of fantastic colors, while a panther-skin encircled the head of the Chief, and extended down his back, these Indians presented a picturesque and imposing appearance. For some reason, those in the rear now retired, leaving Dale and his little party free to attack those in the canoe. The red voyagers, apparently unapprised of their danger, glided gently down the river, sitting erect, with their guns before

---

*Randon was a wealthy Indian countryman, who was massacred at Fort Mims.

them. Dale and his party immediately opened a fire upon them, which they promptly returned. Several rounds were afterwards exchanged, resulting, however, in but little injury, as the Indians now lay flat in the canoe, exposing nothing but their heads. At length two of the latter, cautiously getting into the water, swam for the shore, above the field, holding their guns dry above their heads. They swam near the land, above the mouth of a stream, over whose muddy bottom Austill and Smith crossed with difficulty to pursue them. When near the Indians, the buckskin leggins of Austill, suspended by a band around his waist, fell about his feet from the weight of water in them, causing him to slip and be precipitated down the bluff. At that moment, a ball from Smith's unerring rifle perforated the head of one of the Indians, who immediately turned over upon his back and then sunk. The other gained the bank and ascended it, keeping Smith off with his gun, which he pretended was charged. Austill, who had now gained the top of the bluff, pursued the Indian up the stream, when a gun was fired, the contents of which passed just over his head. Imagining himself among the enemy, and hesitating for a moment, the savage escaped. The fire proved to be from Lieutenant Creagh's gun, who, in the thick cane, supposed Austill to be the warrior, whose pursuit he was likewise engaged. While these things were rapidly transpiring, Dale ordered the large canoe to be manned on the opposite shore, and to be brought over to capture the Indians who were still in their canoe. Eight men sprang into it, but having approached near enough to see the number of fierce warriors still alive and ready to defend themselves to desperation, this cautious party rapidly paddled back to the western side. The exasperated Dale now proposed that some of his men should follow him in the small canoe, which was immediately acquiesced in. Dale leaped down the bank into the boat, and was followed by Smith and Austill. All the others were anxious to go, but it afforded room for no more. The noble Caesar paddled toward the Indian's canoe, and, when within twenty yards of it, the three resolute Americans rose to give them a broadside; but only the gun of Smith fired, for the other two had unfortunately wet their priming. Caesar was ordered to paddle up, and to place his boat side by side with that of the warriors. Approaching within ten feet, the Chief, recognizing Dale, exclaimed, 'Now for it, Big Sam!'* At the same instant he presented his gun at Austill's breast. That brave youth struck at him with an oar, which he dodged, and in return he brought down his rifle upon Austill's head, just as the canoes came together. At that moment the powerful arms of Smith and Dale raised their long rifles, which came down with deadly force, and felled the Chief to the bottom of the canoe — his blood and brains bespattering its sides. Such was the force of the blow inflicted by Dale that his gun was broken near the lock. Seizing the heavy barrel, still left, he did great execution with it to the end of the combat. Austill, in a moment, engaged with the second warrior, and then with a third, both of whom he despatched with his clubbed rifle. Smith, too, was equally active, having knocked down two Indians. Caesar had by this time got the canoes close together, and held them with a mighty grasp, which enabled Dale, who

---
*Dale had long been a trader among the Indians, and, on account of his prowess and large frame, was familiarly called by them "Big Sam."

was in the advance, and the others, to maintain a firm footing by keeping their feet in both canoes. These brave men now mowed down the savages, amid the encouraging shouts of the men on both sides of the river, who had full view of the deadly conflict. In the midst of this unparalleled strife, a lusty Indian struck Austill with a war-club, which felled him across the sides of the two boats, and, while prostrate, another had raised his club to dash out his brains, when Dale, by a timely blow, buried his heavy rifle barrel deep in the warrior's skull. In the meantime, Austill recovered his feet, and, in a desperate struggle with another savage, knocked him into the river with the club, which he had wrested from him. The only word spoken during tthe fight was the exclamation of the Chief upon recognizing Dale, and the request of Caesar for Dale to make use of his bayonet and musket, which he handed to him. Having laid all the warriors low, these undaunted Americans began to cast them into the bright waters of the Alabama, their native stream, now to be their grave. Every time a savage was raised up from the bottom of the canoe by the head and heels and slung into the water, the Americans upon the banks sent up shouts, loud and long, as some slight revenge for the tragedy of Fort Mims. Just as the last body found its watery grave a ball shot by the Indians from the eastern side struck one of the canoes, and was followed by other discharges, but without effect. After the fight had ended eight athletic Indians were thrown out of the canoe. It will be recollected that there were eleven in the boat when first seen, and that two of them had swum ashore, and the other one Austill had knocked out before the conflict ended.

"The Indian canoe presented a sight unusually revolting — several inches deep in savage blood, thickened with clots of brains and bunches of hair. In this sanguinary bark, and the one paddled by Caesar, the nine Americans who had been left on the eastern side were now conveyed across to the opposite bank, where the heroes received the warm congratulations of their companions, who exultingly surrounded them.

"The expedition then marched up to Cruell's Ferry, two miles distant, and, seeing no more of the enemy, and being out of provisions, returned that night to Fort Madison. It is remarkable that no one received the least injury, except Austill, whose head and arms were severely bruised.*

HEROES OF THE CANOE FIGHT

Austill, Smith and Dale, who were participants in the famous canoe battle on the Alabama river, account of which battle will be found on another page in this book, were once citizens of Clarke County; Dale and, perhaps, Smith, resided at Jackson for a short while, and Austill lived about ten miles south of Jackson for many years. The author met Major Austill in this county several years before his death, which occurred in 1881. A history of the lives of these brave pioneers is found in Pickett's History of Alabama, and, knowing that this will be interesting reading to all Clarke countians, we reproduce below what Pickett has to say of them:

---

*Conversations with Colonel Girard W. Creagh, who witnessed the Canoe Fight, while standing in full view upon the eastern bank of the Alabama, and Colonel Jeremiah Austill, of Mobile, one of the heroes. Among the MS. papers of General Claiborne I also found the report of Captain R. Jones, of the First Regiment of Mississippi Volunteers, on the "canoe fight," which fixes the date of that affair.

"Jeremiah Austill was born near the Oconee Station, in Pendleton District, South Carolina, on the 10th August, 1794. His father, Captain Evan Austill, has already been mentioned as one of those who boldly remained to defend Ford Madison after it had been evacuated by Colonel Carson. His mother was the only sister of Colonel David Files, who died in this state in 1820. At the time of the canoe expedition Jere Austill was nineteen years of age, and weighed one hundred and seventy-five pounds, without any surplus flesh. He was bold, active and strong, and had been raised upon the Indian frontiers, having lived some time at the Agency, in the Cherokee Nation. He is still a resident of Mobile, and is regarded as a respectable gentleman. Since the canoe fight he has filled several important offices, and represented the people of Mobile in the legislature. His countenance is open and manly, his form is erect, and his step elastic. Even now, at the age of fifty-six, Colonel Austill is capable of being a very troublesome adversary in a desperate encounter, although one of the most peaceable and amiable men in the country in the ordinary pursuits of life.

"James Smith was a native of Georgia, of low stature, well set, weighed one hundred and sixty-five pounds, and was twenty-five years of age at the period of the canoe fight. He was a brave, daring, frontier man, and died in East Mississippi several years ago. He was a man of great prowess, and had killed several Indians in frontier expeditions. He was admired by every one for his courage, honesty and willingness to defend his country, at all times and under all circumstances.

"Captain Samuel Dale, of Irish extraction, was born in

Rockbridge County, Virginia, in 1772. In 1775 his father moved to Glade Hollow, on the Clinch river, in the County of Washington, Virginia, and was actively engaged in the border warfare of that day. In 1774 he removed, with his family, to the vicinity of Greensborough, Georgia, where e purchased a farm, but, in a short time was compelled to take refuge in Carmichael's Station, in consequence of the inroads of the Indians. Several desperate attempts were made to burn this fort, in one of which Captain Autry was slain. About this time Mr. Dale and his wife died, leaving eight children. Samuel, the subject of this memoir, who was the oldest, placed the children upon the farm and joined a company of troopers, raised by Captain Fosh, to watch the movements of the Creeks, which was soon afterward mustered into the federal service, and quartered on the Oconee, at a place called Fort Mathews. Toward the close of 1794 this troop had several engagements with the savages, in which Dale displayed those traits which so distinguished his subsequent career — vigilance, perseverance, energy, and dauntless courage. At Ocfuskee, on the Chattahoochie, he slew two Indians. Soon after, having been elected colonel, and stationed at the head of a separate command at Fort Republic, on the Apalache river, in Georgia, he rendered efficient service, until the troops were disbanded. Then he became a trader among the Creeks and Cherokees, purchasing his goods in Savannah and exchanging them for cattle and ponies. He also acted in the capacity of guide to many parties emigrating to the Mississippi Territory. He finally established a trading-house in copartnership with a half-breed in what is now known as Jones County, Georgia, where he remained for some time.

He was at Tookabatcha when Tecumseh appeared there, and assured Colonel Hawkins that the mission of that man would result in great evil unless his efforts were immediately counteracted; but the agent did not concur with him in that opinion. His bravery has been seen at Burnt Corn, and in the canoe fight. At the time of the latter Captain Dale weighed one hundred and ninety pounds, was over six feet high, possessed a large, muscular frame, without any surplus flesh, and was in the prime of life. Althtough he will be mentioned hereafter, in connection with the Indian wars, we deem it proper, in further illustration of his character, to insert the following well-written obituary, published in The Natchez Free Trader, from the pen of John H. F. Claiborne, formerly a member of Congress from Mississippi, and the son of the general of that name, whose military services are now under review:

"'I have not observed in your paper any notice of the death of our veteran friend, General Samuel Dale. He died at his residence, Daleville, Lauderdale County, on the 23d ult., with the fortitude of a soldier and the resignation of a Christian. On his dying bed he repeated, as I am informed, a request which he made last summer, that I should make a memoir of his life, most of the particulars I wrote down from his lips. I design visiting Lauderdale in a few weeks to obtain all the materials that remain. Few men have run a career so full of benevolent actions and of romantic adventure, and no man was ever better adapted to the country and the period in which he lived — that country the frontiers of Georgia, Florida and the (then) Mississippi Territory, embracing all the present state of Alabama — the period including nearly all that bloody interval between the close of the Revolution and the termination of the last war. With the story of these times, the dreadful massacre at Fort Mims, the battle of the Holy Ground, General Jackson's Seminole campaigns, and the earlier events of the Georgia frontier, General Dale was closely connected. The most affecting of those scenes of murder and conflagration are as yet unwritten, and live only in the fading memorials of border tradition. In preparing the life of General Dale, I shall seek to put many of them on record. As a scout, a pilot to the emigrants who blazed the first path through the Creek Nation, from Georgia to the Tombigby, with arms in their hands, and subsequently as a spy among the Spaniards at Pensacola, and as a partisan officer during the most sanguinary epochs of the late war, present at every butchery, remarkable for "hair-breadth 'scapes," for caution and coolness in desperate emergencies, for exhibitions of gigantic personal strength and great moral courage, his story is studded over with spirit-stirring incidents, unsurpassed by anything in legend or history. His celebrated "canoe fight," where, in the Alabama river, he, with Smith and Austill, fought nine warriors with clubbed rifles, killed them all, and rowed to shore, would be thought fabulous if it had not been witnessed by many soldiers standing upon the banks, who could render them no assistance. Some years before, he was attacked by two warriors, who shouted their war-whoop as he was kneeling down to drink and rushed upon him with their tomahawks. He knifed them both, and, though bleeding from five wounds, he retraced their trail nine miles, crept stealthily into their camp, brained three sleeping warriors and cut the thongs of a female prisoner who lay by their side. While in this act, however, a fourth sprang upon him from behind a log. Taken at such a disadvantage and exhausted by the loss of blood, he sank under the serpent-grasp of the savage, who, with yell of triumph, drew his knife and in a few moments would have closed the contest. At that instant, however, the woman drove a tomahawk deep into the head of the Indian, and thus preserved the life of her deliverer.

" 'Shortly after the treaty of Dancing Rabbit, our deceased friend settled in what is now known as Lauderdale County; and it is worthy of remark that at the first election (1836, I believe), when he was chosen to the legislature, but ten votes were cast. Now, the county could probably poll 750, and in every direction its fleecy fields, its fine flour-mills, its school-houses and churches indicate a thriving, enlightened and moral population.

" 'One anecdote of the old general is so similar to an event in Roman history that I cannot forbear relating it. The Consul Acquilius, returning from a campaign, was allowed a triumph, but shortly afterward was arraigned for some misdemeanor committed during his foreign service. He called no exculpatory evidence, nor deigned to court the favor of his judges, but when about to receive sentence he tore open his vest and displayed the wounds he had received in the service of his country. A sudden emotion of pity seized the court, and unfixed the resolution which a few moments before they had taken to condemn the accused. Some time ago General Dale, being in Mobile, was held to bail as endorser upon a note. The debt was in the hands of a stranger. Accompanied by an officer, he sought the creditor, and found him in the saloon of Cullum's far-famed hotel. "Sir," said the general, "I have no money to pay this debt. The principal has property — make him pay it, or let me go home and work it out." The Shylock hesitated. "Very well," said the veteran, in tones that rang indignantly through the apartment, "Very well, sir! Look at my scars! I will march to jail down Main street, and all Mobile shall witness the treatment of an old soldier!" These simple words fell like electricity upon that high-toned people. In half an hour a dozen of the brightest names of the city were on the bond, and before morning the debt was paid, and a full discharge handed to the general. I have seen the manly tears chasing down his cheek, as the aged warrior dwelt on these recollections of the generous citizens. In person, General Dale was tall, erect, raw-boned and muscular. In many respects, physical and moral, he resembled his antagonists of the woods. He had the square forehead, the high cheek-bones, the compressed lips, and, in fact, the physiognomy of an Indian, relieved, however, by a fine, benevolent Saxon eye. Like the red man, too, his foot fell lightly upon the ground, and turned neither to the right or left; his face grave; he spoke slowly and in low tones, and seldom laughed. I observed of him what I have often noted as peculiar to border men of high attributes: he entertained the strongest attachment for the Indians, extolled their courage, their love of country, and many of their domestic qualities, and I have often seen the wretched remnant of the Choctaws camped around his plantation and subsisting on his crops. In peace, they felt for him the strongest veneration — he had been the friend of both Tecumseh and Weatherford — and in war the name of "Big Sam" fell on the ear of the Seminole like that of Marius on the hordes of the Cimbri.'

"Captain Dale, with a scouting party, had effectually scoured the swamps of Bassett's Creek, and Major Hinds' horse had routed a small body of the enemy near Weatherford's Bluff, killing ten of their number, when an order from Flournoy permitted Claiborne to advance with the Southern army to the Alabama. His instructions confined him still to defensive operations, requiring him to establish a depot at Weatherford's Bluff, and not to advance further into the Creek Nation until he was joined by the Georgia and Tennessee troops. Claiborne accordingly broke up his camp at Pine Levels, marched across Clarke County with three hundred volunteers, the dragoons and some militia, flanked by detachments under Captains Kennedy and Bates and Lieutenant Osborne, and parties of Choctaws under Pushmatahaw and Mushullatubba. Arriving at the Alabama, the army encamped for the night upon the western bank, and the next day at twelve o'clock had gained the other side by means of rafts. Colonel Gilbert C. Russell, an accomplished and gallant commander in the regular army, marched the Third Regiment of federal troops from Mount Vernon, through Nannahubba Island, by Mims' Ferry, to the head of Little river, and thence to the encampment of Claiborne, with whom he had been instructed to co-operate. In the meantime, Claiborne had made rapid progress in the construction of a strong stockade, two hundred feet square, defended by three block-houses and a half-moon battery, which commanded the river. Before the close of November it was completed, and received the name of Fort Claiborne, in honor of the commander. The town where it stood still bears his name. The general wrote to Jackson, congratulating him upon his victories, and giving him an account of the operations in the southern seat of war, and acquainting him with the fact that an abundance of corn and other provisions were to be obtained in the neighborhood of Fort Claiborne. He also wrote to Governor Blount, apprising him of the arrival of more English vessels in Pensacola, and added that he wished 'to God that he was authorized to take that sink of iniquity, the depot of tories and instigators of disturbances on the southern frontier.' He had a few days before despatched Major Kennedy and others to Mobile, to learn from Colonel Bowyer the particulars of the arrival of the British at Pensacola. They reported, giving satisfactory assurances that a large quantity of Indian supplies and many soldiers had arrived there; and, in addition, that the Indians were committing depredations in Baldwin County, having recently burned down Kennedy's and Byrne's mills.

"Lieutenant-Colonel George Henry Nixon had succeeded Russell in the command at Mount Vernon. At his request, Claiborne permitted him, also, to man Fort Pierce, in the neighborhood of the disturbances.*

"Claiborne, having determined to advance to the enemy's stronghold, the line of march was taken up by an army consisting of Colonel Russell's Third Regiment, Major

---

*Colonel Nixon was born in Virginia, and, living some years in South Carolina, rremoved from thence in 1809 to the Mississippi Territory. He was among the first to offer his services in defence of his country. Durin the Creek War, Colonel Nixon, at the head of a considerable force, scoured the swamps of the Perdido and other streams, and frequently killed and captured Indians. After he had accomplished all he could, he marched to the head of the Perdido, where he divided his command, sending Major William Peacock, with the troops of the 39th, to the Boat Yard, on Lake Tensaw, while he marched the remainder of his command to Fort Claiborne. He was an excellent officer, and served in the war until its final conclusion. He was a member of the convention that formed the constitution of the state of Mississippi, and was, afterward, frequently a state Senator. He died at Perlington, Mississippi, in 1824. He was a large and fine-looking man, with fair complexion, and was very popular.

Cassels' battalion of horse, a battalion of militia, under Major Benjamin Smoot — Patrick May being adjutant, Dale and Heard captains, and Girard W. Creagh one of the lieutenants — the twelve months' Mississippi volunteers, under Colonel Carson, and one hundred and fifty Choctaws, under Pushmatahaw, numbering, in the aggregate, near one thousand men. A few days before, nine captains, eight lieutenants, and five ensigns, signed a remonstrance, in respectful language, against the march to the Nation, and presented it to the general. They set forth that the time of service of many would soon expire, that the weather was cold, that they were too scantily supplied with clothing and food for such a campaign, and that the route to the enemy's towns was entirely a pathless one; but they stated their willingness to obey, if Claiborne should resolve to proceed.

"Claiborne moved in a northeastern direction, until he reached the high lands south of Double Swamp, at the distance of eighty miles, where he built a depot, called Fort Deposit, situated in the present County of Butler, and where he left the wagons, cannon, baggage and the sick, with one hundred men, as a guard. Thirty miles further brought him into the immediate neighborhood of the Holy Ground, which had been reached without the aid of a single path. The pork being exhausted, the troops were in a suffering condition, for they had only drawn, when leaving Fort Deposit, three days' allowance of flour. Econachaca (Holy Ground) had recently been erected by Weatherford, the prophets having assured the Indians that here no white man could approach without instant destruction. It was strongly fortified in the Indian manner, and had for some months formed a point to which those who had been routed in battle retreated, and where a great amount of plunder had been stored. It was situated upon a bluff, on the eastern side of the Alabama river, just below the present Powell's Ferry, in the County of Lowndes. Here many of the white prisoners and friendly Indians were burned to death, by order of the prophets, and when Claiborne was almost within sight of the town with his advancing army, Mrs. Sophia Durant and many other friendly half-breeds were mustered in the square and surrounded by lightwood fires, designed to consume them.

"The troops advanced toward the town in three columns, the centre commanded by Colonel Russell, at the head of which was Claiborne himself, Lester's guards and Wells' dragoons acting as a corps of reserve.

"At noon Carson's right column came in view of the town, and was vigorously attacked by the enemy, who had chosen their field of action. The town was nearly surrounded with swamps and deep ravines, so that the enemy, who afterward retreated, could not be successfully pursued. Major Cassels, who had been directed to form his battalion of horse on the river bank, west of the town, failing to effect such a movement, fell back on the head of Carson's regiment, who, however, advanced and took his position. The Third Regiment, coming up in gallant style, did its duty. Major Smoot assumed his position in a proper manner, and all would have been right if Cassels' cavalry had not failed to obey orders, thereby permitting hundreds of the enemy to escape along the Alabama river, by the western border of the town. The Indians, headed by Weatherford, for a short time fought with considerable fury, but afterward fled with great rapidity. The short engagement resulted in the death of thirty Indians and negroes, whose bodies were afterward counted upon the field. Many must have been severely wounded. Lucket, an American ensign, was killed, and twenty men were wounded.

"Several hours before the battle began the Indian women and children had been conveyed across the river, and were securely lodged in the thick forests of the region now familiarly known as the Dutch Bend of Autauga County. Here the retreating warriors, some of whom came over in boats, while others swam, joined them. Weatherford, seeing that his forces had deserted him, now pushed hard for his own safety. Coursing with great rapidity along the banks of the Alabama, below the town, on a gray steed of unsurpassed strength and fleetness — which he had purchased a short time before the commencement of hostilities of Benjamin Baldwin, late of Macon County — came at length to the termination of a kind of ravine, where there was a perpendicular bluff ten or fifteen feet above the surface of the river. Over this, with a mighty bound, the horse pitched with the gallant Chief, and both went out of sight beneath the waves. Presently they rose again, the rider having hold of the mane with one hand and his rifle firmly grasped in the other. Regaining his saddle, the noble animal swam with him to the Autauga side.*

"Claiborne reduced the town of Holy Ground to ashes. He then despatched the cavalry to Ward's place up the river, who, before reaching there, fell in with three Shawnees of distinction retreating from the battle, whom they

---

*Extravagant tales have often been told of Weatherford's leap, and a bluff at or near the site of the Holy Ground town, which is probably eighty or a hundred feet high, is often pointed out as the one over which he charged. The account I have given is Weatherford's own statement of the affair.

killed. The firing being heard at the camp, Claiborne struck his tents and marched in that direction during the night. Encamping at Weatherford's place in an open field, the cold rains descended in torrents upon the troops, and Christmas morning found them engaged in parching corn for breakfast, which was the only thing left to eat. After destroying some houses and farms, the army marched back to Fort Deposit, and from thence to Fort Claiborne, where, the term of service of Carson's Mississippi volunteers and cavalry having expired, they were mustered out of service.

"Colonel Russell, now left in sole command of Fort Claiborne, preferred charges against Major Cassels for disobedience of orders at the Holy Ground, and a court of inquiry, composed of Captain Woodruff, president; Captain J. E. Denkins and Lieutenant H. Chotard, decided that Sam McNac, the guide; was chiefly to blame for the failure of Cassels to occupy the position which had been assigned to him. Another court of inquiry, composed of Colonel Carson and Lieutenant Wilcox, decided that the contractor of the army was solely to blame for the perishing condition of the expedition, as General Claiborne had given him ample instructions to furnish abundant supplies. The command had been entirely without meat for nine days.

"General Claiborne wrote to the Secretary of War from Mount Vernon, that he had been left with but sixty men, whose time lacked only a month of expiring; that his other volunteers, who had been disbanded, had gone home naked and without shoes, with eight months' pay due them; and that his army, being thus broken up, he intended to return home as soon as he received permission from General Flournoy.*

"Having planned an expedition against the enemy, Colonel Russell despatched Captain Denkins up the Alabama from Fort Claiborne in command of a barge, laden with provisions, and defended by a piece of artillery, with instructions to enter the Cahawba river, and to ascend it to the 'Old Towns,' where his army would shortly join him. Afterward, marching the larger portion of his regiment to the crossroads in Clarke County, four miles north of the present Suggsville, he was there joined by a company commanded by Captain Evan Austill and Lieutenant G. W. Creagh, and Captain Foster's horse company, both under the command of Major Samuel Dale. Leaving this place, with six days' rations, Colonel Russell reached the Cahawba Old Towns, where he was mortified to find that Captain Denkins had not arrived — nor had he encountered on the way a solitary Indian. Despatching Lieutenant Wilcox in a canoe, with five men, with directions to find Denkins and hasten him on, that officer proceeded down the Cahawba, upset his boat the first night, wet his ammunition, and lost two of his guns. Recovering the canoe, however, and proceeding down the river, lying by in the cane in the day time, he was, in the evening of the second day, fired upon by a party of Indians. The two Wilsons, who belonged to this expedition, made their escape, and reached the lower settlements many days after, in a starving condition. One of them, Mathew, was found by Hais Rodgers, on the ridge road of Clarke. Lieutenant Wilcox and the

---

*Claiborne's MS. papers. Conversations with the late Colonel Creagh, General Patrick May, of Greene, and others.

other three were made prisoners by the Indians, who proceeded with them down the Cahawba, into the Alabama. In the meantime, Denkins, unfortunately passing the mouth of the Cahawba by mistake, had ascended some distance up the Alabama, and was now returning to Fort Claiborne, knowing that the army could not wait for him, but would return to that place likewise. The Indians, going down the river also, descried the barge, and fearing to lose their prisoners, tomahawked and scalped Wilcox and his three companions, leaving them in their canoe. When the canoe and the barge came together Wilcox was still alive, but too far gone to give an account of the particulars of his capture, or of Russell's expedition. The body of this gallant young officer, being found upon the Alabama, where it meanders through the region between Canton and Prairie Bluff, the legislature appropriately preserved his memory by giving the county his name.

"Colonel Russell remained two days at the Cahawba Old Towns, in which time one of his men was killed by some skulking savages. Despairing of the arrival of the barge, he began the return march, without any provisions; and, setting the example himself in having his best horse killed, twelve animals of that kind were devoured by the perishing troops. At Bradford's Pond they were timely relieved by wagons, laden with abundant provisions, and arriving again at the crossroads, were disbanded, the regulars marching to Fort Claiborne."*

---

*Conversations with Colonel Girard W. Creagh, late of Clarke County

MIGRATION TO CLARKE

After the famous Canoe Fight the citizens of Clarke County had no further trouble with the Indians. As mentioned heretofore, quite a number of the white families had moved into Clarke County between the years of 1800 and 1813. According to Ball, "about the year 1800 a brisk migration had begun from Georgia and the Carolinas, through the Creek country, to the Mississippi Territory. Samuel Dale, then a Georgian, placed three wagons and teams on this route of migration, transporting families westward and taking back to Savannah loads of Indian produce. In 1809 Caleb Moncrief, with a number of families, settled on the west side of Bassett's Creek. Many others came during these few years and settled near Old Clarksville, Grove Hill, at Suggsville, and in other parts of the county. The names of many of these families will be found among the Family Records and Sketches.

"In 1812 Dale removed Colonel J. Phillips and family to Point Jackson, on the Tombigbee, started his teams back to Georgia, and went himself to Pensacola. West Florida proper, it is to be remembered, was still a Spanish possession, and Spain continued to hold, as a part of West Florida, all south of latitude 31 degrees, between the Perdido and the Mississippi until 1813."

Ball further says that in the fall of 1805 "the Choctaw Indians ceded to the United States five millions of acres of their lands, beginning at the Cut-Off, now the southern limit of Clarke, half-way between the two rivers, running north along the watershed, to the boundary of Clarke, and on or near the second range line east, then west to the Fuluctabuna Old Fields, or to the mouth of Fluctabuna Creek, then crossing the Tombeckbee, west to the Mississippi settlements, south to latitude 31 degrees, called Elliott's line, and east to the Mobile river, and north to the Cut-Off. Thus a grant of land was obtained lying east of the Tombeckbee river where those pioneers, coming through the Creek Nation, might settle and make homes without intruding upon Indian rights. But it appears that for this very strip of territory east of the Tombeckbee and extending half-way to the Alabama, other claimants soon appeared. The Creek Indians claimed that it belonged to them, rather than to the Choctaws, and that the Choctaws had therefore no right to cede to the United States any lands east of the Tombeckbee. Instead of resorting to arms or to diplomacy, the Creeks agreed to risk their claims on the success of a game of ball. Old settlers in Clarke refer to this game as a fact well authenticated and attested by eye-witnesses. John Scarborough, who would now be about eighty-five years of age, if living, was one of those who witnessed it. The contestants in this game laid aside most of their clothing. The Creeks are described as having been slim and straight in person, the Choctaws as shorter but active as cats. It is said that the first game was played by warriors against warriors, and that the Creeks, being vanquished, were dissatisfied. Then the Choctaws offered to let their squaws play against the Creek squaws. This offer was accepted. The women played. And again the Choctaws won. The Creeks now gave up their claims. The locality assigned for this singular game, by the early settlers, is an old playground near the old site of Elam church, and near where the corner-post was finally driven that marked the boundary between Choctaw and Creek. In 1808 the line was surveyed from Hall's Lake to the Choctaw Corner. Previous to this time, in the disputed region, the Choctaws and Creeks had both hunted and fought for the game. The surveyors were on the ground. The Indians agreed to a line that should cross no water. One who has traveled in various directions across this disputed territory would suppose such a line very difficult to be traced. It is said that twenty Chiefs of each party went along with their tomahawks to blaze the trees. The whole space between the Alabama and Tombeckbee, and further north than Clarke County extends, even to the mouth of the Black Warrior, had been ceded by the Choctaws to the British, in a treaty made at Mobile, March 26, 1765. Now, for the last time, after the decisive game between the Indian squaws, this strip came into the possession of those who proposed to hold it against Creeks or any other claimants or invaders. For a few years they had been coming from Georgia, South and North Carolina, Kentucky and Tennessee, and continued to come rapidly until 1812."

INDIAN BALL GAME

A description of the ball game mentioned above is found in Ball's History of Clarke County, and runs as follows:

"It must suffice here to say, that eighty or a hundred warriors were chosen upon each side. The ground was previously prepared, in the center of which were two poles between which poles the ball must pass to count one. The players were distant from the poles about one hundred and fifty yards, each furnished with two rackets having wooden handles about three feet long, and furnished with a kind of hoop net, the netting made of strips of rawhide or some animal tendons. When the ball, which was covered with buckskin, was thrown into the air, the players rushed to catch it, and he who caught it ran and hurled it into the air, to get it near the poles. While so doing he might be tripped, seized hold of and the ball wrested from him, or any means adopted to prevent his making a successful throw. Thus the ball might pass from one to another, he who caught it and those who came near, of the opposing sides, exposed alike to the danger of being thrown to the ground, trampled upon, and severely injured, in the fearful struggle that would at once take place. When at length the ball passed the two poles the side from which it came was declared the winning side.

"From twelve, usually, to twenty times the ball must thus pass the poles, and the game would last for hours. The women in the meantime were watching with their gourds of water to refresh their favorite players. Ponies, jewels, wearing apparel, would be staked upon the issue of the game. These Indians would gamble on the strength and endurance of Indian muscle, as their civilized white brothers gamble on the speed and endurance of horseflesh. This Indian ball play, dangerous as it must have been, suited well the peculiar training of Indian warriors, and is said to have been the most exciting and interesting game imaginable, ... the admiration of all the curious and learned travelers who witnessed it."

The years of 1813 and 1814 seemed to be years of strife

and bloodshed, but there were no conflicts between the whites and Indians of Clarke after the close of the year 1813. The battle of Horse-Shoe Bend occurred in 1814 and resulted in the utter defeat of the Indians at that place. After this battle the Indians began to weaken and to realize that they were doomed. At the close of 1814 the Creek War ended, and on the 24th day of December a treaty of peace was signed between Great Britain and the United States, known as the Treaty of Ghent.

After the dispute between the Indians was settled, resulting in favor of the Choctaws, the county began to progress rapidly, and a number of towns sprang up, among them being Jackson, Suggsville, Coffeeville and Choctaw Corner. In 1815, three years after Clarke County had been established by an act of the Legislature of the Mississippi Territory, and two years before Alabama was made a territory, the town of Pine Level was launched, but in the following year the name was changed to Jackson, as will be seen from the following sketch of the old town:

JACKSON IN 1816

In 1815 a stock company was organized and styled "The Pine Level Land Company." This company purchased all of Section 8, Township 6, north, Range 2 east, except the southeast quarter. This land was laid off in lots, streets and alleyways. A sale of lots was advertised in the Georgia papers, and on the day set for the sale there were men here from Tennessee, Georgia, North Carolina, and South Carolina, and every lot was sold. Soon the woodman's ax could be heard from the peep o' day until the mantle of darkness shut out the light. The town sprang up like magic, reaching a population of about fifteen hundred, and drawing trade from a hundred miles distant. "Pine Level" was the name first given to the town. In 1816 the commissioners of the town changed the name to "Jackson" in honor of General Andrew (Old Hickory) Jackson, who was the man uppermost in the minds of the people at that time. Jackson was then nearly at the head of navigation on the Tombigbee. Boats plied the river from there to Mobile. Several boats were built and launched here to care for the heavy river traffic. Mr. Ball, speaking of the old town, says:

"Of the first actual settlement near what is now the village of Jackson, in the old French and Spanish times, no certain knowledge remains. And it is difficult now to ascertain who were the first American residents here. Evidently, about the year 1800, settlements were made on the east side of the river opposite St. Stephens and below. The little village that sprang up, at first called Republicville, and afterward Pine Level, was incorporated in November, 1816, under the name of Jackson, a name which was given, very naturally, in honor of the distinguished general. The officers of the town were five commissioners, a constable, a treasurer, an assessor, a collector, a town clerk, and 'when necessary,' a clerk of the market. The new town soon became a thriving, prosperous place. The population at length reached the number of fifteen hundred. The main thoroughfares were Carrol, Washington, Commerce, Broadway, Florida Avenue, and other smaller streets. Trade came from a distance of a hundred miles. The streets were lined with shops, in which were carried on various trades.

It was at that time a manufacturing and commercial town. Among other branches of industry there was a large tannery; there were shops for tinware, for the manufacture of saddles, of hats, of boots and shoes, and of other articles of household and family use. Before the days of steamboats twenty sail of vessels at one time sometimes lay at the landing, and after steamboats began to navigate the river they were repaired and almost rebuilt, in these enterprising and manufacturing times, by the mechanics of Jackson, A large academy with a spire and bell, was erected and used also for a church. There were French residents at Jackson in these palmy days, among them families who had in 'sunny, vine-clad France,' seen other and, to, them, better times, were the M'Tongs, Dido who was a merchant, Morio who became a shoemaker, and others whose names are lost. The names given may not be correctly written. There was one small tradesman, a bachelor, living alone and being his own housekeeper, who had a genuine Three-waters to help him in household affairs. This was a little dog, who, it is said, performed the whole duty of washing the dishes, thus saving his master from no little trouble.

"There were also as residents at that time Pennsylvania Germans and Quakers. Among the former was Sebestian Hauk, a very ingenious man. He had a tame black bear trained to do the churning of the family, instead of what some of his countrymen elsewhere have employed a New foundland dog. How well the bear liked the occupation and whether he feasted on the buttermilk tradition has not said. John Hauk, a relative of Sebastian, was an ingenious draughtsman. Machinery for a mill, according to his design, was cast at Philadelphia and brought to Jackson and set up. And it worked well."

Like the grass, the old town sprang up in the morning and was cut down in the evening. The old town flourished for a while and then went down. Other trade centers opened up, navigation forged higher up the river, and the citizens of Jackson moved to other points, some of them pulling their houses down, taking the materials with them, and erecting houses at other places.

HOME OF DR. DAVID TAYLOR

On the opposite page will be seen a picture of the Taylor home, erected in 1816, and in which Walter Taylor, son of David Taylor, was born in 1817. This house is still standing and is perfectly sound. It is now owned by E. S. Fleming, and is occupied by G. W. Fleming and family.

The following Agreements, Resolutions, etc., are taken from the old Minute Book of the Commissioners of the town of Pine Level, alias Jackson:

Articles of an agreement made and entered into between the undersigned, subscribers for the Pine Level Purchase, witnesseth, that the same shall be conducted, planned & governed in the manner hereinafter stipulated, to wit.

Art. 1st. The five following persons is Perregrin F. Bayard, Benjamin I. Bedell, David White, David Taylor & Ruben Saffold, are hereby constituted, appointed and recognized as a board of commissioners whose duty it shall be to cause the said purchase to be made; and in all things

HOME OF DR. DAVID TAYLOR

appertaining to the same, to govern themselves according to the instructions contained in these articles.—

2nd. The aforesaid commissioners shall convene in the Pine Level, at such time & place as a majority of them may appoint five days previous notice thereof being given, to the rest of the commissioners, requesting their attendance, a majority of the whole number shall be necessary to constitute a Quorum to do business a majority of the quorum to any determination of the board.—

3rd. The said commissioners when so organized shall have power to appoint a Secretary and Treasurer removable from office at their pleasure, for neglect of duty breach of confidence or any other cause which a majority of the whole number may deem sufficient, as also one of their own body, and fill the vacancy occasioned thereby; or by death, resignation of removal from the county; the said Secretary and Treasurer when so appointed, to govern themselves agreeably to the stipulations contained in these.

4th. At the time the said Secretary and Treasurer may be appointed, each of them shall enter into bond with good and sufficient security, to be approved of by the said commissioners in the penal sum of one thousand dollars payable to the commissioners in the name and style of "The Commissioners of the Pine Level Company" Conditioned truly and faithfully to perform their duty in all things appertaining to the Pine Level Purchase, according to the true intent & meaning of the articles agreed on; and signed by the said company for that purpose, and agreeably to the directions of the said commissioners not repugnant to any thing contained in the aforesaid articles; and shall the said bonds or either of them be forfeited the same shall be put in suit by the commissioners and the amount recovered thereby applied toward the indemnification of the subscribers respectively, in proportion to the interest each, at the time of the breach as aforesaid.

5th. The purchase for which these articles are agreed on, shall consist of two quarter sections most eligible or convenient for a town and the Stringers Ferry fraction & be bid off by the said Secretary, under the directions of the Commissioners and paid for at the times here in after mentioned, with money to be drawn from the treasurer, out of a fund to be created in his hands by the subscribers to these articles.

6th. Each subscriber shall have an interest in said purchase proportioned to the number of shares respectively subscribed for; provided that no one person shall be at liberty to subscribe for more than ten shares, and the number in the whole purchase shall not exceed Two hundred shares.—

7th. Where the a-fore-said purchase shall be made agreeably to the foregoing Articles, th epart most eligible & convenient, shall be laid out according to the most approved plan of a Town, and the ballance surveyed into lots under the direction of the Commissioners and by some fit and proper person employed by them for that purpose. In laying out the plan of the Town as a-fore-said, regards only shall be had to the situation of the ground and when ever it may so happen that houses or other improvements shall obstruct the street or lot lines or shall be on lots which may be purchased by other persons than the proprietors, at the Company sale to be made of lots as herein after provided in that case the proprietors of said improvements shall have thirty days to remove the same in after being notified of a resolution of the board of commissioners, that the same is necessary to be done, and in case of failure to remove the same within the limited time such improvements shall be forfieted by the owners, and such as obstruct the streets on said lines shall be at the disposal of the commissioners for the use of the company and such as remain the limited time for removal on lots purchased by others shall rest in the purchasers respectively.

8th. In order to create a fund for the purchase a-foresaid each subscriber shall at the time of subscribing pay into the hands of the Treasurer two dollars for each share so by him subscribed; within twenty days after the purchase may be made as a-foresaid each subscriber shall pay in the same manner his proportion of the first in statement together with office fees &c. having regard to the interest of each, which amount shall appear by a statement signed by the secretary containing the calculation, and deposited by him with the Treasurer for the information of all concerned, free to their inspection at all times. A receipt particularly specifying the amount paid, time when and number of shares for which the payment are made, shall be given by the Treasurer to the persons respectively paying the same and an entry shall be made by the Treasurer in a book to be kept by him for that purpose, of each subscribers interest in the aforesaid purchase, which entry shall be subject to the order and inspection of the commissioners at all times.

9th. The secritaty shall for the purpose of the purchase a-fore-said draw from the Treasurer at all times, any monies in the Treasury by virtue of a resolution of the board of commissioners to that effect, first had and obtained and giving a receipt for the same, specifying the amount and for what purpose, the same is drawn.

10th. If it shall so happen tthat any subscriber shall fail to make punctual payments according to the provisions in the foregoing articles—or such as may be made in pursuance of the stipulations contained in the following this and in that case, every such subscriber shall forfiet his interest in the purchase a-fore-said, together with the money he may have advanced towards the same, and the shares so forfieted to the company, shall be liable to be entered by the whole number, so many of the other subscribers as may choose to except in equal proportions according to their respective interests in the purchase, on such notice as may be deemed necessary and published by the board of commissioners, requiring all who choose to appear and signify their disposition except and interest, in the forfieture as a-fore-said.

11th. At the time when the lands directed by these articles to be purchased shall be exposed to sale, it shall be the duty of the Secritary to bid the amount for the same to which he may be limited by a resolution to be passed by the board of commissioners for his instructions therein, before the time of the a-fore-said sale — The deposite of one twentieth part together with the office fees and other expenses, shall be paid down at the time of purchase, by the secretary the ballance of the first installment, within the time allowed by law for making the first payment, and as soon after the twenty days allowed for that purpose, as there shall be sufficient funds raised in manner aforesaid for its completion.

12th. When the purchase shall be made agreeably to

the intentions of these articles & the plan of the Town laid out, and discribed, and all the lots surveyed in the manner herein directed payment in full shall be made for the whole purchase or any divisionable part there of as soon as practicable on the principals contained in the articles, and at such time, or times and under such rules and regulations as the board of commissioners may establish, immediately after the first payment shall be completed and patents received by-order the Secretary for the a-fore-said lands there the same shall be exposed to public sale by the secritary under the directions of the commissioners, and such rules & regulations as the said board may have previously established, for the government of the same. For the lots so sold at the company sale the secritary shall make to the purchaser respective by their heirs or assigners absolute and complete titles, under a general warranty in facsimple.—

13th. The Secritary shall keep a registry containing particular entries of all monies received and paid out by him in his official capacity the amount at which he may have bid off the lands directed by these articles to be purchased & the amount of payments made from time progressively, and of all other duties assigned him by these articles, and rresolution of the board of commissioners, which registry shall at all times be subject to the order & inspection of the commissioners, The secritary & treasurer, shall take receipts and keep particlar accounts of all monies which may pass from one to the other, and of all other transactions between them.

14th. The board of Commissioners shall and may prescribe such further regulations in the manner of conducting the aforesaid purchase, in the manner of keeping books &

accounts between the Treasurer & secritary and for the government of their own body as to them may appear necessary & proper, in order fully to carry into effect the provisions of these articles.

15th. The proceeds of the lots whenever sold at the company sale, in the manner directed in the preceding articles, shall be paid in to the Treasurer there to remain a common fund subject to a fair and equitable distribution among all the subscribers in proportion to the number of shares which may be held by each respectively at the time of the distribution under the direction of the board of Commissioners.

```
Subscribers Names.    No. of shares)/(Subscribers names   No. of shares
Rubin Saffold            (   do     10)/( 1--to 18 Deld. W. Goodrich.
Nathaniel T. Goodrich.   (Green     18)/(19 to 24  do.   W. Bodgood.
William Walton,          (   do      6)/(25 to 34  do    Joel E. Cannon
Benjamin I. Biddell,     (   do     10)/(25 to 48 ─────────────────────
Josuah Carney            (   do     14)/(49 to 51 deld T. Barnby
David White              (   do      3)/(52 to 61 deld him.
                         (          )/(

Joel E. Cannon    S. given(   2  ) 62 to  63
Percy T. Bayard       do  (   5  ) 64 to  68
William A. Robison    do  (   2  ) 69 to  70
Nathan Nabours        do  (   1  )  "  to  71 Deld Wm N. Thompson
David Taylor          do  (  10  ) 72 to  81 delvd from
Daniel Campbell       do  (  27  ) 82 to 108 Delivd him
Neal Smith            do  (  20  )109 to 128 Delvd him
Thomas I. Strong      do  (  10  )129 to 138
Thomas Langham        do  (   5  )139 to 143 delivered him
Robert Caller         do  (   1  )    to 144 delivered Creagh
Doct N. Smith         do  (   1  )    to 145     "      him
James P. Price        do  (   1  )    to 146
Able Farrer           do  (  10  )147 to 156 Delivd him
Henry Potts           do  (   5  )157 to 161 delivd him
George Buchanand      do  (   5  )162 to 166
Walter Beale          do  (   3  )167 to 169 delivered him
John G. Creagh        do  (   4  )170 to 173
Benjamin Clemints     do  (   1  ) "  to 174     "       "
Henry Howell          do  (   2  )175 to 176     "       "
```

Henry Houpt	do (12)	177 to 188	
Neal Smith	do (2)	189 to 190	delivered him
Joel E. Cannon	do)(__22__)	__ to 192	del Howel
Henry Howel	do)( )		
Doctr Neal Smith	do (1)	to 191	Delivered him
	( )		
William Lechlan	)( )		
assigned to Neal Smith	)(___6___)	193 to 198	del N. Smith
	( )		
William Wilson	(1)		deld him
Rubin Trayman	(1)		200 deld, him
	((( )		

Wilson Esqr
Decr 25.

(pp. 15-16)

Jackson (alias Pine Level) 31st, Jul816

A Board consisting of the whole number of commissioners, to wit. P. F. Bayard Benjamin I. Bedell David White, D. Taylor and R. Saffold having met for the purpose of making further regulations for the government of the Town purchased by the Pine Level company, have ordained & established, the following additional articles To wit.

1st, Resolved that the plan to which the names of the whole number of commissioners were this day subscribed to and the same is hereby adopted that the town thus planed, and heretofore called Pine Level Shall hereafter be called and known by the name of Jackson, and that the Avenue, Broadway, and several streets be always known and called by the names assigned to each of them respectively in the plan adopted as above mentioned.

2nd, Resolved that in all cases where there are one or more persons being subscribers situated on the same lot as described in the Plan adopted, he she or they shall be entitled to the peaceable enjoyment of the same until other wise ordered by the commissioners and that no other person shall obtrude on any lot or lots thus improved and occupied provided that nothing herein contained shall be so construed to prohibit any subscriber belonging to this company from building or making improvements on any naked lot subject to the future order and regulation of the commissioners.—

....Com.

At a meeting of the undersigned commissioners in the Town of Jackson on the 17th, Feby. 1816.

Resolved that the street leading through this Town being a common highway cannot in our opinion be varied in its course, or in any manner obstruded by the citizens of the place. That the commissioners never conceived they had the power nor intending to grant such permissions untill other streets were opened equally suitable to the commerce of the public, and for the time being all such acts are in violation of the laws of the Territory and regulations of the commissioners.

      P. F. Bayard
      David White
      B. J. Bedell Com.
      R. Saffold

(Copied from pages 41, 42 and 43)
Milidgeville, Georgia 14th, of March, 1816.
Dear Sir:—

By the last mail we forwarded you a paper containing the address of the commissioners of the Town of

Jackson. We have exhibited for inspection the plan sent and those who have seen the plan are very much pleased with the elegant style in which it is laid off and if nothing prevents I calculate you will have a number of Georgians to visit your sale. After taking a full examination of the plan, and considering the many advantages that does, and will be derived from the settlement of your part of the country, we have concluded if a fair opning for a Printing establishment would offer, we would move our office to your Town, and indevor to conduct a Republican paper of this, we would be glad to get your advice, and beg that you would inform us of the population of the adjacent county: your early attention to this will confer a favor on. De Sir. your most

      Obb Humbl servents,
         Jones & Hightowr

A. Farrar Esqu.
Town of Jackson.

      Milidgeville 1st of May 1816

Dr. Sir Yours respecting the population of your parts of the country and the views you have of a printing establishment has been duly recieved. As to a final decision on the establishment of a press in your Town, we cannot yet make up since the reciet of your very friendley letter, we have sold our interest in the establishment we had in this place and are trying to bring our business to a final close here before we can finally make up our minds. In order to settle up our business, we are in want of all the

Cash we can possibly get. We have threrfore enclosed you a bill for printing the address you sent which amount, we will thank you to forward as early as possible

    Respectfully yours & c.

        Jones and Hightower,

The commissioners of the Town of Jackson.
  1816   to Jones & Hightower Dr.

March 13 to publishing addresses to the
    Publick and sale of lots
    2 Towns 10 squares $13.00

   (Copied from pp. 43-44-45)

       Jackson 15th, of May 1816

Gentm. Commissioners secretary and Treasurer of Jackson. Permit me to congratulate on the flatering sales of your lots on Jackson. I herein close you letters on business which was received during the time I had the honor of serving you as Secretary. You will see the necessity of attending to and complying with the requisition of the letters. I. have done considerable business for you and been at some expense previous to our sales, and as ever have served you faithfully. If in your wisdom, and generosity you take into, consideration, and pass a resolution complimenting me with the lot which I purchased, price $80 It will not pass unnoticed, and be greatfully reicved by Gentlemen. Your Obt St.

         Able Farrar.

Mississippi Territory)
Clark County   )

Know all men by these presence that we Henry Potts, Arthur Foster, and Robert Callier all of the county and Territory aforesaid acknowledge our selves held and firmley bound unto Perigrine F. Bayard, Benjamin J. Bedell, David White, David Taylor and Reubin Saffold commissioners of the Pine Level company and their successors in office, for the use of the said company, in the penal sum of two thousand dollars, for which payment well and truly to be done and made, we bind ourselves and our hiers unto the said commissioners in manner aforesaid, firmley by these presence. Singned with our hands and caled with our seals this 14 day of October 1815. The conditions of the above bond is such that if the above bound Henrey Potts who is appointed Treasurer of the Pine Level company, by the commissioners there of shall truly and faithfully perform his duty as Treasurer as aforesaid, in all things appertaining to the Pine Level purchase according to the true intent and meaning of the articles, agreed on and signed by the said company for that purpose and agreeable to the directions of the said commissioners not repugnant to anything contained in the aforesaid articles, then the above bond to be null and void. Otherwise to remain in full force and virtue, and be recoverable in any cost of competent jurisdiction according to its term and effect. In presence of
    Neal Smith.

Henry Potts	(Seal)
Arthur Foster	(Seal)
Robert Callier	(Seal)

(Pages 46-47)

No.	Purchasers name.	Sum	Paid	Discount.
1	Peregrine F. Bayard	1.12	3.25	50.00
2.	Peregrin F. Bayard	101	....	....
3.	Edward Smith	104	2600	....
4.	Henry Potts	162	....	40.25
5.	Benjamin J. Bedell	150	....	37.50
6.	Daniel Campbell	99	....	24.75
7.	Benjamin J. Bedell	100.25	....	25.
8	J. Hearne	100	94	....
9	Walton and Bidgood	75	56.26	18.75
10.	Joseph Warnuch	71	....	17.75
11.	J. H. Harwell	75	18.75	....
12.	J. Hearne	81	76.14	....
13.	Reubin Saffold	95	....	23.75
14	Reubin Saffold	58	....	14.50
15	Reubin Saffold	52	....	13.00
16	Daniel Campbell	1.50	....	37.50
17.	Jacob Forguson	210	....	52.25
18	N. Branson	69	....	17.25
19	J. Crockess P. F. Bryand & Co.	80	20.00	....
20	L. Wood	95	89.30	....
21	A. & M. Magilvery	95	89.30	....
			47299	
22	N. Branson	61	....	15.25
23	Ishamael P. Harwell	75	....	18.75
24	I. Hearne	90	84.70	....
25	N. Branson	81	....	20.25

26	Reubin Sacold 62	....	15.50
27	Potter and Bidgood 81	....	20.25
28	Joseph Thompson 81	20.25	....
29	Evingham 112	28.00	....
30	John Thomas 91	84.54	....
31	John G. Creagh 101	....	....
32	John G. Creagh 112	....	....
48	John Long 151	....	37.75
68	J. Hearne 100	94	....
69	William Robinson 162	10	30.50
70	J. McGoffin		
71	Thomas Langham 206.50	....	51.62
79	J. P. Price 65		16.25
81	Benjamin Clements 80	100	19.00
82	J. Ranaldson 76	71.44	....
83	A. McAlpin 90	....	22.50
84	H. Hibert 200	50.00	....
85	John G. Creagh 200		

444.93

(pp. 48-49)

	Purchasers Names	Sum	Paid	Discount.
86	John G. Creagh 90			
87	William Wilson 157			
88	Walter Chiles 100	25.00		
89	" " 20	....	5.00
94	Thomas Brumby 100	....	
95	Able Farrar 80	....	20.00
96	E. Ethridge 83	20.75	

97	Benjamin J. Bedell	130.25	....	32.50
98	Reubin Saffold	50.00	....	12.50
99	Pearson and Triplet	13.00	3.25	....
103	Walton and Bidgood	144	4.00	
104	Benjamin J. Bedell	200		
105	" " "	190		
106	Josiah Carney	112	....	28
107	Josiah Carney	205	....	28
108	Daniel Campbell	213	....	53.25
109	Charles Ivy	79	....	19.75
110	William Bass	58		
111	William Cochran	58	14.50	
116	J. P. Price	55		
			42.10	
119	Walter Chiles	25	625	
122	Francis Collier	141	....	35.25
124	David White	170	1250	30.00
123	Eddin and Nicholson	150	37.50	
125	Barney Cahall	101	25.25	
126	Walter Beall	114	....	28.50
127	Thomas Langham	114		28.50
128	Francis Collier	131		32.75
129	L. Wood	101	952	
130	L. Wood	80	75.20	
138	David Taylor	205		51.25
139	Walton and Bidgood	75		18.75
140	Joel E. Cannon	102		25.50
141	Joel E. Cannon	60		15.00
142	Thomas Brumley	60	15.00	

143	George Buchanan 120		30.00
144	Thomas Brumley 103		
145	David Taylor 60		15.00
146	Josiah Carney 205		51.25
147	H. Howill 104	1.00	25.00
148	Josiah Carney 150	28.00	9.50
149	Walton and Bidgood 160		40.00
150	Josiah Carney 153	38.25	

333.97

(pp. 50-51)

At a meeting of the Board of commissioners in the Town of Jackson on the 24th of August 1816.

Resolved, that the time for removing houses and other improvements from the streets & alleys in the plan of the Town of Jackson, be and the same is hereby extended thirty days longer than the time heretofore limited by a resolution of the Board of commissioners for that purpose and that on Monday the thirtieth day of September next all such improviments shall become forfieted to the use of the company and sold by the secretary in the manner directed by the resolution of the Board of Commissioners dated 20th, July 1816 unless sooner removed.

And be it further resolved that where it so happens that such improvements remain on lots belonging to other persons than the proprietors of the improvements the same may by concent of the two parties interested remain there on until thirty days after requested to remove the same by the owner or owners of the lots respectively and no longer anything in any former resolution to the contrary notwithstanding.

And be it further resolved that the Secretary enter the foregoing Resolutions of record and advertise the same immediately in three places in the Town of Jackson.

Present.

    Reubin Saffold
    David Taylor Commissioners.
    Neal Smith.

The promoters of the old town of Jackson evidently had visions of a great city here on the beautiful plateau overlooking the Tombigbee. An examination of the original plat of the town shows that they planned for a large city. It shows that the commissioners set apart quite a number of lots for public use. There was a large public square, lot for a market place, three church lots, a school lot and a large parcel of ground for a cemetery. A school building was erected, but no other public buildings were erected, as the old town soon began to wane. All of the old settlers departed this life many years ago. None of the promoters of the old town are represented here now, except two. David Taylor has three granddaughters residing here, and Josiah Carney has a great-grandson and a great-granddaughter.

JACKSON FERRY

On the opposite of this page will be seen the Southern Railroad bridge, and just north of it is the Jackson ferry, where Generals Jackson and Claiborne, with their armies,

JACKSON FERRY

crossed the Tombigbee river in the early part of the nineteenth century. This ferry has been in constant use since the latter part of the eighteenth century.

"GENERAL PEACE"

Ball says:

"General peace now prevailing, the settlers between the rivers had opportunity to promote more rapidly the growth of their settlements and to build up the various forms and institutions of their civilization.

"St. Stephens at this time was their principal town. The courts of Washington County were held in the town of Rodney, at the close of the war, William Jordan having built a court-house for the county, but in 1815 the courts were ordered to be held at the house of Robert Caller until new commissioners arranged new public buildings. It was also ordered that the courts of Clarke be held at the house of John Laundrum, Joseph Phillips, Samuel Hill, Moses Larrele, William Easeley, and Warham Easeley being appointed commissioners to locate the public buildings. It seems that these commissioners did not make rapid progress, for in 1819 it was ordered that the courts be held at the house of William Coate, near Clarkesville.

"Educational interests were not neglected.

"In December of 1814* Lewis Sewall, James Caller, George S. Gaines, Joseph Phillips, Thomas Malone, Joseph Carson, Thomas B. Creagh, Benjamin S. Smoot, Reuben Saffold, Benjamin J. Biddill, and John Dean, were constituted a body corporate, as trustees of the Washington

---
*Turner's Digest, p. 55.

Academy, to establish such academy in Washington or in Clarke County. The academy was finally located at St. Stephens. It was quite flourishing for several years. Here the young ladies of those two counties received their first academic education.

"In 1817 Mississippi Territory was divided, the western part being admitted into the Union as the State of Mississippi, and the eastern being organized into a territorial government March 3d, 1817, and called

ALABAMA TERRITORY.

"Of this territory, St. Stephens, as the center of the oldest settled portion, became the seat of government.

"In 1818 an act was passed to establish the Tombeckbee Bank in the town of St. Stephens.

"Also in the same year, February 10th, an act was passed to incorporate the St. Stephens Steamboat Company. Directors: James Pickens, B. S. Smoot, Silas Dinsmore, David Files, Henry Bright and D. P. Ripley.

"It had been ascertained that there were salt springs near the Tombigbee river in Clarke County, and in 1819 an act was passed to lease these springs.

"The men who engaged at this time in the manufacture of salt were probably Ball and Bayard. They do not seem to have continued it many years.

"Thus improvements were going forward, but as yet mills and gins and workshops were few in number and distant from each other. Some of the settlers had brought with them whip-saws. By means of one of these saws the lumber was obtained for erecting the White-House. This was built by General J. B. Chambers about the year 1818. It was about three miles north-east from Grove Hill, on the Peach Tree Road. It was two and a half stories high, and in size about twenty-four feet by fifty. Not only was the lumber all sawed by hand, but the nails, it is said, were all made by a blacksmith. This house has been the residence of several families, retaining its name after it lost its color and its first imposing appearance. It is still standing, but is no longer white, and no longer inhabited. It will soon be a ruin and be removed.

"One of the first frame houses was built by Eskridge in 1815. The stone chimneys of this house still remain.

"At the close of the war of 1812, and as late as 1817, there were, comparatively, few families between the rivers. The larger settlements were on Bassett's Creek, around Magoffin's Store, south of Suggsville, near Pine Level, on Jacksons Creek, and at West Bend and Coffeeville. James Magoffin, who had settled at St. Stephens in 1809, had a store on what is now the Allen place in 1817. In 1819, according to the acts of Alabama, there were in Clarke six places for voting: Campbells, Coffeeville, Magoffin's Store, Jackson, Suggsville, and William Coate's. The last was made the returning precinct, as there the courts were held.

"As early as 1812, so near as can be now known, Greenlee had a store, the first store, at the mouth of Cedar Creek.

"Near Suggsville John Slater erected one of the first grist-mills, probably in the same year. And in 1813 Jonathan Emmons started the first cotton gin in the vicinity, on Smith's Creek, two miles south of Suggsville. Robert G. Hayden had one of the first tanneries. He also started a small shoe factory about three miles south of Suggsville.

The probable date of this new enterprise is 1815. Hayden's tanner was a colored man named Solomon. Robert Caller had a mill and a water gin, and an iron screw for packing cotton by hand or horse-power, on what became afterward the Barnes place, as early as 1816.

"To the year 1816 may be assigned Walker's mill on Bassett's Creek, five miles east from Jackson, and six west of Hickory Hall, near the Dale Ferry and Jackson road; also Jackson's mill, some six miles south from Suggsville on a little stream. To the same period belongs The Mud Tavern. This house of entertainment was some seven miles from Suggsville between Dale's Ferry and St. Stephens. The name is said to have been given, not from any peculiarity of the building, but from the fact that some mud was found in a bale of cotton sent off from this primitive hotel. The first goods were taken to Claiborne in January, 1817. The earliest towns and villages in Washington County west of the river have been named. The town of Jackson was incorporated in 1816, Coffeeville, by legislative act, was incorporated in 1819, and Claiborne in 1820. These three places were named in honor of three of the generals in the Creek War, but there is no evidence that Jackson was ever at the place which bears his name, or that Coffee ever camped at Coffeeville.

"The question whether General Jackson was ever in Clarke County will by and by receive due notice.

"Suggsville was a trading point for the neighborhood, containing one store in 1815. Town lots were laid out and sold in 1819. Families were now beginning to locate on some of the streams in the northern part of the county, a few having settled along Bashi and Tallahatta before the

Creek War. Many of the older families of Clarke date their residence from the year 1818. Millwrights and some carpenters now came, physicians and ministers came, civil, social, educational and religious institutions were established, and the foundations in the newly organized territory were rapidly laid, for a large, prosperous and vigorous state. At this time a large part of the county was covered with a dense growth of canes. Along the bridle pathway from Claiborne to Suggsville in 1808 the saddle-bags of the travellers had worn the canes on each side of the trail, so narrow was the track, so dense the cane. This cane was as high on each side of the trail as a man on horseback could reach with an umbrella. Pasturage was excellent, and for many years the county was a great stock region. McGrew in 1818 had a drove of about one thousand head of cattle. In the dense cane deer and bears were abundant, and also wolves, yellow and black, and catamounts or panthers. Game of various kinds abounded, droves of hogs and flocks of sheep were brought from Kentucky and the Carolinas, cotton, corn and sweet potatoes were cultivated, and food was abundant.

"St. Stephens was a cotton market. "Supplies" could be obtained there, although many sent to Pensacola, to Mobile, and also to New Orleans. Barges from forty to fifty feet in length, were running on the rivers, propelled by long poles furnished at one end with a spike and at the other with a hook. Such was the beginning of transportation facilities in the heart of the cotton-growing belt, when the second decade of the nineteenth century was about to close.

"The census gives for Clarke County, mentioned first

in 1820, three thousand seven hundred and seventy-eight white inhabitants.

"In 1810 Washington and Baldwin in the south, and Madison in the north, were the three counties in what soon became Alabama.

"When the Alabama Territory was organized in 1817 there were seven counties — Mobile, Baldwin, Washington, Clarke, and Madison, Limestone, and Lauderdale. When the first territorial legislature met in January, 1818, with one senator and about a dozen representatives, eleven new counties were established. The governor recommended the advancement of education, the construction of roads and bridges, and the establishment of ferries.

"St. Stephens did not long continue to be the Alabama capital. The second session of the territorial legislature met there in the fall of 1818. New counties were formed. The St. Stephens Bank was authorized to increase its capital stock by selling shares at auction. Ten per cent of the profits was to go to the stockholders, and the excess, if any arose, was to be appropriated to the St. Stephens Academy.

"The next session was appointed to be held at Huntsville, Governor Bibb being empowered to lay out a seat of government and erect a temporary capitol at the mouth of the Cahawba.

"One 'Seminole War' had just ended, and in the words of Pickett, 'The flood-gates of Virginia, the two Carolinas, Tennessee, Kentucky and Georgia were now hoisted, and mighty streams of emigration poured through them, spreading over the whole territory of Alabama. The axe resounded from side to side, and from corner to corner. The stately and magnificent forest fell. Log cabins sprang, as if by magic, into sight. Never, before or since, has a country been so rapidly peopled.'

"In 1819 a convention assembled at Huntsville to form a state constitution, twenty-two counties were now represented, and soon Alabama was a state."

COFFEEVILLE

The town of Coffeeville was incorporated in 1819, and was named in honor of General Coffee, who was with General Jackson at the battle of Horse-Shoe Bend in 1814, and other places. Jackson was named in honor of General Jackson previously, else Coffeyville might have been named in honor of him.

"Coffeeville is situated on the east bank of the Tombigbee river, and has a fairly good farming country surrounding it. It has several stores, two churches and a school building. There was, perhaps, more business done there fifty years ago than there is now. Its principal merchant was Mr. Foscue, father of the late Judge Clayton Foscue. Among the old settlers there were Lankfords, the Scruggs, the Foscues, the Yorks, the Dawsons, and many others whose names we do not recall just now. In the good old days of steamboating on the Tombigbee, Coffeeville was quite a shipping point.

SUGGSVILLE

Suggsville is one of the oldest towns in the county. It is more than 100 years old. It was once a great educational center. Its citizens were wealthy and progressive and believed in education, but at the close of the Civil War and the freeing of the negroes, the old town began to wane. We are indebted to Mrs. Emma Rivers Krouse for the following information concerning the town:

"There are about six buildings here that are between seventy-five and one hundred years old. Among them is the Methodist parsonage, the Pritchett home, now owned and occupied by Mr. George Whisenhunt and family; the home Mr. George Clothier built, owned and occupied by Miss Mattie Deas; the Cogburn home, where Mr. Jere Cleveland and family now live. All these have changed owners many times, but my own home, built by my father, Dr. T. B. Rivers, has never changed owners — at least, has been occupied by some member of the family — for eighty-three years this month, and owned by them. Neither of the academies is standing in its original form. One (the male) academy was torn down, moved to another site, and made into a dwelling. The female academy was moved and made into a one-story public school building. Miss Bessie Cleveland is teacher this present session. There are five pupils in the high school at Grove Hill from this place, thirteen in this school.

"Dr. B. S. Barnes was born August 20th, 1838, and died March 9th, 1911. Colonel John W. Portis was born September 9th, 1818, and died April 7th, 1902. Mr. G. W. (Gerard Walthall) Creagh, who lives here, is a son of the G. W. Creagh who figured in the famous battle of Burnt Corn. He is in his eightieth year, and has one brother, a few years older, who lives in Selma, the only remaining children. Both served four years in the Civil War."

ALABAMA A STATE

Ball says:

"Alabama was now a state, admitted into the Union December 14, 1819. No longer did Clarke County, with its surroundings, the original Washington County, contain the sole American residents of those mighty forests and large watercourses. Mobile on the south was now at length American, and along the beautiful Alabama, where DeSoto had found waving cornfields and populous Indian villages, and far up along the Coosa and Tallapoosa, and up the winding Tombeckbee, the stream of the Box-Maker, and along the banks of the Warrior, enterprising American citizens had pitched their tents, erected their cabins, located their homes. But Clarke County, although no longer environed by Indians and Spaniards, is yet first in its historic associations, and to it we may soon give a less divided interest.

"The whole state now contained over eighty-five thousand white and over forty-two thousand colored inhabitants. Of these, in Clarke and the surrounding region were about one-fifth, or sixteen thousand, of the white inhabitants.

"The first chartered academy of the state was at St. Stephens, the charter having been granted in 1811, although the academy was not fully organized until 1814.

"The first steamboat company was also organized at St. Stephens in 1818. But as late as 1820 nearly all the river transportation was on barges and flatboats.

"Clarke County extended eastward only to the Choctaw line; but by act of the Alabama legislature, November 28,

1821, the eastern part of Suggsville was transferred from Monroe to Clarke. Other additions were made at three different times until the limits of the county became what they are now."

POPULATION OF CLARKE

In 1820 Clarke County had a population of about four thousand whites and two thousand negroes. Ball further says that in 1820 there were "some four hundred American families now south of latitude thirty-two degrees, and between the Tombigbee and Alabama rivers. Although at this time that portion lying east of the watershed was called Monroe, as it afterward became a part of Clarke, the inhabitants there may frequently be found mentioned in these chapters as early settlers of Clarke. Among these were Greenlee, who had the store on Cedar Creek; J. King, who married a daughter of General Joseph Chambers; Bronson Barlow, the large Wilson family, C. Worley, Thomas McConnel, Charles Stokes, and Noah Agee, having plantations on or near the river between Gosport and Gainestown. There were also, south of Suggsville, the families of John French, of H. Finch, of W. Ezell; in Suggsville the Portis and Rivers families; and, in the neighborhood, the families of Hayden, Slater, Fisher, Emmons, Creagh, Barnes and others, whose names will appear somewhere in these memorials. There were also in the 'forks' three families of much earlier date, the Holder family, natives of the territory, the Bates family, Joseph Bates, it is said, having been born in Washington County about a hundred years ago, and the Duncan family. Benjamin Duncan, who married a

Holder, was considered to be a man of unusual common-sense.

"No one can reasonably expect to find here the names of even the four hundred families of 1820. Many of them, and of those who became residents in later years, may be woven into the narrative as it proceeds.

"Suggsville seems to have been at this period the most advanced town in the county in respect to cultivated and wealthy families, educational and religious interests, and general enterprise.

"Early physicians here were Dr. Alexander Tucker and Dr. Huston. Also Dr. Whyte, a son of Judge Whyte, who was shot in the town in consequence of a game of cards, a game which he was induced, with great reluctance on his part, to play.

"Dr. Stewart probably succeeded Dr. Tucker. He commenced raising the castor-oil bean and manufacturing oil. He had ten acres in this bean, probably, in the year 1825.

"Leaving for a time the growing interests, the tannery and shoe-factory, the gins and mills, the oil factory and the cotton plantations, the pleasant families, the increasing wealth, comfort, and refinement, centered around Fort Madison, we may now glance along the boundary line between Marengo and Clarke.

"It is somewhat singular that so late as 1877 few if any of the citizens of Clarke knew exactly their northern boundary. Even the officials of the two counties, the tax assessors, were uncertain which border-families belonged to the jurisdiction of Marengo and which belonged to the jurisdiction of Clarke, and some families, it was said, because of this uncertainty, paid tax in neither county. This uncertainty must have arisen from the nature of the boundary line. Before the United States survey, in 1805, as elsewhere stated, the Choctaw Indians sold to the United States lands bounded by the Tombigbee and Alabama watershed, and an east and west line running from a post, in a mound, called in this history the Choctaw corner, westward to the Fulluctabuna Old Fields on the Tombeckbee. This boundary line does not seem to have fallen upon a section line in the United States land survey; along it many fractions exist, and no record has yet come to light of a regular survey of that east and west line.

"The watershed line between Monroe and Clarke was retraced by a surveyor, John Jones, who said it was about as easy to follow that line as it would be to follow the trail of a dog with a tin-pan tied to his tail.

"The proper Choctaw corner-post, according to the best maps, should be near the range line between ranges two and three east, in township twelve, and near the southeast corner of section twenty-four. This location gives to Clarke County two rows of sections in the ranges of township twelve. The assessor of Marengo County for 1877 allows to Clarke County two and two-thirds rows of sections across the south part of township twelve, range two east.

Leaving this singularly uncertain line we may now look for the inhabitants.

"The northern part of Clarke and the south of Marengo, the strip of country lying between the settlements of 'the fork' proper, and the French colony near Demopolis, remained, to quite an extent, unoccupied for some years after the Creek War ended. The bottom lands of Bashi and Horse Creek were covered with heavy cane-brake as late as 1824. Some of this cane was so large that one joint, it is said, would hold a pint, and that travellers used it for carrying water.

"Among the early residents near Bashi were John Loftin and William Williams; settling in 1819.

"The first mill on Bashi was built by Nathan Lipscombe a short distance below the Choctaw corner. Two years afterward a saw-mill was erected on the same creek. Before the erection of this mill puncheons were used for floors, or plank cut by a whip-saw. The chimneys were made of sticks and clay, the builders using lime obtained from the cave shells and from the rocks. Large quantities of shells were in these earlier years of the Lime Hills' settlement taken from the caves and made into lime for building purposes. The rock was not suitable for the erection of chimneys like that in the central parts of the county. The saw-mill just mentioned was started by Joseph Hearn, who sold it afterward to Barney Pope. The first cotton gin in the north of the county, so far as tradition asserts, was built by W. Williams for John Loftin in 1825. The same year Archibald and M. Campbell established the first store in the north of Clarke. Dr. Earle, the first physician here, located on the Tombigbee, is assigned to the year 1824. He did not confine his attention to his profession, but brought from Georgia large droves of cattle that they might enjoy the luxuriant pasturage and also increase his resources. He seems to have been a trader, and was state senator in 1827. The first school in this Bashi region, according to tradition, was taught by Lewis Spinks, in 1829. The chestnut trees were abundant then over these lime hills, furnishing, in the autumn months, much pleasure for the children, as they and the squirrels would gather the brown nuts. These trees very generally died out about 1836.

"In 1824 settlers had begun to come more rapidly into this part of the county. Among others the following family names belong to this period of immigration: Anderson, Merriweather, White, Dewitt, Crenshaw, Knight and Paine. The Noble family and others on Satilpa were earlier settlers.

"There were now in the county three principal neighborhoods, the upper, the central, the lower; called the Loftin, Magoffin and Fort Madison settlements.

"The villages of Coffeeville, Jackson, Clarksville and Suggsville were also in existence. In these days persons at a distance were neighbors. Many would go ten miles to help their neighbors roll logs.

"At this time bears were abundant, and large gray and black wolves, in the cane-brakes. It was dangerous to be exposed, and dangerous to be lost. The old settler relate that a colored woman was lost in the dense woods and could not be found. She chanced to escape the bears in her wanderings, and, at last, almost famished, reached in the forest a lone settler's cabin. Here she was cared for, and reached her home after an absence of three weeks.

"An amusing story is told by some, who are yet living in Clarke, in which a supposed bear is concerned. The occurrence is located eastward, toward Lower Peach Tree. A planter had a field of corn, not very securely fenced. His neighbor had a drove of forty hogs, and these were accustomed to break into the cornfield, doing no little damage. One day the planter caught one of the hogs (the swine of those days had long limbs and were swift of foot), and fastened a bearskin securely on the prisoner. The bearlike hog was then let loose and endeavored, of course, to rejoin his companions. They, however, mistaking him for a true bear, started immediately from the field on that swift gallop characteristic of the half-wild pioneer hog. Thirty-nine were counted, one in wild pursuit after the other, the fortieth, with the fierce-looking bearskin, bringing up the rear. And here tradition divides. One story is that the owner chanced to see them and turned the line of flight toward home; and the other is, that the wearied ones dropped out of rank and took refuge in the woods, and that the last ever seen of the forty corn thieves was a passing glance which a distant neighbor caught of one lone, frightened, almost exhausted porker, still runninig as for dear life, and close behind him was something that looked like a bear but was running after the manner of a woods hog. Both accounts agree that the cornfield suffered no further depredations.

"A sad narrative is also given, on Bashi, connected with wolves. Mike Johnson was about ten years of age, and, like little Red Riding-hood, he left his home to go upon some errand in the broad light of day. He went alone into the forest and the wolves came upon him. There was no human ear to hear his cry for help. His feet could bear him to no place of safety. His hands had not the strength to do battle with the savage monsters. Ravenous and fierce and pitiless, they gathered round him. It was hard thus to yield up his young life, but no rescuer came. The sharp fangs tore his flesh, and red tongues lapped his blood; and all that his friends could find of this active boy, when later in the day they began a diligent search, was some mangled bones which the hungry wolves had not devoured. This event is placed by early settlers as late as 1828; and this record is that mangled and wolf-eaten boy's only monument. Such boys can pass the forest pathways now in safety. Those denizens of the woods are gone. Let the name of him that thus perished live.

"Returning now to the central part of the county, and to the administration of civil affairs, we may briefly notice some items concerning the Orphans' Court and County Court of Clarke County. And, although extending beyond the limits of the history belonging to this chapter, the names of the judges and their terms of office will be here inserted, coming up to the present time.

"Records of Orphans' Court, and County Court of Clarke County, Ala.

"First court held in 1813 — minutes headed as follows:

"At an Orphans' Court begun and held for the County of Clarke, in the Mississippi Territory, at John Landrum's, on the first Monday in February, A. D. 1813. Present: The Worshipful John Caller, Esqr., Chief Justice of said Court, and John Dean, William McGrew, and James Kirkpatrick, assistant justices.

"The last court presided over by Chief Justice John Caller was held the 18th May, 1813. Minutes signed:

"John Caller, Chief Justice.
"James Bradberry, Clerk.

"The next term of the Orphans' Court was held 25th and 26th March, 1814. The 25th 'at the house of John Landrum,' opened by John Dean, Sen. Justice, and 'the Court adjourned until to-morrow at ten o'clock, to meet at Pine Level on the 26th.' 'The Court met according to adjournment. Present: The Worshipful Joseph Phillips, Esqr., Chief Justice, and John Dean and William Cochran, Justices of the quorum.'

"Said Court was held 11th Dec. 1815, 'at the house of Dr. Biddlix in the Pine Level, before Joseph Phillips, Esqr., Chief Justice.'

"The last court presided over by Chief Justice Phillips was 'held at the house of John Landrum, deceased, on the 6th May, 1816.'

"L. J. Alston as Chief Justice presided over the Orphans' Court and County Court from November, 1816, till May, 1821, during which time the names of John Dean, William Cochran, William Murrel, Elijah Pugh, Nathan Christmas, Ida Portis, William L. Paris, Jamerson Andrews, Joseph B. Chambers, Samuel B. Shields, Thomas Matlock, Thomas Portis, and James Kirkpatrick, appear as 'Justices of the quorum.' The senior Justice present presided in the absence of the Chief Justice.

"During the year 1817 this was changed from Mississippi Territory to Alabama Territory — and from November, 1817, to August, 1819, these courts were 'held in and for Clarke County, Alabama Territory.' Alabama became a state in 1819. From February, 1813, to ——— the courts were held at private houses. The first court-house for Clarke County was erected in 18—,at Clarkesville, seven miles west from Grove Hill, and the courts were held there till the county seat was moved to Macon (now Grove Hill) in 1832. First court held at Macon 28th December, 1832.

"Previous to January, 1824, the 'Minutes of the Orphans' Court, County Court, and Court of Commissioners of Roads and Revenue, were kept in the same book; but in separate books from and after that date.

"Prior to September, 1821, only two regular terms of the Orphans' Court were held in each year. Occasional special or intermediate terms were held. Monthly terms since September, 1821.

"1. From September, 1821, to January, 1823, John G. Creagh presided in the Orphans' Court, as judge thereof.

"2. Robert Lee was judge from January, 1823, to January, 1824.

"3. Edward Kennedy was judge from February, 1824, to January, 1827.

"4. Samuel Wilkinson was judge from April, 1827, to November, 1833.

"5. William R. Hamilton was judge from January, 1834, to ———, 1838.

"6. William T. Jones was judge from January, 1838, to December, 1838.

"7. Joseph P. Portis was judge from January, 1839, to December, 1844.

"8. Terrell Powers was judge from January, 1845, to May, 1850.

"9. H. W. Coate (judge Probate Court)' was judge from May, 1850, to May, 1856.

"10. Z. L. Bettis was judge from May, 1856, to February, 1866.

"11. Isaac Grant was judge from February, 1866, to May, 1866.

"12. R. J. Woodard was judge from May, 1866 to 8th August, 1868.

"13. J. R. Wilson was judge from 8th August, 1868, to November, 1880.

"For the above records of the courts and judges the author gratefully acknowledges his indebtedness to the patient research of Judge R. J. Woodard, whose carefulness and intelligent familiarity with the records are a sufficient guarantee of their correctness.

"The blanks above should probably be filled by the date 1820 or 1821; for it seems that in 1818, in November, Lemuel J. Alston, Alexander Kilpatrick, Joseph Hearn, Solomon Boykin, William Coleman, William Anderson, and William Goode, Sen., were appointed by the territorial legislature to select a location for a court-house. And again in 1819, these not seeming to have agreed upon any locality, William A. Robertson, Joseph B. Earle, John Loftin, Samuel B. Shields, William F. Ezell, Robertus Love, and Edmund Butler, were appointed commissioners to locate the county seat. In this same year the courts were ordered to be held at the house of William Coate. A place was selected not far from the residence of William Coate, and named Clarkesville. Here a village soon commenced to grow, and here the courts were held and county officials and lawyers resided until 1832.

"According to Brewer, Clarke County did not extend south of the line of township five, or four miles south of Jackson, until about 1822.

"The road from Choctaw Corner to Grove Hill was opened in 1825. The road from Choctaw Corner to Wood's Bluff was opened in 1828. These are traditional dates, and this latter road is said to have been only a path in 1834. It is now one of the best carriage roads in the county. The landing at the Bluff was established about 1826.

"Among the Lime Hills, in the Bashi or Loftin neighborhood, the first family carriage was introduced about 1830. In this Mrs. Upchurch and her two daughters were accustomed to ride when going to make visits or to attend church.

"As yet, in this chapter, little mention has been made of that locality which finally became the county-seat, bearing the names of Smithville, Macon, and Grove Hill.

"Magoffin's store, a little north of the town locality, was a place of considerable business in 1817 and some families had opened plantations in different directions around this center; but no village had started on that plateau now called Grove Hill. Some fine groves of oak still remain, which were not cut down for the first plantations there. The existence of Fort White is evidence that several families had settled, before 1813, around, and perhaps upon, this level height. In 1824 the Dickinson family were residing near the present location of the 'Male and Female Academy'; Mrs. Wright lived, in 1826, about where the court-house now stands; one mile east Hiram Tommy was living; General Chambers had built the 'White-House'; and Chapman and Pugh families were already in the edge of that range of hills on the west of the tableland. Probably village life was beginning in this locality as early as 1830; but few traces of a town or village appear in the memorials here gleaned, until the establishment of the county seat in 1832.

About thirty-nine hundred white and thirty-seven hundred colored inhabitants are now in the few villages and upon the hundreds of plantations scattered over the county.

The ten years which close with 1830 have been years of progress and improvement, but not years of active immigration or of much increase of white population; for the number of white inhabitants added during the whole ten years has only been one hundred and sixteen, the United States census reports being taken as authority. The colored inhabitants, however, in the same time, have increased in number one thousand six hundred and forty.

"It thus appears that this region, trodden by Spaniards, inhabited or first settled by French and Spanish rovers, by British royalist refugees, and by enterprising American pioneers, is in some sense already becoming 'old'; that its four hundred families, having established themselves as permanent holders of the soil, are giving their attention to the increase of wealth, and to building up a prosperous planting community.

"The solitudes of Alabama were fast awaking from the sleep of unnumbered ages."—Brewster, 1830.

Ball says: "No doubt, in many parts of the great State of Alabama there were remaining in 1830 magnificent solitudes (there are such still); but busy life, varied forms of industry, a prospering planting community, were now in the heart of the Alabama Pine Belt, along the streams and on the broad uplands and among the lime hills.

"In 1831, by act of the legislature, that part of Wilcox lying west of the middle of range four, in townships eleven and twelve, including the Choctaw Corner settlement, was made a part of Clarke County. The Choctaw line or watershed had before this time been the county boundary.

"In 1832, as elsewhere mentioned, the county seat was

rermoved from Clarksville to Grove Hill, then called Smithville or Macon; the court was first held there December 28th of that year.

"The principal villages were now Suggsville, Jackson, Coffeeville, the declining Clarksville, and the new and growing Macon; also, commencing village life, Choctaw Corner and Gainestown.

"The first hotel at Grove Hill was kept by Tom Brown, a free colored man. At his hotel Governor Bagby and other lawyers made their home when attending the courts.

"In the course of the ten years included in this chapter new enterprises were commenced, improvements were made, and incidents and events occurred, a brief record of which will form the staple of the narrative for the present.

"William B. Travis, who was a lawyer at Clarksville, instead of establishing himself at Grove Hill, removed to Texas and became there one of the heroes of the Alamo. Dr. Samuel Wilkinson, an early settler at Clarksville, a man of respectable talents and of good education, who was judge of the County Court from 1827 to 1833, removed to Grove Hill. In 1834 he became state senator. He was gentlemanly and affable, and had an extensive practice as a physician. He had several sons and one daughter. The daughter was a young lady of uncommon intelligence. After residing in Grove Hill a few years this family removed to Union Town, in Perry County.

"Educational interests in these years received attention, while the plantations were becoming larger, the hands to work them more numerous, and the material interests were gaining rapidly.

"Pendleton Academy at Coffeeville was incorporated in

1833. How long it continued in existence or how succesful it proved has not been ascertained. An institution about which more is known, called the Franklin Academy, at Suggsville, was opened in the fall of 1836, 'B. H. Sturges, Rector.' At the same time or a little earlier the Female Academy at Suggsville was first opened, 'a superior and fine-toned Piano Forte' having been procured for this school in the fall of this year, when instrumental music seems for the first time to have been regularly taught.

"The Suggsville Institute for young ladies, by Mr. and Mrs. Pilate, seems to have opened in July, 1837. They advertised to teach music on piano, guitar and harp. Vocal music with piano and guitar was at the rate of one hundred dollars a year. The same with the harp was one hundred and twenty dollars.

"The rates of tuition in this school were, by the year:

EXTRAS

"General instruction	$32
"French	$24
"Italian	40
"Spanish	40
"Botany	24
"Drawing and Painting	24
"Board and Washing	120

"Mrs. McCary, wife of the editor of the Clarke County Post, was Principal of the Female Academy. The Institute did not continue in existence long; but the two academies were permanent institutions, accomplishing under various teachers a large amount of educational work.

"Although the great agricultural interest was raising

cotton, the rearing of silk-worms and making silk, which at this time enlisted the interest of many in the North, reached the enterprising citizens of Suggsville, and to feed these worms the Morus Multicaulis, or many-stemmed mulberry, was extensively cultivated around the village in 1835.

"The people of the county took a lively interest in the Texas struggle of 1836, as they also did in the Florida or Seminole War, which began the year before. In this a number of the citizens had taken an active part. On the 18th of May, 1836, a meeting was held in Suggsville to express the sentiments of the community concerning their patriotic fellow-citizens who had 'volunteered to suppress the ravages of the Indians in Florida.' Of this meeting Colonel G. W. Creagh was chairman and W. F. Jones, Esq., secretary. The object of the meeting was explained by Colonel B. C. Foster. Commendatory resolutions were adopted and a committee was appointed to invite Lieutenant B. R. Mobley to partake of a public dinner at Suggsville in 'evidence of the high esteem in which' he was held by his fellow-citizens. The festivities of this occasion were held on Friday, May 27th. After the formal reception 'W. F. Jones, Esq., addressed him on behalf of the citizens in a brief and appropriate style, to which Lieutenant Mobley as briefly and happily replied.' The company then proceeded to the residence of J. P. Portis and partook of a sumptuous repast. The following sentiment was offered by Colonel B. C. Foster: 'Lieutenant B. R. Mobley — Long may he live to partake of the reward due to virtue, bravery, and patriotism.'

"Colonel Foster, and probably most of the prominent men of that eventful period have ceased to mingle in the social and political affairs of earthly life; they sleep with their fathers; but Lieutenant, now known as Colonel, Mobley, is still living at an advanced age, a resident now of Choctaw Corner, at the home of his son, Dr. Mobley.

"In this same year a new Creek War called forth the patriotic services of the citizens. Orders came from the state authorities for men from Clarke County to march into the Creek Nation. The Macon Cavalry of Clarke County had been requested to attend at Suggsville in full uniform on Saturday, May 28. The request was issued by Thomas Hearin, Cornet. On that day, however, a large concourse of citizens assembled at the court-house. Colonels G. W. Creagh and B. C. Foster raised a company of volunteers. One hundred names were soon enrolled. G. W. Creagh was chosen captain; B. C. Foster, lieutenant; and J. M. Chapman, ensign. On Monday, May 30, the volunteers assembled at Suggsville, on their way to Claiborne, where they were to receive their arms; and at eleven o'clock they were ready for marching orders. After forming in line of march, the Honorable W. R. Hamilton, of Suggsville, 'delivered a short and appropriate address,' at the conclusion of which, amid 'the deafening huzzas of the assembled multitude,' the order was given to march, and these young men of Clarke started for the scenes of Indian strife.

"How little did any then think that in twenty-five years there would be gatherings and partings on that same spot for a much more stern and bloody conflict. (The waters, in the latter part of this month of May, were unusually high. Heavy rains had fallen. The streams on Saturday, May 28th, were so swollen that many citizens were unable to reach Grove Hill. The Alabama river, on the 27th, was some thirty feet above low-water mark, rising about fifteen feet in twenty-four hours.) On Friday, August 12th, the Clarke County troops having returned from this Creek War, a dinner was provided for them by the patriotic citizens of Coffeeville and vicinity. John G. Creagh was president of the day, and Richard Q. Dickinson vice-president. Seventeen toasts were offered, representing the various sentiments of that day. The following was the ninth:

"'The Constitution of the United States — Before we will consent to its violation we will act the part of Virginius.'

"On Thursday, August 18th, another dinner was given at Choctaw Corner 'by the patriotic citizens of the neighborhood, as a mark of honor to their fellow-citizens, late Volunteers and Drafted men in the Creek campaign.' Nine toasts expressed the sentiments of this assembly.

"The following is a copy of most of them:

"'1. Washington — The soldier's study in camp; the soldier's pride and glory in moments of recreation.

"'2. The Soldiers of the Revolution — They taught the valuable lesson, that it was only necessary for man to will his freedom and it was achieved.

"'3. Our Country (most of this is missing).

"'4 Our Militia — In the hour of danger our country's safeguard and protection.

"'5. Our Guests — Who at the sound of the war-whoop nobly seized their arms and rushed to the rescue.

"'6. Texas — May her government be free and enlightened as her troops were brave and chivalrous in the battle of San Jacinto.

" '7. Education — Let a people know their interest and they will preserve it.

" '8. Liberty.' (A part of this and the ninth are wanting.)

"The following sentiments were toasts at one of the dinners above mentioned; and the probability, amounting almost to a certainty, is that they were adopted at Suggsville, May 27th.*

" '1. The late officers and soldiers of Clarke County — They will long live in the hearts of their fellow-citizens.

" '2. The State of Alabama — May sound politics and virtue grow with her growth and strengthen her with strength.

" '3. The Union of these States — May it ever continue.

" '4. The Navy of the United States — The strongest arm of American power, may it never be paralyzed.

" '5. President Jackson — May his declining days be crowned with peace.

" '6. Our Virtuous Fair — Always lovely, but most so in the domestic circle.

" '7. The Heroes of Seventy-six — We believe their patriotic blood still flows in the veins of their progeny.

" '8. May Texas continue as she began, and never cease until she is free.

" '9. The noble fabric of our Republic — Reared by the hands of sages, cemented by the blood of patriots, may it last till the dissolution of all earthly governments.'

"Such were some of the sentiments which the Indian troubles and the Texas struggle for independence called

---

*The copy was unfortunately mislaid among the author's notes.

forth from the liberty-loving citizens of that generation. Forty years, bringing many changes, have passed away, and their descendants love civil and religious freedom still.

"Agricultural pursuits were now carried steadily on. But the speculative tendency of the times reached even among the pines of Clarke. A Southern writer has humorously portrayed what have been well called the 'Flush Times of Alabama.' As conveying to the citizens, especially to the young men of Clarke, some idea of these flush times just before the great financial crash of 1837, the following advertisement is inserted, taken from the Clarke County Post of August 1st, 1836:

" 'TO CAPITALISTS

" 'Extensive Sale of Valuable Real Estate. On Monday, 30th of September next, will be sold at public auction, on a liberal credit, in front of the Exchange, in Suggsville, one hundred and twenty-one splendid building lots, situated on the following streets, viz: Broad, Mulberry, Pearl, Depeyster, Van Rensaleer, Van Buren, and Tennessee — Also, immediately after the sale of the above, will be offered, one hundred and ninety lots, of ten acres each, suitable for gardens, country residences, and mill seats. None of said lots being more than ten miles from town; and their contiguity to Bassett's Creek, which is navigable by law for boats not drawing over six inches water — on this stream will undoubtedly be located the depot for the contemplated rail road connecting the waters of the Alabama and Tennessee—this renders them peculiarly valuable. To distant readers we will observe, that Suggsville is a beautiful village, situated in the very centre of Clarke County; and is only nine miles from Gosport, fourteen miles from Gainestown, twelve miles from Smithsville, and ten miles from Talbert's wood yard. The State of Alabama, will undoubtedly establish a bank and place a branch of the same with a capital of one million here, and we look confidently for its operation to commence early next fall. Lithographic maps of the property may be seen at most of the book stores in the State, and at the store of T. Brown, Esq., in Smithsville.'

"As another example, four hundred valuable lots were advertised for sale, on the 19th of December, 1836, in the town of Soda Springs. This town was situated in township 12, range 3 east, section 23, near the heads of Turkey, Beaver, Horse, and Bashi Creeks, on an elevated sandy hill, 'where a vast deal of business must and undoubtedly will be done.' 'Terms of sale — one and two years credit with approved security. Commissioners, G. W. Gilmore, Charles E. Woodard, Wm. McClure, N. Harrison, T. B. Hawkins, John B. Anderson, J. E. J. Macon.'

"Other illustrations: Four hundred acres of swamp land, seventy under cultivation, some buildings on the place, advertised for sale 'at the low price of twenty-five hundred dollars.' Situated six miles from Lower Peach Tree. Also, a tract of land on Hawkins Creek, number of acres not given, seven miles west of Macon, now Grove Hill, advertised for five thousand dollars.

"It will be interesting and instructive to turn aside for a moment and to look southward at the city of Mobile in this year of large prospective wealth and expansion. The following is an extract from the Christian Index, a large religious paper of Georgia, published March 10th, 1836, and written from Mobile:

"'About one hundred and twenty years ago, a few Frenchmen came here, and made the first little opening in the pine forest. Previously to 1817, it was occupied principally as a place of deposit and trade with the Indians. There were then but two American houses, and about 600 inhabitants. Now the population is not far from 10,000. Its exports of cotton last year were 197,000 bales. The present year there will be not less than 250,000, and the probable increase for ten years to come, will not be less than 30,000 bales per year. Nineteen years ago, 5,000 bales was the whole amount raised in the state. Then the population was 30,000. Now it has more than 400,000. The city revenue nineteen years ago was $1,500; six years ago, $25,000; and the present year it will be about $70,000. During the last year 300 stores and dwelling houses have been erected. No less than 4,000 seamen were employed in the trade of Mobile last season; about 500 of whom were in port during the business months. Eighteen years ago, a single steam boat found her way to this port; now 45 are employed in the Mobile trade. At the wharves there are probably 40 vessels loading and unloading; and in the bay I counted at a single view 55 sail.'

"Subscription books were opened at Grove Hill, in charge of Isham Kimbell and Terrel Powers, to receive subscriptions for capital stock of the Tennessee and Mobile Rail Road.

"This was only three years after the road from Augusta to Charleston was opened, a road extending one hundred and thirty-five miles, and then 'the longest continuous line of railroad in the world.'* The financial crash came, and the Tennessee and Mobile road is not completed yet.

"About this time exporting timber seems to have become quite a business, G. D. Wilson of Suggsville advertising for men whom he could hire to cut cedar. The inhabitants near the great cedar 'hammocks' had formerly made rafts of cedar timber and on these had floated their cotton to Mobile, selling both cotton and timber at good rates. But about this time a steam-boat, called the Native, was built by Major Wilson, on Cedar Creek, and employed in the carrying trade.

"J. R. Wilson engaged largely in shipping cedar to Mobile. It is said that he in a short time sent down fifty thousand dollars' worth. An extensive tract of this timber now lies in township 7, range 4 east, including section 33 and adjoining sections, formerly a part of the Darrington plantation, originally owned by Joseph Phillips, and sometimes known as the Forbes tract. It is now owned by Osceola Wilson.

"It will be of interest to some to look over the following record of medical charges for 1837:

"A day visit $1.00.

"A night visit 2.00.

"Letters of advice 5.00

"Verbal advice 1.00.

"Consultation 10.00.

"Riding per mile .50.

"Double rates in the rain, at night, and for over ten miles distance.

---

*The author remembers well his first introducetion to railroad cars in passing over this road in the fall of 1833, going from his Georgia home at Applington to Charleston, South Carolina.

"Medical attendance per day $10.00.
"Medical attendance per night 12.00.
"The persons of Ordained Ministers.of the Gospel, Pensioners, and the Poor, attended gratis.

               Signed,   "T. B. Rivers,
                              "W. W. Wilson,
                              "C. Lindsay,
                              "A. B. C. Dossey,
                              'S Gayle,
                              "A Denny.

"The physicians at Suggsville at this time were: A. Denny, A. B. C. Dossey, T. B. Rivers, and probably W. W. Wilson; at Jackson there was W. H. Calvert; and at Grove Hill Samuel Wilkinson was probably still residing.

"Merchants at Suggsville were, in 1836: G. W. Creagh, and Cogburn & Lensir; in 1837, Portis and Finch; at 'Gosport Retreat,' Forwood and Fleming; at Grove Hill, T. Brown. The names of those at Jackson, at Coffeeville and at Choctaw Corner, at this period, have not reached this page of record.

"S. S. Brittingham located at Smithville, now Grove Hill, in 1836, and opened a shop for 'carrying on the carriage-making business in all its various branches.' He remained there as a citizen and a mechanic until after 1852.

"The Commissioners' Court of Clarke County received proposals in February, 1837, for the erection of a fireproof brick building 'for a county and circuit court clerk's office, for the safe keeping of the records of said county.'

"The building was to be twenty-five feet long, fifteen feet wide, and ten feet high, with flagstone or brick floor, and with slate or tin roof. It was no doubt erected that same year. The roof was slate. It was rebuilt and enlarged in 1877.

"The familiar brick building with its two rooms, in which have been held so many probate and commissioners' courts, where for so many years Judge Coate was postmaster, has therefore stood just forty years.

"The Macon Cavalry have been mentioned incidentally. The date of organization of the company is not known. In June, 1837, another company, called the Clarke County Cavalry, was organized at Suggsville. Fine horses had been raised on the Alabama river by the Weatherfords and other Indian planters and traders many years before, and now in Clarke County were some excellent saddle horses. Colonel John Darrington was keeing thoroughbred colts on his Cedar Creek plantation in 1836. Militia musters were in all these years common, and a military spirit was kept up by means of independent companies and the state militia regulations until about 1850. General musters ceased, it is said, in this region, in 1848.

"The divisions of the county, it may here be observed, are called beats, instead of towns or townships as in many older and also newer states. The term suggests a military origin. The place within the beat where the citizens meet to vote is called a precinct. School trustees are appointed for congressional townships, but political matters and voting are connected with these civil divisions called beats.

"The road from Grove Hill to Tallahatta Springs was opened about 1838. It passes over many hills and through a region that seems even now like the native wilds.

"The last three years of this decade, from 1837 to 1841,

are mentioned by some of the older citizens as a period of emigration. The new lands of the regions lying west were beginning to attract settlers from what was now becoming 'old Clarke.' Some thirty families, forming a single party, are said to have met near Clarksville and started together in their wagons for Louisiana and Texas. Among these were members of old families bearing the names of Chapman, Pugh, Cox, Daniels, and Calhoun. At different times from then till now Texas has had attractions for many of the enterprising sons and daughters of Clarke. Some have succeeded well in their new homes; and some have wished themselves again among the sheltered valleys and beside the bright streams of their youth.

"Between the two dates which stand at the beginning of this chapter, as its two landmarks of time, there came into many of these peaceful, pleasant, and Christian homes, where no Muscogee war-whoop could penetrate again, little ones, perchance from Paradise, and 'trailing clouds of glory,' some of whom are active men and women now, some of whom had beauty as their birthright, some of whom had fine endowments of mind and heart, and whose names will by and by have gone back to Paradise. Their presence added rich sources of enjoyment to their parents, whose union Christian marriage had sanctified and blessed; and they were the jewels, more precious than all the material wealth, finding a commencement of existence among the flowers and fruits of this favored clime, destined to shine as a part of the true glory of this growing civilization.. The story of their childhood years amid these homes is unwritten history, with lines as beautiful as romance, as strange as fiction. . Could their budding lives be traced we might well say, looking back to the wild freedom of the Spanish times and to the days of those river settlements eighty and one hundred years ago, let us rather dwell where Christianity 'spreads the nuptial couch and lights the household fires.'"

CLARKE COUNTY, 1850-1860

Ball's History says that in 1851 "Clarke County, like the rest of this great country, seems to have a career of large prosperity opened full before it. And the ten years upon the history, events and records of which we now enter are years of peace and plenty, of joyous home life and home love, of regularly developing resources and of rapid increase in population.

"Suggsville, still a center of wealth, refinement and culture, shares now with Grove Hill, the county seat, in influences that mold opinions and that build up the higher interests of communities. The establishment of a well-conducted paper, containing vigorously written editorials, and having quite a large circulation, aided in making Grove Hill more thoroughly the intellectual center of the county; and so long as D. Daffin and J. T. Figures conducted the Herald, its influence as a political and news periodical seemed to continually increase.

"In 1851 Edward A. Scott took charge of the Franklin Academy at Suggsville, and T. H. Ball and his sister, Miss E. H. Ball, of the Male and Female Academy at Grove Hill. At the latter school the choice selection of philosophical and chemical apparatus formerly mentioned was now for the first time brought into use, having arrived in the summer from Boston.

"Miss Virginia Yarrington, of Marion, Alabama, soon became the teacher of music. She was fair and delicate, but far too frail for much endurance. She was more indisposed than usual, and her father and mother came to see her. The other teachers left her at their boarding-house in the morning, in her parents' care, and in a few hours a message came to the academy that the teacher of music was dead. The sad tidings came unexpectedly to all. It was probably the only sudden death that ever took place at Grove Hill, except a death by violence. Her remains were conveyed to the town of Marion for burial. Her place as teacher was at length filled by Miss Laura S. Walker, who afterward became Mrs. Dewes."

MULE TRAFFIC IN CLARKE

According to Ball: "About 1840 the mule traffic, from Tennessee and Kentucky into the county, began to be quite a business. The first mule drover, whose name tradition presents here, was James Bottoms, assigned to the year 1843. The cultivation of the many large plantations soon required more than a thousand mules, and year by year additions to this number were needed.

"Some time within this decade the Tallahatta Springs became a place of resort. This place was first called the Lowder Springs, from George Lowder, the first occupant. He was brutally murdered, by members of his own family, in 1844, with attending circumstances of atrocity. The odium of the deed rests upon his wife, who is said to have formed a criminal connection with another man. Such licentiousness is very sure to harden the heart.

"Colonel Foster, who had resided for some years near Suggsville, came to Bashi in 1840. He soon obtained the Lowder place, improved the spring locality, opened a house for guests, and had sometimes one hundred, invalids and rest and pleasure-seekers. The water contains sulphur and has been considered excellent for invalids. The roads leading there are not at present in good order for carriages. Few, therefore, now resort to these waters for health.

TALLAHATTA SPRINGS.

"In June, 1847, the proprietor, B. C. Foster, published the following: 'The Tallahatta Springs are in a broken and healthy section of the country, surrounded by mountains and high hills, between Wood's Bluff and the Lower Peach Tree, fifteen miles from the former and twenty-two miles from the latter. The Proprietor has erected a number of outbuildings and offices for the convenience and accommodation of boarders, and will furnish his table with the best that the Mobile market affords.' Board was at this time five dollars by the week, and eighteen dollars a month.

"The location of this, then called, 'celebrated watering-place,' is the same as it was; and it ought to be made again a place of resort.

"During these years the planting interest went steadily on; the people were recovering from the speculative tendencies and the reverses which preceded and followed the financial crisis of 1837; the closing up of the branch banks in Mobile, Montgomery, Decatur and Huntsville, in 1842, and of the parent bank in Tuskaloosa in 1843, by means of which banks the state had for some twenty years supplied its citizens with currency, did not very materially affect the planting community;* the commission merchants at Mobile furnished their supplies and sold their cotton; home comforts were readily procured; and thus ordinary life, and pleasure, and business, went on.

"Lawyers in 1845 were, at Grove Hill, Terrel Powers and J. S. Anderson; at Suggsville, W. R. Hamilton, Pickett, and J. S. Williams; at Gosport, Frederick S. Blount.

"Felix G. Christmas graduated at the University of Alabama in 1841, and Archibald H. Pope in 1846. Not many of the young men of Clarke seem to have graduated at that university. The following additional names have been found: Jacob Bryant in 1857, W. James Thornton in 1872, and L. Earle Thornton graduating in 1877.

"The home academies furnished a sufficient course of instruction for most of the young men, and also for the girls; a few of the latter graduating at older or larger institutions at Marion and Selma and Camden.

"The county seat was in these years improving.

"The Macon Male and Female Academy was first opened in September, 1846. Rufus H. Kilpatrick, A. M., Principal.

"(This school has continued, with some suspensions, until the present time. Quite a number of teachers have been connected with it. The trustees and citizens furnished it with valuable philosophical and chemical apparatus obtained from Boston. The care of this was finally neglected, and when the war closed, and in 1865 the trustees returned

---
*A few sheriff's sales were advertised in 1847 to satisfy executions "in favor of the Branch of the Bank of the State of Alabama at Mobile."

home, nothing was left in the once well-furnished apparatus room but the bare walls.)

"The war with Mexico, which broke out in 1846, and which sent waves of excitement, of interest, and of opposition, over the country, enlisted the sympathy and aid of citizens of Clarke.

"The following are the names, so far as known, of the volunteers from the county: C. D. Hamilton, F. B. Whatley, Henry Bell, T. Bell, John Brooks, John Ewing, Robert Taylor, Jeremiah Drinkard, Lemuel Drinkard, Jesse Robinson, James Robinson, Richard Montgomery, Marion York, Robert Bradley, F. W. Baker, A. R. Lankford, and James Gilbert. On the return of the troops, in 1848, Judge Meek delivered by appointment an oration at Mobile, on the 4th of July, called 'National Welcome to the Soldiers Returning from Mexico.' In this he reviewed, in beautiful language, some of the leading events and incidents, expressing the interest which the inhabitants of this whole rergion had taken in the contest, and paying deserved tributes to General Shields.

"Some of those whose names are recorded above, survivors of the thousands who performed such brilliant actions in Mexico, are still residing in the country, especially C. D. Hamilton and F. B. Whatley.

CIVIL WAR

In the year 1860 war-clouds began to cast their dark shadows over this fair land; the war dogs began to show their teeth and men began to take their places north and south of the Mason and Dixon line, according as their sympathies led them. When the first cannon was fired at Fort Sumter in 1861, the  organization of troops was begun in haste, and soon the mighty struggle was on.

Several companies were organized in Clarke County. These were as follows: Grove Hill Guards, J. M. Hall, captain; Suggsville Grays, Rufus Lankford, captain; Clarke County Rangers, S. B. Cleveland, captain; Dickerson's Guards, Daniel McLeod, captain.

Little did anyone suspect that this conflict would continue for four long years, but it did. We shall not now undertake to go into the history of this war. Fifty-nine years have passed since its close and the Blue and the Gray are now dwelling together in peace and harmony.

"The gray line" is growing thin and in a few more years all of the old veterans will have answered the last roll call. Below we give a list of Confederate veterans living in Clarke County on October 1st, 1923:

Allen, M. V. B.	Brewer, J. W.
Anderson, T. J.	Burge, C. W.
Brandenburg, M. E.	Bradford, M. D.

Bedwell, J. D.	Pugh, J. E.
Burroughs, Bryant	Little, O. M.
Bolen, John A., Sr.	Mathews, Eljah
Coleman, W. W.	Moore, T. L.
Creagh, Gerard W.	Monk, Angus
Chapman, E. M.	Miles, W. M.
DeWitt, R. J. W.	McFarland, C. B.
Davis, W. M.	McLendon, J. T.
Drinkard, J. L.	McCasky, T. H.
Davis, H. C.	McCurdy, A. J.
Drinkard, G. W.	Pippen, E.
Evans, Jehu	Rocker, W. E.
Friddle, D. L.	Rutledge, L.
Fendley, J. H.	Roberts, M. I.
Gordon, J. A.	Roberts, A. J.
Grayson, A. H.	Shepherd, J. W.
Graham, John S.	Soloman, T. H.
Gwin, C. E.	Smith, C. L.
Holder, Willie	Stifflemire, G. W.
Hendley, L. B.	Stringer, A. R.
Jackson, W. R.	Smith, H. H.
Odom, J. B., Sr.	Tolbert, F. M.
Pugh, J. P., Sr.	Turner, T. J.
Pritchett, Chas. G.	Tucker, Wm. S.
Philen, Madison	Wiggins, J. C.
Pugh, W. S.	White, John

WAR RECORDS OF CLARKE COUNTY VETERANS

Following are the war records of the old veterans, according to their own statements:

J. H. Fendley, Fulton — Enlisted March 28, 1862, at Bethel, in Company B, Thirty-eighth Alabama Regiment. Was in the following battles: Chicamauga, Lookout Mountain, Missionary Ridge, Dalton, Resaca, New Hope Church, Jonesboro, Peach Tree Creek, Atlanta, Franklin, Nashville,

Spanish Fort and Blakely. In every battle and every march of the Thirty-eighth Regiment; slightly wounded at Chicamauga; was never taken prisoner; was made a lieutenant after the battle of Chicamauga; was paroled at Meridian, Miss.; got home May 17, 1865.

(Civilian; was married on July 6th to Harriet De Witt, who is still living; bought a home on the 20th of July, 1865, on Bassett's Creek, and went to farming; was ordained in 1869 as Baptist preacher and preached for nearly fifty years; preached in every community in the county; said to have baptized and married more people than any one in Clarke County; has nine children — four boys and five girls; is in his eighty-eighth year, wife in her seventy-ninth year.)

Charles W. Burge, near Thomasville — Enlisted in March, 1862, in the Alabama State Troops, Company A. Derusha Daffin was captain; Isaac Grant, first lieutenant; John C. Foscue, second lieutenant; George F. Fontaine, third lieutenant; John H. Higley, colonel. Served his time out and was honorably discharged. In September, 1863, enlisted in Wirt Adams' cavalry and served until the surrender. Was in the following battles: Brownsville, Franklin, Decatur, Bear Creek, Yazoo City, Port Gibson, Little Sypsy River; was in all the battles or skirmishes after joining the company. Was born April 4th, 1846, near Jackson.

L. B. Henley, Fulton — Was born May 12, 1845, in Clarke County. Enlisted in Company F, Twenty-first Alabama Regiment, at Point Clear, Baldwin County. D. C. Anderson was colonel of the regiment; was with the regiment at Fort Gaines when the Yankee fleet ran into Mobile Bay. Colonel Anderson surrendered the fort and his men to the Yankee fleet and they were taken to New Orleans and kept there two months, then taken to Ship Island and kept there two months; was exchanged in Mobile Bay on January 1, 1864, and given a seventy-five-day furlough; after furlough expired went back to Mobile; regiment reorganized and sent across the bay and joined to Holtzclaw's brigade; went down to Hollywood and met the Yankee army, then fell back to the breastworks at Spanish Fort; fought the Yankees twelve days and nights, when the place was evacuated; waded through the marsh up to Blakely, thence to Mobile by steamer; remained in Mobile a few days, then went to Meridian, Miss., and there paroled.

T. H. McCaskey, Fulton — Born in Clarke County, May 22, 1838; age now eighty-five years. Enlisted in March, 1861, at Natchitoches, La., in Company 5, Third Louisiana Regiment; was in the following battles: Springfield, Mo.; Elkhorn, Ark.; Iuka, Miss., where wounded and taken prisoner; was in battle at Vicksburg, Miss., and Spanish Fort; was in several skirmishes; was paroled at Meridian, Miss., May 10, 1865.

J. W. Brewer, Coffeeville—Was born in Wilcox County on November 24, 1840. Will be eighty-three years old the 24th of next month. Joined Joe Robins' cavalry company, Company C, Third Alabama Regiment, at Clifton, on the Alabama river; company met at Choctaw Corner, went to Grove Hill and ate dinner, then to Jackson, crossed the river there and went to Mobile, and were there sworn into service, and from there sent to Grand Bay; stayed there until March, guarding the bay; went to Corinth and stayed there a while and then went to another place (name forgotten), then to Shiloh, where we had our big fight; was in battle of Chicamauga; was wounded at Rocky Fall Mountain February 24,

1864, and was not sent to the front any more, but was put on provost duty at Macon, Ga., and remained there until the close of the war.

(Mr. Brewer says he lived two years in Wilcox County after the war closed, coming to Clarke County in 1867, and has lived here since. He also states that he was in Wheeler's brigade; got transferred to Company B, Thirty-eighth Alabama Regiment. Rip Welch was captain of Company B, and he was killed in the Chicamauga fight. Brewer says that he had a brother killed and one wounded at the battle of Chicamauga.)

Richard Ott, Campbell — Was born in Dale County in 1844; moved to Clarke County when about fourteen years old, and has been in the county since. Enlisted in the war in 1864; went to Mobile with Captain Girard, and from there was sent to Montgomery; stayed there a while and took erysipelas in his arm and was sent home two months before the war closed.

G. W. Drinkard, Thomasville — Was born in Marengo County, April 23, 1837; lived there until 1857, then moved to Clarke County; volunteered in Captain Powers' company, Company K, Twenty-third Alabama Infantry; served through the war; was taken prisoner at Port Gibson on May 2, 1863, and was carried to Alton, Ill., and kept there until the last of June, 1863, then exchanged at City Point, near Richmond, Va.; was in the following battles: Port Gibson, Holly Springs, Missionary Ridge, Lookout Mountain, Chattanooga, Rock Face Mountain, Atlanta, Ga.; Franklin, Tenn.; Nashville, Tenn.; Bentonville, N. C.

John D. Bedwell, Coffeeville — Was born in Mississippi February 5, 1841, and lived there thirteen years, then moved to Clarke, where he has since resided. Enlisted in Mobile in Company B, Twenty-second Alabama Regiment; was in the service four years; never wounded or taken prisoner, but served until the surrender.

W. E. Rocker, Alma — Enlisted in September, 1862, in Company A, Thirty-eighth Alabama Regiment; W. J. Herrin was captain of the company. His service was in Tennessee, Alabama and Georgia; was in the following battles. Chicamauga, Missionary Ridge, Rock Face Mountain; in the big battle at Atlanta; after the big battle of Atlanta the army divided, some went east and some went west. Rocker went with the army going west; crossed the Chattahoochee river below Rome, Ga., and marched through the northern part of Alabama, and crossed the Tennessee river at Florence, Ala., and started north to Nashville, Tenn.; went from Nashville to Franklin, having numerous skirmishes on the way, and a fierce but short battle at Franklin, but Rocker says they routed the Federal army and chased them to Nashville, Tenn. Then there came a heavy snow and they could not move the artillery and wagons. The enemy reinforced their army and made fight again, and we retreated, falling back to Corinth, Miss. From Corinth they went to Mobile, then to Blakely, and from there to Spanish Fort; was at the Spanish Fort at its downfall. He was not wounded or taken prisoner. Rocker was born September 12, 1843.

C. L. Smith, Chance — Was born in the northern portion of Clarke County, where the postoffice Chance now is; enlisted under Ben Anderson of Whatley on April 15th, 1862, at the age of fifteen years; afterward put in the Thirty-eighth Regiment, Company D; was drilled around Mobile

WAR RECORD OF VETERANS 155

for ten months and then sent to Tennessee, where they began to fight immediately, under General Braxton Bragg. Mr. Smith says they were afterward put under command of General Joseph E. Johnston, who, with his great skill and dauntless courage, led them to victory in many places along down the line as they were compelled to fall back on account of the odds being so great against them, which must have been ten to one. They reached Atlanta, and there had some pretty hard fighting. Smith was wounded in the head on August 5, 1864. He says that he did not do any more soldiering. He says that General Hood took the army from Atlanta back to Franklin, Tenn., and there the South lost thousands of brave and good men. I have not told you much about the fighting from Missionary Ridge to Atlanta, but you have doubtless read the history of those great fights that took place up there, such as two days at Resaca and New Hope Church. At Resaca our colors were twice shot down and were picked up both times by Colonel R. A. Lankford of the Thirty-eighth Alabama Regiment, and there we lost some of the best blood of the South. I have lived in Clarke County all of my life. Mr. Smith says he was fifteen years old when he joined the army in 1862, therefore, he must have been born in 1847.

Martin E. Brandenburg, Scyrene — Enlisted in Company A, Thirty-eighth Alabama Regiment at Suggsville, March 22, 1862. William Herrin was captain of Company A and —— Ketchen was colonel of the regiment. Mr. Brandenburg was in the following battles: Chicamauga, Atlanta, Dalton, Resaca, Jonesboro, Missionary Ridge, Nashville, Franklin, Lookout Mountain and New Hope Church; was captured at Nashville and carried to Camp

Chase, Ohio prison, and kept there until the close of the war. Mr. Brandenburg was born in Clarke County in 1843 and now lives within a mile and a half of where he was born; was married in 1866; his wife is still living; they have thirteen children, all of whom are married and away from home.

John Collins Wiggins, Dickinson — Says he enlisted in the Home Guards in May, 1861, at Tallahatta Springs, and drilled under Colonel Ben Foster, and then joined the Dickinson Guards at Grove Hill October 15, 1861, which was Company E, Twenty-fourth Alabama Regiment (or known as Thomas I. Kimbell's company), and in May, 1862, joined as a Confederate soldier, the second time belonging to the State Troops and the last time in the regular army. His first battle was at Murfreesboro, Tenn.; next was at Resaca, Ga.; then captured at Atlanta, Ga., off the picket line, together with Lut Stephen, P. Chapman, Sergeant Billy Calhoun, Duge Stewart, Pink H. Pogue, Lane and Ben Bumpers, and Billy Hall, and carried to Camp Chase; there released June 11, 1865. He was never wounded. He was born six miles above Lower Peach Tree, October 5, 1842, and moved to Clarke County in 1859.

E. Pippin (now in Baldwin County) says: I enlisted in the Confederate army in the year 1862, at a little town called Skipperville, Dale County, Ala., in Company E, Fifty-ninth Alabama Regiment. I was first under General Grace, who was the brigadier-general, and General Buckner was the division general. We went out to East Tennessee and stayed there nearly a year. Then we were ordered out, then went in a battle at Chicamauga, the 19th, 20th and 21st of September, 1863; then ordered back under General Longstreet to the State of Virginia; then went in battle at Knoxville, Tenn. Then we went in winter quarters at Bristol, Tenn. Then in the early part of 1864 we went on to Richmond, Va. Our next fight was at Drewry's Bluff, Va. On June 17 we went into another fight at Petersburg, Va. Then went into the ditches for nearly nine months on the 17th day of June, 1864, and came out on the 14th of March, 1865. Then on March 25, 1865, we went in at battle at Hatcher's Run, Va. There I was captured and taken to Pine Lookout, Md., and was paroled on June 27, 1865. I was never wounded. I came to Clarke County in 1874 and lived there until 1922, then moved to Baldwin County, Ala.

Willis Holder, Jackson — Was born in Clarke County September 16, 1846. He worked on gunboats at Oven Bluff in Clarke County from June, 1863, until January 10, 1865, Lieutenant Blackford being in charge of the work.

William S. Tucker, Whatley — Was born December 30, 1846, in Warren County, N. C. Enlisted at Lower Peach Tree, in Wilcox County, about April 10, 1864. Went from there to Dalton, Ga., and joined Company B, Thirty-eighth Alabama Regiment. Was with his command in all the battles from then on and was wounded at Marietta, Ga., and was in hospital about ten days. He then went into the siege at Atlanta, Ga., for about a month, and was flanked out of that place by the Yankees, and then went with Hood to Tennessee, where they were defeated, returning to Tupelo, Miss. His command then went to Mobile, and from there was sent to Spanish Fort. He was captured at Spanish Fort. He was paroled at Vicksburg about May 1, 1865.

R. J. W. DeWitt, near Jackson — Was born December 11, 1840, in Pine Hill, Wilcox County, Ala. Moved to

Clarke County in 1857. Enlisted in Company E, Thirty-second Alabama Regiment, in the spring of 1862. Alexander McKinstry was colonel of the regiment and Harry Maurrey was lieutenant-colonel of the regiment. Bandy Kilpatrick was captain of the company. Was in every battle in which his regiment was engaged from the time he enlisted until the close of the war. Among the many battles he was in were the following: Chicamauga, Murfresboro, Lookout Mountain, Missionary Ridge, Luverne, Resaca, Dalton, New Hope Church, Stone Mountain, Atlanta, Jonesboro, Franklin, Nashville, and Spanish Fort. He surrendered at Lauderdale Springs, Miss.

Daniel Louis Friddle, Jackson — Was born thirteen miles south of Greenville, Ala. (Butler County), January 11, 1845. Joined the Confederate army in December, 1861, at Greenville, Ala. Joined the cavalry in 1862 at Montgomery, Ala. Joined under Captain Sanderson in 1863 the Alabama Cavalry Regiment, Company I; M. W. Hammon was commander of the regiment. According to the records kept by Adam C. Whetstone of his brigade, he fought in one hundred and seventeen battles. He fought in Alabama, Georgia, Tennessee and Mississippi. Was shot eleven times, though wounds were slight, and was captured while in service. The following are some of the important battles he was in: New Hope Church, Tuscumbia, Athens, Chattanooga, Chicamauga, Missionary Ridge, Okolona, Huntsville, Dalton, Atlanta, Franklin; last battle April 24, 1865, against odds of forty to one. Fought from Bear Creek to Lovejoy, seven miles. Paroled April 25, 1865.

A. H. Grayson, Bashi — Was born November 25, 1844, near Springhill, Marengo County, Ala. Enlisted in Clarke

County, 1863, in the Sixth Alabama Cavalry, Company H. W. G. Campbell was captain; C. H. Colven, colonel; General James H. Clanton's brigade. He was never captured or wounded.

G. Pritchett, Thomasville — Born in Wilcox County January 25, 1848. Enlisted in the service at Greenville, Ala., January 23, 1865. The company he joined was composed of state troops. He was wounded at Columbus, Ga., April 16, 1865. Was taken prisoner and was in the hospital four weeks at Columbus. The company he joined was not united with any regiment.

John Elijah Pugh, Grove Hill — Was born two and a half miles northwest of Grove Hill, Ala., April 4, 1844. Enlisted in the summer of 1862 at Montgomery. He served with Company I, Fifth Alabama Regiment. He was struck by a bullet once; during the battle of Gettysburg a bullet struck his pack and went through his blanket and fly-tent, and lodged in his oilcloth; this knocked him down. He was never a prisoner.

H. H. Smith, Salitpa — Born in 1846 in Dale County. Enlisted in Company A, Alabama Regiment, in 1862, Captain —— McCray; George Newman, first lieutenant, and Mike Holmes, second lieutenant. Later transferred to Company E, Captain Vaughn. Was in the battle of New Hope Church, at New Hope, Ga., and was shot through the clothes and blankets, and was also in the battle of Spanish Fort and Tensaw River Landing; was captured at Tensaw River Landing and sent to Ship Island; was later exchanged and sent to Vicksburg, Miss., and from there to his old command at New Hope, Ga., and was with them until the surrender.

T. J. Anderson, Dickerson — Was born near Dixon's Mills, Marengo County, January 29, 1844. Came to Clarke County when very young. Enlisted in the army in April, 1862. Was wounded at Chicamauga September 20, 1863. Was in the battles at Rocky Face Mountain, Resaca, New Hope Church, and was captured at Atlanta, Ga., July 22, 1864. Was in Company E, Thirty-eighth Alabama Regiment, General Holtzclaw's brigade, Stuart's division, Army of Tennessee. Was discharged at Camp Chase, Ohio, June 12, 1865.

W. M. Davis, Nettleboro — Was born on the line between Clarke and Wilcox (but was reared in Clarke), August 14, 1841. Enlisted in Company K, Twenty-third Alabama Regiment, commanded by Colonel Frank Beck. Was never wounded or taken prisoner. Was in about ten battles, the last one being at Bentonville, N. C. Stacked arms at Salisbury, N. C., about April 6, 1865.

J. W. Shepard, Coffeeville — Was born near Eufaula, Barber County, Ala., October 23, 1843. Enlisted in Company K (Poe's company), Colonel Beck's regiment, Pettus' brigade, Stephenson's division, and Johnston's corps, near Atlanta, Ga. Was wounded at Missionary Ridge and taken prisoner at Nashville, Tenn.

O. M. Little, near Jackson — Was born September 10, 1845, in Dale County. Was reared in Clarke County. Enlisted in Company J (Thirty-eighth Alabama Regiment. Rufus Lankford, colonel; Charles Bursey, captain, in March, 1864. Was wounded slightly in the leg and head. Was in the battles at Rocky Face Mountain, Spanish Fort, Jonesboro and Franklin. Was paroled in May, 1865.

A. R. Stringer, Grove Hill — Was born about ten miles

north of Jackson, near old Union, February 14, 1845. He enlisted in Company F, Twenty-first Alabama Regiment, May 20, 1861. The captain of his company was Benjamin Franklin Dade, from Baldwin County. His regiment was in the following battles: Shiloh, Fort Morgan, and later at Spanish Fort.

Walter S. Pugh, Grove Hill — Enlisted at the age of sixteen years in Company E, Twenty-fourth Alabama Regiment, in Mobile, on October 18, 1861. Served thirteen months in General Bragg's army, and being a non-conscript was honorably discharged. Was not engaged in any battles while a member of this command. Enlisted in Company I, Woods' cavalry, on September 21, 1863, and served in that command until the close of the war. Was surrendered by General Dick Taylor, near Gainesville, Ala., where he received his parole. Was engaged in quite a number of little cavalry fights, nearly all being in Mississippi.

Dr. Bryan Burroughs, Jackson — In response to an interview as to his war record, says as follows: Early in 1863 I was considering volunteering in the Virginia army. I was sixteen years old. Those having authority over me thought it best that I should have some training in the art of war. I was sent to the University of Alabama, which was an officers' training camp. These military schools were encouraged by President Davis, who was a West Point graduate and military man. The Universities of Alabama, North Carolina, and Lexington, Va., were expected to furnish military officers for the embryo government. The intensive military training and discipline enforced caused some of the students to leave for the front in Virginia or the Western army. In June, 1864, we were called to Montgomery by Governor Watts. Farragut's fleet had captured Fort Morgan, and there were raids in North Alabama, which we were called on to meet and turn back. We were camped on the Coosa, enjoying the fine climate, when we were ordered to Blakely, Spanish Fort and Saluda Hills, where Governor Thomas Watts had ordered the entire militia of the state to assemble. Boys sixteen to eighteen years old, and men from forty-five to fifty. We drilled this large body of raw troops during July, August and September. The Yankees did not land an army to march from the eastern shore to Montgomery, but an army of mosquitoes invaded our camp and nearly all the cadets had malarial fever. There was also typhoid fever. We went out 285 strong but were reduced to thirty or forty by sickness. We were ordered back to Montgomery, there given furloughs home, and to report back to Tuscaloosa for service, which we did, and we served until April 1st. During Claxton's raid we exchanged several volleys with their Yankee troops, but we were withdrawn and marched to Marion, Ala., and disbanded, as the university had been burned and General Lee surrendered.

J. B. Odom, Allen — Says that his record is the same as that of Dr. Burroughs.

Elijah Mathews, Grove Hill — Was born three miles southwest of Grove Hill on December 13, 1841. Enlisted in the army March 4, 1861, in Company I, Wirt Adams' cavalry. Was never wounded or taken prisoner.

H. C. Davis, Chance — Was born in Clarke County, 1843, on November 29th, near Lower Peach Tree. Enlisted in the army in Company B, Thirty-eighth Alabama Regiment, under Captain W. R. Welch, at Yellow Bluff, on the

Alabama river; Colonel Ketchman in command. Was in the following battles: Chicamauga, September 19-20, 1863; Missionary Ridge; Resaca, Ga., New Hope Church, Atlanta, Ga.; Columbus, Tenn.; Nashville, Tenn.; Spanish Fort. Was never taken prisoner, but was slightly wounded one time at Spanish Fort, in April, 1865. Was discharged May 15, 1865, at Livingston.

Angus Monk, Grove Hill — Was born in Henry County August 7, 1847. Enlisted in the army at Pollard, Ala., in Company A, Fourth Alabama Regiment. Was slightly wounded in the forehead.

E. M. Chapman, Grove Hill — Was born near Grove Hill, December 20, 1846. Enlisted with State Troops August 6, 1864, and was stationed at Mobile and Blakely for two months. Had pneumonia and was sent home. Enlisted again in Company I, Wirt Adams' cavalry, Wood's Regiment, and was with that command until he laid down arms. Was never wounded or taken prisoner.

All of these old veterans are nearing the sunset of life. Their ages range from seventy-five years and upward. They have played a noble part in this life, in time of war and in time of peace. All will soon cross over the "valley of the shadow of death." It is to be hoped that when the "roll is called up yonder" they'll be there.

All the world loves a brave man, a man who will walk into the very jaws of death when duty calls. Such were the Confederate soldiers. No braver soldier ever wielded a sword or pulled a trigger than the Southern soldier. He displayed his courage not only in time of war, but in the time of peace as well. When the war was over and the smoke cleared away he returned to his home and began to battle for a livelihood.

The dark days of reconstruction was a period that tried men's souls, but the brave old Confederates of many hard-fought battles rose above all difficulties and came out victorious. Speaking of the days following the close of the Civil War, and old veteran who followed Forrest through all of his many hard-fought battles has the following to say of

RECONSTRUCTION:

"Much has been said and written of that unhappy period immediately following the Civil War — unhappy for both the North and the South, because its memories delayed the reunion of our sections through many years. The humiliation and grief of that frightful era left far deeper scars than all the sabers and swords and bullets from Bull Run to Appomattox. The flame of war had burned out the lives of thousands of our brave sons and consumed our homes and wasted our lands, but the embers of reconstruction seared their mark upon the very souls of our people.

"We do not charge that horror to the great nation to which we are as true and loyal as any beneath the flag today, but to individuals who abused authority and misrepresented the spirit of the North toward the South.

"I for one thank God that our people themselves settled the problem of reconstruction by the application of a righteous courage to a desperate situation; but there was one influence in that settlement that was never generally appreciated. Across the closed chasm, above the graves of all the soldier dead, the great men of the North and the great men of the South looked at each other in silence and understood, when the oppressors were driven from the South.

"As soon as the insidious tongues of a few intermeddling, ignorant, vicious men and women, seeking to be the ministering angels of the former slaves, were hushed by the stern policy of the representative Southern people, the happy and natural relations of the two races were restored; and today, after nearly sixty years of freedom, the black man of the South knows that the Southern white man is his truest friend, because he alone understands him and sympathizes with his natural and legitimate needs.

"As one who in a very humble way helped to make that sad history, as the representatives of a family who owned slaves, I desire to here record my opinion that in the trying period following the war it was the Christian fortitude of our people that saved the day for us. Out of the ashes of material wealth, out of anguish and humiliation, we came with honor; and the unbroken spirit of the Old South, serene amid its earthly poverty, is the unquestioned and priceless heritage of our sons.

"Whenever and wherever I meet a soldier of the sixties, no matter whether he wore the blue or the gray, I think of his life as the figure and symbol of a sad, eventful day. His youth represents the morning, and it was filled with golden dreams. Achievement and success smiled before him, and his heart leaped with love, just as young hearts leap today. But, before he could realize his dreams, a great storm — that awful war — came and swept away his fairest prospects. The noontide of his life found him busy with the wreckage of the morning, and then it was that there rose in his soul a far greater courage than that which had sustained him on the bloodiest field — the courage to meet and conquer adversity, the divine grace to cast away his bitterness and to love his former foes.

"My comrades, out of the ruined morning and the rebuilding toil of the noontide we have come at last to the evening and the twilight. Time has placed upon our heads his crown of silver and of snow. For us the long day of life is near spent, and the world can never chide us if, in the spirit of fraternity and forgiveness, we find ourselves dreaming backward toward the blood-billowed years of Shiloh and Chicamauga and all our other fields of mutual and glorious memories.

"All of us who are now living in the true spirit of liberty and union know that out of our great war of sixty years ago has come a greater peace than our nation could have ever known had we not cut away, with the sword, the great mistake of the fathers of our country.

"Let us pray that our sacrifices, now far back in the years, may be truly recorded, to be the living evidences of American courage — that tried and true courage which is our greatest asset, an asset of national wealth outweighing the value even of our vast material wealth.

"Embodied in our sons and grandsons, only a little while ago, the whole world glimpsed that same spirit of courage and patriotism on the battlefields of Europe, when the 'Blue and the Gray' turned to 'Olive Drab' and our boys, millions strong, crossed the ocean to defend the ideals of our country — ideals of national life which are rapidly becoming the ideals of all truly civilized peoples of the earth.

"I rejoice that I have lived to see the greatness of America dawn upon the world. I rejoice that when the hour struck for the flag of universal liberty to 'go over the top,' it was carried there by the substance of our fields, by the power that came from our mountains of coal and iron, by the whirring wings of our Liberty motors, and by the unbeaten and unbeatable soldiers of the United States.

"For one hundred and forty-seven years the individuality of the American soldier has defied the analysis of military critics and upset the theories of every nation that has met him on the battlefield.

"Since his first far-off shot of Lexington, the makers of war maps have been unable to chart his power from his visible numbers, for in his unconquerable spirit there is the might of unseen legions and the unmeasured force of just and democratic purpose, as an armed host, is bivouacked in his soul.

"You may follow his history from his advent into the world of political contention, through his almost unbelievable and unbroken line of successes, and you will find him, always and everywhere, the one unbeatable force which cannot be weighed in the scales that determine the military values of all other peoples. If other evidences were lacking to establish these facts, certain incidents of the World War alone would prove them. In no case did he fail to meet the test of fire; and the anxious world stood aghast when the German staff reduced the question of fighting ability to an absolute test in the hope of proving the weakness of our 'raw recruits' when pitted against soldiers not only trained, but bred and born in the iron atmosphere of the 'Great Empire.' The Germans, confident of their superiority, man for man, felt that such a test would weaken the morale of the American soldier and boost the waning German hope at Berlin.

"On April 20, 1918, at Seicheprey, in the Toul sector, a picked German column, the product of a century of militarism, assaulted an American force of approximately equal numbers.

"Not only was it a clash of men; it was the deadly embrace of principles — the death grapple of human systems.

"The world knows the result. The individuality of the American soldier was asserted before the astonished eyes of all nations, and the Stars and Stripes floated triumphantly over that field of death.

"Unafraid of all the military camps of the earth, this strange civil soldier, while fostering and guarding the greatest of all republics, has eschewed the damning principles of militarism, ever preferring to keep his sword sheathed in the peaceful scabbard of industry, drawing it only when Liberty is endangered.

"Of that deadly war, which, directly or indirectly, involved every square inch of the earth's surface and the fate of every human being, living and yet to live, Hendrick Van Loon has beautifully said:

"The human race was given its first chance to become truly civilized when it took courage to question all things, and made 'knowledge and understanding' the foundation upon which to create a more reasonable and sensible society of human beings. The great war was the 'growing pain' of this new world."

AMERICANISM TRIUMPHANT

"That Americanism which today is a dominant world force is not alone of North or South or East or West. Out of the blended greatness of all the sections of the United States came the hope of peace and universal democracy in that dark hour when the allied armies of Europe were backing doggedly toward the tottering gates of Paris. That hope was born of the reunited blood of the gray and the blue armies.

"As it was Americanism that tipped the doubtful scale of victory on the field of battle, so it was Americanism that inspired the war-sick world to seek the great League.

"And now that all eyes are turned toward Geneva as the chosen capital of the earth, the fascinating history of that far corner of Switzerland will be lifted by a thousand pens from the dust of neglect. Poured into the stream of current literature, it will add mellowness and flavor, as if a flagon of old wine were resurrected from some long-deserted cellar and poured into the spiritless punchbowl of today.

"This new seat of world deliberation has ever been a home of thought — a place of dreams. From the brain of a dreamer who dreamed there more than a hundred years ago there issued a ghost — the most monstrous and terrifying that ever looked from the pages of fantastic literature — for a century considered only a gloomy fancy of a wonderful imagination, but now revealed in the light of the world revolution as a hideous prophecy of the terror and agony of the great war. Perchance the prophecy was an accident. It may be that there was nothing miraculous — no inspired vision back of the dream; and still it may be that some yet undiscovered force of mind and soul mirrored in the brain of that bright dreamer the troubled future of the world and caused its expression in the mental creation of a monster

"In reviewing this ghost of accidental or miraculous prophecy, as the case may be, it is well to remember that this country of landmarks has ever held a charm for the restless spirits of genius. The hill of Geneva is cathedral-crowned. Its unique and historic river, born of snow and ice and reborn of a crystal like, divides the city like a stream of blue and trembling light, and the lands that sustain its countryside are a succession of orchards, gardens and vineyards.

"The beautiful Lake of Geneva, touching the city with its westerly extremity, stretches eastward for more than forty miles. Great spirits of many centuries have gathered about this place of dreams to sing their songs to all the future or work out their messages to mankind — poets, philosophers, painters, sculptors, theologians, astronomers and scientists.

"There Calvin lived and taught and died. There Rousseau was born to be the siren of free thought, and from that base of dreams went forth to lead his life of wonderful, dissolute, and brilliant vagabondage.

"And so the list of the great whose lives have touched this charmed and charming place could be extended on and on; but let us leave this to the research of the interested, while we pass to the immortals who are linked with our strange story.

"In the eventful summer of 1816, while all Europe was being adjusted to the new sensation of living without fear of the great Napoleon, then just settled in his cage at St. Helena; when Germany, at last free from his dominating genius, was already beginning to steel the national heart for a career of supermilitarism, there came to the lonesome shore of this famous lake Lord Byron, the poet Shelley, and Mary Godwin (afterward Mary Shelley).

'Mutually possessed with the spirit of mysticism which seemed to brood over the moss-grown city, the beautiful lake and its environs, these impressionable children of nature entered into a playful contest to determine which could write the most harrowing story dealing with the supernatural. At least, it is known that Lord Byron, Mary Godwin and Byron's physician entered the contest. So supremely terrifying was the story of Mary Godwin that Byron never finished his story, and the story of the physician is unknown to the world of literature.

"Her story tells of the secret ambition and dreadful realization of a German student of science in the University of Ingolstadt. Pushing his clandestine research into the realm of the unknown until he discovered the secret of human life, ambition kindled in his soul to mimic the master work of God. He created a soulless body of a man, and by the application of his discovered chemical, infused into the cold, dead form, the vital spark. It did not step from his touch as Adam stepped from the Divine Hand — in beauty and in grace — but came groveling into consciousness, a distorted monster. The student fled from his work; but in the silent hours of the night that followed, his horrid creature stood, with bloodshot eyes, above his bed, and, with hideous face and wildly waving arms, cursed the daring intelligence which had called it from the night of nothingness into an unnatural and miserable existence. Again the student fled, and continued to flee from the awful work of his hands; but ever the monster followed, penetrating the barriers of his most secret lodgings, begging death at the hands of its creator, or silently pressing against the pane of his window a face of suffering and rage. It murdered his friends and the members of his family. It pursued him through life, and at last stood and shrieked above his coffin — a terrible witness to the folly of his wisdom. Its work of vengeance ended, it stepped into a self-kindled fire and perished.

"Could it not have been that this monster was more than a fantastic dream of Mary Godwin's brain? Did not this imaginary German student, misusing the discoveries of science to ape the power of God, foreshadow the mighty German nation harnessing every art and discovery of civilization for the creation of a monster a thousand times more terrible than that of the strange story — the monster of militarism? Have we not seen this German-created monster, with body of steel and breath of fire, go forth to terrorize the world? Failing in its unnatural purpose, have we not seen it, like the awful ghost, turn upon its creator and hound a dynasty to its death? And is not this monster, like the other, now perishing in its self-built fires?

"Beautiful Mary Shelley! You cannot arise from your long sleep to answer our anxious question and tell us whether your uncommon story was the picture of a dream or the record of a vision!

"Ring on, the soft bells of your golden past, O Geneva, and keep the sweet cadence of their ancient song to mellow the newness of your greater life to come! The heart of the world will beat within your gates; and may truth and liberty, clear and changeless as the waters of your Rhone, flow from the deliberations of your gathered wisdom."—Recollections of Thomas D. Duncan.

Thomas D. Duncan and the author of this book were neighbor boys in Corinth, Miss., when the Civil War began. He enlisted in April, 1861. He was but fifteen years of age when he first enlisted (in the infantry). He was transferred to Forrest's cavalry and with that command served throughout the entire war, receiving only one slight wound. He was engaged in fifty-two battles and was in many close places.

These two men have never met since the close of the war, and neither had any knowledge of the fate of the other until October, 1923, when the writer came into possession and read the "Recollections of Thomas D. Duncan." Mr. Duncan is a prominent and highly-respected citizen of Corinth, Miss., having rreturned to that place after the close of the war, and has resided there ever since.

He is a forceful and fluent writer and his book is intensely interesting.

OVEN BLUFF

It is, perhaps, not known to many Clarke countians that gunboats were built at Oven Bluff, in this county, during the Civil War, but such was the case. Just how many boats were built there the author is not informed, but there was a force of men stationed there for quite a while. Above is shown a picture  of a cannon which was located at Oven Bluff, and which was brought to Jackson a few months ago and placed on the public square at Jackson. It was through the efforts of Representatives J. F. Boykin that this cannon was procured from the Department of Archives and History. This cannon was brought to Oven Bluff in the early part of the war. It appears that the Confederate government anticipated an attack on Mobile, and in order to provide relief in case that point should fall, they conceived the idea that the placing of a fort of defense on the lower waters of the Tombigbee might serve as protection against a river fleet. In consequence thereto it is probable that some of the old United States guns which had been mounted at Pensacola and at Mobile (Fort Morgan) were sent up the Mobile river to these points, one of which was Fort Stonewall, named in honor of Stonewall Jackson. Neither of the points was ever developed. The embankments were started in both cases, without being completed.

JACKSON, 1875

The author of this book first set foot on Clarke County soil in the lovely month of June, 1875, coming from Mobile, where he had resided since September, 1872. He came by way of the Tombigbee river on the old side-wheel steamer Atlanta, arriving at Jackson on the morning of the first Sunday in June. He was met by Porter Wainright, "porter" of the Wainright House, kept by Captain Luck Wainright, of whom we shall speak more fully elsewhere. There were no taxi-drivers to meet you with a glad smile in those days, and no other conveyance was available that morning, but walking was good and the writer was young and active, so

HEMPHILL LUMBER CO. MILL, AT JACKSON

he hit the trail and he soon landed at the hotel, or boarding house.

He found in Jackson the remains of a once live, hustling, bustling town of about fifteen hundred people. There were about fifteen families living here, namely: Doty, Smoot, Chapman, Kimbell, Stringer, Dahlberg, Taylor, Walker, Wing, Parker, Dubose, Wainright, Baker, Denny and Dolbear.

E. J. Doty lived near the river landing and he and his wife kept a boarding house for the accommodation of river travellers. S. Smoot and wife lived where what is now known as the Hicks place. John C. Chapman, his wife and several children lived in a house where the Goff Hotel now stands. Isham Kimbell, two children and two grandchildren, where J. C. Rivers now lives. S. P. Stringer and F. W. Dahlberg and wife, daughter of Mr. Stringer, lived in what is now known as the old Dahlberg house. Walter Taylor, wife and three daughters, lived where J. C. Stewart now lives. S. P. Taylor lived where Mrs. Wing now lives, and they lived in what is now Mrs. Wing's dining-room and kitchen. Calvin Walker and wife lived in a house back of where Dr. Chapman now lives, the house having been torn away. A. M. Wing (wife not the present Mrs. Wing) and one or two children lived where Horace Frisbie now lives. W. S. Parker and wife lived where Charles Howard now lives. Mrs. Peter DuBose, two sons and three daughters, lived just back of the store of the Beville Mercantile Company. Luck Wainwright lived where Skip Coale now lives, with wife, one son and two daughters. Mrs. Drake Dolbear, one son and one daughter, lived where Mrs. Drake Dolbear now lives. Sewall DuBois, wife and, perhaps, one

LOCK NO. 1 ON TOMBIGBEE RIVER AND OTHER SCENES

child, and his mother-in-law, Mrs. Denny, and daughter, lived where M. E. Wilson now lives. F. W. Baker and two sons lived where Mr. Mason now lives.

It will be seen from the above list that there were less than sixty white people living in Jackson in 1875. Of those mentioned above there are not more than ten or fifteen now living, five in Jackson and others elsewhere. Those in Jackson are: Mrs. Cora R. Wing, Mrs. Carrie H. Neville (nee Taylor), Mrs. Josie D. Prosser (nee Taylor), Miss Sarah Taylor and James Monroe Chapman. Those living elsewhere are: J. E. DuBose, Selma, Ala.; Sewell DuBose, Mississippi; F. W. Dahlberg, Suggsville, this county; Mrs. Stella Johnson and her sister, Miss Mattie DuBose, Mobile; Miss Julia Wainright and Mrs. L. O. Hicks, Mobile. We are not informed as to Mrs. J. C. Chapman and children; they may be living.

Forty-eight years have rolled by since 1875 and all of these persons are getting down toward the evening of life.

In 1875 Mr. Wing was merchandising in what is now known as the old Bolen store. S. P. Stringer was keeping the postoffice on the south side of Commerce street, the northwest corner of Miss Alice Kimbell's yard, east of the driveway. Calvin Walker's blacksmith shop was right in front of where Dr. Chapman now lives. S. Parker Taylor had been doing business where Charles Howard is now doing business. This was about the extent of the business being done here in those days.

There were two churches here, Methodist and Presbyterian. These church buildings were erected before the Civil War. There was no school building here then, and no school.

RED CROSS

The American Red Cross was organized first in Jackson in the summer of 1917. There were four active chapters in the county at that time — Jackson, Grove Hill, Fulton and Thomasville. The territory assigned Jackson by the division representative extended from West Bend to Gainestown. Committees from this chapter visited and organized every community and town, resulting in a large and working organization. Miss Ella Sewall was elected chairman and served in that capacity until, by instructions from headquarters at the close of the war, all chapters in the county were consolidated. A meeting of the members of the executive committees of each chapter was held in Grove Hill in October, 1919, to vote on a chapter for county headquarters. Jackson was unanimously elected, as the membership was more than the other three combined. Shortly after reorganization Miss Ella Sewall was elected executive of the county chapter, and still holds the position.

Clarke County should be proud of the work of the Red Cross. During the war it went over the top in every quota assigned; more than doubling relief funds; sending money and clothing to European sufferers; has never failed to respond to every relief call at home and abroad. Thousands of garments have been sent to storm sufferers in our state and Mississippi. Many disabled ex-service men in this and Washington County have cause to bless the Red Cross for the aid given in filing their claims for hospitalization and compensation. The Clarke County A. R. C. has a high rating with headquarters; in the division none has ever ranked higher — not in membership, but in efficiency, the various activities being kept up practically the same as during the war. When it is known that the little chapter is held up as an example to other states comprising the southern division, all should take pride in joining and keeping it up. The Red Cross has helped to put Clarke County on the map.

WORLD WAR SOLDIERS

Following is a list of World War soldiers who are honorably discharged from the service, and who had their discharges recorded in the Probate Office of Clarke County. The letter "x" indicates those who saw service overseas:

WHITE

Lewis H. Sewell
William L. Scruggs
Erby L. McLeod
William G. Jaris x
Hendrick C. Smith
Garfield Morgan
Arthur Harrell
Charles S. Mathers
Daniel E. Jones
Shellie Lee
William Ward
George P. Few
Willie Dukes x
Thomas W. Larrimore
David D. Larrimore
Albert S. Deas
Gary M. Coleman
Thomas M. Anderson
William Lester Reeves
George B. Reeves
Durry Lee Dorman
Dan L. Coleman
Adlie Bell
Erby V. Pugh
William G. Robinson
Hiram General Haskew
Claude Hawk
Condie Chancey
John Thornton
Wesley Beck Kennedy
Grady Purvis
Robert Curtis Guy
Robert L. Downey
William B. LaFlore
Charlie Coble May
Herbert A. Calhoun
Ivy J. Griffin
John M. Drinkard

WORLD WAR SOLDIERS

John C. Dortch
William E. Phillips x
James J. Brooks
Elbert Reeves x
John Foscue
Elvin C. Monk x
Ocie L. Downey x
Robert L. Champion x
Mit C. Etheridge
Agnew Etheridge
Lester L. Coates x
William C. Snell x
Clifford J. Snell x
Connie Long
Fred W. Benson
Curtis McVay x
Sidney A. Payne x
Eddie G. Pugh
Clarence Beck
Bowman Wilson x
Nettles D. Coats x
Ervin Lamberth x
Jesse A. McLeod x
Samuel B. Milstead
Sol Fleming
Bonner C. Wiggins x
Acie E. Hill
John R. Sanders x
William Sanders x
Morgan B. Pugh x
Enoch M. Garrick x
Bernard C. DeLoach
Manah Dozier
William C. Davis
Henry C. Poole x
Donnie A. Vickers
Earl Pugh

Howard K. McClure x
Roy W. Kimbrough
Monroe Gates x
Willard E. Hudson
Dr. W. Estis
Frank Q. Tompkins x
Cecil S. Chapman
Napoleon Fendley
Harry H. Miller
Paul C. Wilson
Howell Brooks x
Nelson C. Wing x
Willie Ray Guy
Steve E. Bullock
Charles A. Jordan x
Elmore E. Agee x
John W. Agee x
Robert E. Gwin x
Erby A. Leonard x
Solomon Tarleton x
James R. Gregory x
Willie M. Robinson x
Elmer E. Hoven x
Evie C. Leonard x
Amos Brooks x
John B. Brewer x
James Williamson
William A. Bagley x
Arthur J. McClinton x
John B. Barnes x
James E. Hoven x
Thomas Motes
William F. Odom
Albert G. Raybourn x
William W. Bagley x
Fred Dumas x
Leander Joiner

John D. Henley x
Leo DuBose
Fred'k L. Danzey x
Dacy B. McVay
Jesse B. Doyle
William B. Doyle
Albert V. Pugh x
Thomas K. Boyles
Shellie A. Wilson x
James K. Ashley
Pearl Furr
John R. Bolen x
Gordon B. Vickers
John C. Spinks
Eddie Bishop x
Arthur Bishop x
James H. Brunson x
Bettis Anderson x
Johnnie Roberts
Robert Jordan
Ellis McNider x
Chauncey Moore
Jim M. Sellers
William C. Boswell x
Hadden S. Pritchett
James N. Dunning
Foster R. Treaster
Charles P. McLain x
Thomas B. Gwin x
Elmore Raybourn x
Thomas E. Glenn x
Gus T. Gates
Robert E. Rice
Ewell D. McIntyre
Welton G. Hicks x
John C. Bolen
Walter J. Amerson x

Marion Stabler x
George Faile
Joe D. Lindsay
John H. Hendricks x
Floyd A. Garrick
Henry Blackman x
Chester L. Allen
Robert B. Mosley x
Ashland C. Spinks x
Buster Coats x
Cecil B. Kirk x
Thomas Williams x
Leo H. Hoven
Marion M. Mott x
Ellis G. Griffin x
Elbert Reeves
Atwood Hoven x
Robert J. Fendley x
Felix Wixey x
Wayman D. Keil
Jim H. Turner x
John B. Keel x
James D. Calhoun x
Emmett W. Garrick
Ivy Griffin
John C. Stewart x
George G. Garrett
Charles W. Gwin x
John H. Webb
Thomas H. Steele x
Mark B. Weston
Edward G. Adams
Woodie T. Simpkins x
Joe R. Pickens x
Charles L. Warner
Joe T. Lockhart
Brasell Bradford

Bennie M. Glenn
Floyd C. Mott x
Thomas Cross Wilson
Wiley D. Bagley x
Hugh H. Lisenbe x
Clay A. Davis
Thomas J. Kirven
Clement C. Hill x
John D. Gill x
Watt T. Jordan
John E. Robinson
George C. Pugh
Jesse H. Daughtry x
Evey R. Goodman x
John F. Tucker
Alfred Bettis Pugh
Thurman C. Waller x
Henry L. Brandenberg
William T. Day x
Albert Fendley
W. T. Godbold x
Otha H. Dunning x
John E. Marshall
Ocie W. Kinman x
Emmett M. Lyles
Wallace A. Tompkins x
John T. Baugh
Lewis H. Phillips x
August F. McFadyen x
John F. Roberts x
Creagh B. Mathers x
Henry E. Knight
Thomas J. Larrimore
Fate J. Brunson x
Searcy M. Parker x
Sidney A. McDonald x
Connie Smith x

Robbie B. Pugh x
David T. Reid x
Edwin B. Davis
Ned D. Lee x
John B. Lee x
William B. Fendley x
Amos L. Overstreet x
Earl F. Cobb
Thomas B. Jowers x
John Webb x
James S. Webb
Monroe Rush x
James Mayton x
Joseph McNider x
Ocie B. Pugh x
Mayben B. Pugh x
Earl E. Pugh
Leslie White x
Condie W. Mathews
Hilton K. Joiner
Robert L. Lamberth
Henchie W. Stephens x
Walter E. Roe x
Stonewall J. Roberts x
Carlos Overstreet
Manley B. Griffin x
David T. Mott
Raleigh J. Bumpers x
Henchey M. Skinner
William B. Burge x
Joe Hare
Plez A. Holtam x
John C. Wilson x
Enoch C. Gates x
Geo. W. Cunningham x
Willie G. Bolen
Joseph E. Bell x

Harvey B. Stanley x
Coble H. Stanley x
Guy W. Foreman x
Orie S. Rivers x
Robert Wade x
Solon Day
Franklin H. Coxwell
Mitchell C. McVay x
John N. Wiggins
Joseph S. Cleveland x
Henry F. Overstreet x
George D. Hicks
Sam Overstreet
Henry F. Bradley x
Theo. W. Megginson x
Sullivan Shehan x
Koss U. Shehan x
Thomas K. Mayton x
Nathaniel B. Jackson x
Robert L. Sewell
Ivy C. Deas x
Gross Hoven x
Alvin Rotch
Johnnie Pugh x
Erby A. Dungan x
Sam R. Jones x
Paul S. Jones x
Albert R. Milstead x
Daniel E. Fendley x
Albert Williamson x
James M. Harper x
Edward J. Davis x
Willie Edge x
Grady B. Dungan
Robert M. McVay
John T. Coxwell
Henley B. Jones x

Colonel M. Ott x
Carlos T. Parker x
Reuben F. McKinley x
Massey A. Gwin x
Fred Boroughs x
Charles W. Calhoun
Clarence C. Etheridge
Tollie E. McIntyre
Ocie A. Jackson
Edward O. Lynch x
Ormand L. Davis
John F. Waite
Connie E. Jordan
Fletcher F. Brassell x
Sollie Hoven x
Henry G. Tucker x
Ormond O. Mobley
Reuben R. Singleton
John H. Gunn
James C. Dortch x
Bernard Jackson
John L. Williamson x
George Kelley x
Sidney B. Faile x
Ellis N. Armistead
Owen B. Armistead
Howard L. Bumpers x
Henry J. Dunn x
Emmett Schultz
Wallace E. Calhoun x
Ollie S. Henderson x
Felix Hill
Percy C. Megginson x
Travis R. Dungan
Arthur S. Davis x
George T. Spinks x
Raymond Dumas x

WORLD WAR SOLDIERS

Columbus E. Benson x
John D. Wilson
Clarence Beck
Wyatt F. Anderson
John Wimberly x
Sidney Shehan x
Samuel L. Spinks x
Jack Furr
Edwin B. Davis
Marion C. McMullen
Agnew A. McIntyre
Frank McMullen
Bryant Day
William C. Brady
Thomas M. Findley
Maynard Carl
Geo. A. P. McWhorter
Christopher C. Beverly
Marion Sheffield x
James A. Autrey
James G. Bedsole
Roland E. Adams
Walter W. Andrews
Robert G. Martin x
Alfonso B. Hill
Ellis B. Calhoun
Thomas F. Bradford
Roland C. Heard

Cory L. Calhoun
James L. White
Thomas P. Tompkins
William L. Garrick
Charles L. Morgan
Ernest W. Wimpee
Jesse R. Lamberth x
Jerry W. Favor
Benjamin F. Adams x
Gross S. Turner
David M. Spinks
Lafe C. Calhoun
Earl C. Nichols
Robert S. Bradley
Clinton J. Morgan
Jesse T. Anderson
James Lawlis
W. C. Wiggins
William A. Wiggins
Robert A. Lamberth
James E. Edison
Agnew A. McIntyre
Lemon D. Weaver
Harry L. Oliver x
Henry Bowen Odom x
Clayton W. Knight
William Elbert Smith
W. W. Clay

COLORED

Caleb Chapman
Clarence Pendleton
Charlie Coate
Charlie Robinson
Simon Morris
Eddie Horn
Arthur Black

Belah Pugh
Nick Peavy
Raymond Chapman
Manuel Nobles
Bob Hill
John Craig
Lem W. Finch

Arthur Fluker
Henry Thomas
Sullivan Chapman
Roger Daffin
John W. Lynam
Henry Martin
Lon Stallworth
George Marshall
Tommie Jackson
Lee Williams
Allen Davis
Lige Robinson
Alf Howze
Albert Malone
Senah Beckham
Alfonso Borroughs
Willie Cleveland
Nick Green
Nathaniel Snell
Carrie L. Borroughs
Miles Robinson
Mancy Denson
Eugene Denson
Ocie Bass
Robert L. Callier
Leijurd A. Walker x
Tillis Love
Cossie Chapman x
Albert Morris x
Gilbert Morris x
Harry Howze x
Henry Howze
Robert H. Taylor x
Elijah Pugh x
Colonel Dickerson x
Reuben Pugh
Steve L. Pugh x

Frank Ezelle x
Arthur L. Chapman
Elijah Chapman x
Agee Chapman
Sol Chapman x
Joe Williams
Isaac L. Williams x
Joseph Thornton, x
President Dickerson
George H. Frowner x
William E. H. Parker x
Merrida Allen x
James Allen x
John Horn
Joe Turner x
Edward Fluker
Ed James, Jr.
Fred Robinson
Archie A. Pugh x
Charlie J. Dickerson x
David T. Wilson
Gross Rainey x
James Chapman x
John Kennis, Jr. x
James Todd x
Odell Todd
Portland Nichols
Carvin Hawkins x
Harris Williams x
John W. Wallace x
Caleb Boroughs
Robert Lynum x
Aberdeen Hayden x
Perry Johnson
Raymond Calhoun x
Alec Howze
Alonzo Brown

Carson Law
Thomas Shelly x
Joe Taylor
Otis Bunn
Robert J. Buck

Mitford Chapman
George Law
Russel July
Emmitt Goodwin

THOMASVILLE

Thomasville is one of the largest business centers between Selma and Mobile. It is situated ninety-seven miles from Mobile and sixty-eight miles from Selma. It draws trade from a large territory and its business men are wide awake. The rise of this town was the fall of old Choctaw Corner, which is one and a half miles distant.

Thomasville has had two newspapers, which are mentioned elsewhere.

We are indebted to Mrs. Bettie Forster, one of Thomasville's most intelligent and accomplished ladies, for the following history of the town of Thomasville:

Rumors of a coming railroad blew the sails of progressive men to a favored spot in Clarke County, where, in the summer of 1887, among its cradling hills, was born a fair little city.

Trouble arose when they said, "Name this child." 'Twas thought fitting to christen it "Choctaw," from the Indian tribe, it being near the corner of the boundary line established in a division of territory between the Creeks and Choctaws. This line now runs through the town, and to-day the Jackson National Highway is being constructed along this historic Indian boundary.

There was confusion with the old town of Choctaw Corner, near by, and the new town Choctaw, so this name was abandoned. Someone next suggested "Birmile," a contraction of Birmingham and Mobile; but, no, this was not pleasing to all, and it, too, was laid aside.

One morning a large placard bearing the name "Eureka" was conspicuously displayed. All now thought they had found it; but not all agreed to this. Next name given was "Folsom City," in honor of Mrs. Grover Cleveland, first lady of the land; but not this. Woman had not yet come into her own. The final choice was "Thomasville," in honor of General Samuel Thomas, of the firm of Brice & Thomas, of New York, the financiers of the new railroad. In recognition of this signal honor, General Thomas authorized the town to draw on him for $500 for a high school. With this gift and contributions from the people a beautiful school building, the Thomasville Institute, was erected on a high peak on the south side of Wilson avenue. The building was completely destroyed by fire before the contractors turned it over to the trustees. 'Twas said the loss was caused by a match and a boy's cigarette.

The rumbling wheels of progress were now heard in the distance. The road known as the Mobile and West Alabama Railroad, with Colonel T. G. Bush as president, was completed to Thomasville in the latter part of 1887, and was opened for traffic in 1888. The name of the road was then changed to "Mobile and Birmingham," and again in 1899 to the Southern Railway, when it was taken over and became a part of the Southern Railway system. Prominent among the promoters of the new town was Mr. W. L. Henderson, who was assistant to Colonel Bush, and in reality the original founder of the town.

Mr. Henderson is still a valued official of the road, and

is still one of Thomasville's best boosters. We recall with pride the name of one Mr. James White, from Illinois, who was a prominent member of the railroad family, and a highly respected citizen, who also very ably served the town in the capacity of mayor. The town and railroad still have closely allied interests. Hon. A. W. Clements, who has efficiently filled the agency here for a number of years, is also the city's chief executive.

The town site selected was in the midst of a dense forest. A tremendous task lay before the founders. The sound of the axe, the saw, plane and hammer was to be heard on all sides. Mills, shops and homes were hurriedly built. These were the busy, earnest people, exultant in the building of a new and prosperous community.

The first white child born at Thomasville was a little Eggleston. The event was celebrated by the donation of a town lot. The family came here from Mississippi. The father was a carpenter and built many houses here. Soon the new people felt the need of a house of worship. A hall was erected on the spot where now stands the residence of Mr. Albert Johnson, our city attorney. Union services were held here from time to time. Mr. Fisher, of Presbyterian faith, was superintendent of the first Sunday school. This hall was also used for all public entertainments. It was familiarly known as the Thomasville Opera House. There were frequent magic lantern shows. By way of contrast we point with pride to our school auditorium and the splendid senior plays and the many lyceum attractions secured by different organizations. The population increased and ways and means were devised for the building of needed churches. In the fall of 1889 the Methodist church was built. Mr. Frank Adams was a prime mover in that he gave the land on which to build, did a goodly share of the work, and gave further financial aid. Rev. Mr. Martin was the first pastor. Later this building was used for a school and a larger and better church built, which now stands on Wilson avenue.

On the third Sunday in March, 1890, the First Baptist church was organized. At this meeting Rev. W. B. Crumpton of Marion served as moderator, with Mr. I. A. White, of McKinley, as secretary. Rev. W. A. Parker was chosen the first pastor. Some of the charter members are still on the roll. Among them are Mrs. Mott, Mrs. V. J. Kimbrough, Mr. and Mrs. W. H. Hinson, Mr. Alex. and Miss Callie Hall. On the following fifth Sunday the Baptist Sunday school was organized with forty-two members. They built a large church on the lot now occupied by the pastorium. This was burned some years after, but replaced by a handsome brick structure on Wilson avenue and West Second street, the pride of the community.

In 1900 the Presbyterians built a church. Mr. S. P. Noble donated a lot for the building. The congregation was small and it was found burdensome to keep up a church, so in after years it was sold and converted into a residence, which is now owned and occupied by Mr. V. M. McDonald.

The first school was taught in a crude little cabin on the Moseley place, where now is the H. H. Williams residence. The teacher was a young man from Choctaw County, one Charley McCall, who afterward became judge and a man of prominence. Many have followed in his wake, among them will be remembered Prof. Collins, Mr. Norman Gunn, Prof. McIver, Messrs. Henley, Smith, Pugh, Rozier,

Kersh, Hunt and Hardy. Today we have a consolidated school, a commodious building taking care of near four hundred pupils, with a splendid corps of teachers, eleven in number, headed by Prof. Bennett, of Evergreen, as principal.

New industries were springing up, the volume of business so increasing as to necessitate the facilities of a banking system, hence in 1894 three Camden men, Messrs. Jule and Walter Alford and Pete Horn, came over and organized the first bank. The next year this was taken over by Mr. J. W. Tucker. The First National Bank, absorbing the Tucker private bank, was organized in 1901, with $25,000 capital stock, and J. S. Hanley of Tuscaloosa as president. In 1904 the Citizens National Bank was organized, with capital stock of equal amount, with J. H. Wood, president, and J. W. Tucker, cashier. Then in 1907 these two banks were merged into one, the Farmers Bank and Trust Company, with a capital stock of $100,000, J. W. Tucker, president, and James G. Cuninghame, cashier. Later Mr. Cuninghame, having been elected probate judge of the county, his place has been filled by Paul Clarke, a capable and efficient officer. This bank's resources are now far past the million dollar mark.

Lumbering has ever been an important industry. Virgin forests of long-leaf yellow pine surrounded the town. Pioneers in this business were the Halls, the Williams, the Scotts and Mrs. Livingston. Today the town is enjoying added prosperity from the operation of a number of stave mills.

Its agricultural interests are varied. Before the days of the boll weevil Thomasville took high rank as a shipping point for cotton, handling in a season as many as 10,000 bales.

The mercantile business thrives and flourishes. Prominent among the first merchants were Messrs. Poole and Robison, N. B. Boyles, the Adams, Mr. Billy Wilson and J. W. Brand. The first milliner was Mrs. Mott, conducting a successful business. As a trimmer she was an adept at copying hats of visitors from various points. To satisfy the trade today we have well-equipped establishments, trained trimmers and Parisian patterns. We boast of a number of splendid shops, equal in style and quality to those of any town quadruple its size and age.

The automobile business looms large. To Mr. W. W. Bettis, a prosperous citizen, belongs the distinction of having the first automobile in town.

In the summer of 1889 the town was visited by a dreadful scourge, a fever that baffled the skill of the physicians, a malignant type of typhus fever. Many young persons died from it. A peculiar feature of the disease was that it attacked only young men and women, not a single child nor an old person being stricken. The state health officer, Dr. Saunders, came to investigate the cause. He reported that the water was contaminated by so much decaying timber. The town was almost depopulated for a time. Those who could not leave would spend the nights at Choctaw Corner, returning in the day. The scourge passed and things were not long in assuming the normal. All things went well for some years, but the town was destined to receive another blow. In November, 1899, a most disastrous fire swept away the business part of town, leaving only one building, the brick store east of the railroad. Little undaunted, all set to work in dead earnest to rebuild, this time with brick and stone.

With its advancement along religious, educational and commercial lines, the social side has not been neglected. Thomasville as a social center has no peer. Her sons and daughters are filling high places in church and state. Her professional men measure up to the highest standard. The benefit of organized fraternalism is a source of enjoyment to many. The federated clubs and societies sponsored by the good women of the town are a means of social culture and wield an uplifting influence on the community.

Let us not look mournfully to the past, but find our life in the fidelities of the present, and with a manly heart go forth to meet the future.

CHOCTAW ENTERPRISE

In December, 1887, the Choctaw Enterprise was established by J. F. Meyers and C. W. Hudson. In a short time the name was changed to Thomasville News; it was called the Alliance Reporter; then again Thomasville News. It has had many editors and publishers — Doyle & Desha, Poole, Henry Nixon, Rev. F. H. Von Kon, Robert Carter, Nelson C. White, and others.

JACKSON SPRING (NEAR THOMASVILLE)

It is, perhaps, known to very few people in Clarke County that there is a spring near Thomasville named in honor of General Andrew Jackson. To be frank, the writer was unaware of it until he received a brief historical sketch below, furnished us by Mrs. Eugene P. Stutts:

HISTORIC FACTS CONCERNING JACKSON SPRING AND THE OLD LINE ROAD

"Jackson Spring is just under the hill from this road, which is now a part of Jackson Highway, about one hundred yards east of the residence of Dr. Eugene P. Stutts. This spring flows freestone water every day and night of the year, and forms the head of Hayden's Creek. This spring derived its name from General Andrew Jackson.

"In 1815, on January 8th, the battle of New Orleans was fought, soon after which General Andrew Jackson marched his army from that place to Pensacola, Fla. He occupied Pensacola, which was then a Spanish possession, until the latter part of the summer of 1815, when he started on his homeward march to Tennessee, where his army was mustered out of service and disbanded. It was an unbroken wilderness through which his army had to pass and the road was cut as they marched, and was laid off by the engineers of the army.

"They marched in a northwesterly direction, crossing the Alabama river at Fort Claiborne, which was located on its eastern bank, on the western boundary of what is now Monroe County. They followed practically the same direction, making what has been called the Old Line road to where now stands the town of Thomasville. There the army camped for a few days and the general's headquarters were located on the top of the ridge, just above this spring.

"After breaking camp here the army marched nearly due north and passed through the village of Elyton, which is now Birmingham.

"It was related of the Indians who were with Jackson in

establishing the boundary that they marked every tree for a space of fifty yards on either side of the Line road, and that neither the Choctaws nor the Creeks would cross the boundary into the others' territory."

GROVE HILL

In 1832 the county seat was removed from Clarkesville to Grove Hill and a frame court-house was built. Grove Hill was called Macon, in honor of a Mr. Macon, who resided about two miles west of the town. When the citizens attempted to establish a postoffice they found that there was another Macon in Alabama, so the name of Grove Hill was given to the postoffice, while the town was called Macon. Gradually as the old people died and new citizens moved in the name Macon gave place to Grove Hill. In 1899 the old frame court-house was torn down and a new brick structure was erected at a cost of $13,500. The marble tablet in the hall bears the following inscription:

TABLET
Clarke County Officers
1899

John M. Wilson	Probate Judge
N. E. Drew	
R. L. Ezell	
A. J. Pace	Commissioners
W. L. Williams	
W. W. Daffin	Clerk Circuit Court
Clayton Foscue	Clerk Probate Court
W. J. Taylor	Sheriff

COURT HOUSE

GROVE HILL

W. M. Mobley - - - - - Tax Collector
N. P. Burge - - - - - - Tax Assessor
John M. Agee - - - - - - Treasurer
J. F. Gillis - - - - Register in Chancery
R. C. Heard - - Superintendent of Education
W. D. Dunn - - - - - County Solicitor
Isaac Grant - - - - - - - Senator
T. A. Long - - - - - ⎱ Representatives
J. W. Mathews - - - - ⎰
G. E. Robinson - - - - ⎱ Surveyors
Henry Nixon - - - - ⎰
Hull & Ewing - - - - - - Architects

In a few years this building was found to be too small and an annex was built at a cost of $10,000. The cornerstone on its front has this inscription:

CLARKE COUNTY
Established
December 10 — 1812
Stone laid by
L. H. Lee, Grand Master
A. D. 1911   A. L. 5911

The reverse side bears the following:

Commissioners Court
1911
Clayton Foscue, Judge of Probate, Chairman
J. W. Davis   D. W. Robinson
J. S. Henson   W. J. Tompkins
Commissioners

When the first court-house was built in 1832 a jail was built of hewn logs on a stone foundation. In 1870 the prisoners then confined in this jail tried to burn a hole in the log wall through which they might escape, but the fire got out of their control and the building was burned down, but not before help arrived and the prisoners saved. A new brick jail was erected that year, around which a wooden wall was built, eighteen feet high, in the following manner: A ditch was dug around the jail, two feet wide and four feet deep, and twenty-four feet from the jail. Into this ditch was placed fat-pine bars hewed out seven by ten inches, in an upright position and touching each other. The soil was then filled in, leaving a solid pine foundation about eight inches above the surface. To this foundation was nailed planks two inches thick and twelve inches wide, both inside and outside, making a double wall eighteen feet high. This was then covered with two-foot boards so as to preserve the wall from decay.

In 1887 new steel cells were installed at a cost of $3,100. In 1910 the jail was again repaired. A reinforced concrete two-story addition was made to the brick part, the old cells taken out and new ones installed, bathrooms installed, and the best sanitary fixtures placed in every room.

In 1909 the citizens tore down the old school building, put up in 1856, and erected a house on the state school plan. In seeking funds to build this house they presented the subscription list to Mr. M. Van Heuvel, the agent and partner of the Sage Land and Improvement Company, a real estate company owing at that time many thousands of acres of valuable timber in Clarke and Choctaw Counties. The company, through Mr. Van Heuvel, gave $20,000 for the

COUNTY HIGH SCHOOL BUILDING AT GROVE HILL

erection of a high school building at Grove Hill for the benefit of the two counties. The citizens completed the grammar school building with their own money and then built a high school building at a cost of $10,000, setting aside $10,000 as an endowment from which they receive from the state $600 each year. In 1910, under an act passed at the last legislature, the state located the Clarke County High School at Grove Hill, and the school was organized with Prof. W. F. Puckett as principal, and Prof. L. Y. McLeod and Miss Marion McClellan as assistants.

Grove Hill has built up rapidly for the last twenty years. It has a number of business houses, two churches — Methodist and Baptist, two thriving schools, one being a state high school; two up-to-date drug stores, a telephone system and a picture house, and last, but not least, a prosperous bank.

Prominent among the families in and around Grove Hill for the last century are the Chapmans, Pughs, McLeods and Calhouns. These families are all more or less related, either by affinity or consanguinity. We shall not undertake to give their individual names, for they are "too numerous to mention." About the middle of the nineteenth century Grove Hill came near being depopulated by a scourge of yellow fever.

ROCKVILLE

There is no town at Rockville, but there is a schoolhouse, a church and a postoffice. There is now under course of construction near the church at that place a three-room school building. The citizens of that neighborhood believe in education. Mr. Ball speaks of teaching school at that place about seventy years ago. Living near that place now are the Blackwells, the Howells, the Allens, and others.

CHOCTAW BLUFF

Choctaw Bluff, where the Indian village, Maubila, was supposed to have been situated 383 years ago, there is nothing except a postoffice and a store.

CHOCTAW CORNER

Choctaw Corner was one of the old towns of Clarke. It was quite a thriving place before the Civil War, and for some years after the close of the war. When the (now) Southern Railroad came through the county, leaving that place a mile and a half from the road, and Thomasville sprang up, Choctaw Corner disappeared from the map. We are told that there is one old "landmark" still left there in the person of Baldwin Stutts.

ALLEN

Allen is situated two miles west of Suggsville and is the station for Suggsville. There are two or three business houses there, and a school and church near by.

GAINESTOWN

Gainestown is one of the oldest towns in the county. Much business was done there before the Civil War. There are several stores there now, but there is not the business done there now that there was in ante-bellum days. Dr. Henry G. Davis, Reese Norris, J. S. Lambard were among the prominent men living there fifty years ago.

WHATLEY

Whatley is about six miles southeast of Grove Hill, and is the shipping point for that place. Whatley was named in honor of a Mr. Whatley who owned the land on which the depot is situated. Quite a lot of business is done there. There is a church and a school there. Quite a lot of lumber is shipped from that point.

FULTON

Fulton is a saw-mill town. There is a very large saw-mill there, owned by the Scotch Lumber Company, a corporation.

The citizens of Fulton are wide-awake, progressive people. They have churches and a good school.

DICKINSON

Dickinson is situated about six miles northeast of Grove Hill. It sprang up with the railroad. Quite a lot of business is done there and the people of that place believe in churches and schools.

WALKER SPRINGS

Walker Springs dates back about fifty years, but there was very little known of it until after the coming of the railroad. It is quite a little town. It has several stores, a school, two churches and several industries. The old settlers of that community were the Gills, the Gwins, the Myricks, the Colemans, the Jones, the Drews and others. The pioneer merchant there was John F. Murphy. H. J. Savage, of Perdue Hill, Monroe County, moved there after the railroad was completed, erected a dwelling house out in the hills north of town and built a store-house in town, and opened up a general store, and did a flourishing business there for quite a while, when other merchants came in. The town is supposed to have been named in honor of a man by the name of Walker, who settled near that place over a hundred years ago. His name was William Walker, and he was the grandfather of Hodges Walker, who resides about two miles north of Jackson. Walker owned a mineral spring, or overflowing well, just back of the present town, hence the name Walker Springs. Mr. Savage brought in an overflowing well near his store, which was very strong of sulphur and other medicinal properties. Mr. Murphy and Mr. Savage departed this life many years ago.

SALITPA

Salitpa is situated in the southwest corner of township 8, north range one east. This town sprang up about forty years ago. It has several stores, two churches, a good school, and has a good farming country surrounding it. Some of the old settlers there were the McCorquodales, Moltons, Atchisons, Yorks, Pughs, Mitchels, Cleilands, Porters, McVays, Robinsons, Berrys, Dawsons, Whites, Doyles, and many others.

TALLAHATTA SPRINGS

Tallahatta Springs is located in the northern portion of the county. Ball says this was a health resort about eighty-five or ninety years ago. There is nothing left but the spring. There is nothing there now to indicate that there had ever been a town there. Its former glory has all departed.

JACKSON CHURCHES

On the opposite page will be seen pictures of the three churches in Jackson — Methodist, Presbyterian and Baptist. Rev. S. U. Turnipseed is pastor of the Methodist church; Rev. W. G. Greenlees, pastor of the Presbyterian church, and Rev. T. B. McPheters, pastor of the Baptist church.

When the old town of Jackson was laid out over a century ago the town authorities set aside three lots for church purposes, one for the Baptist, one for the Methodist, and one for the Presbyterian, but no house was erected on either lot. About seventy-five or eighty years ago Mr. Walter Taylor erected a small church near the present cemetery, in which the Methodists worshiped awhile. Later on, the exact date not known, but some time before the commencement of the Civil War, a more commodious building was erected near the same spot, and the Methodists used that church until some time in the early nineties, when a new building was erected on the north side of Commerce street, just opposite the home of J. C. Rivers. That church was used for a few years, when the present church was built.

The Baptists organized a church and erected a building

JACKSON CHURCHES

on the lot where the Presbyterian church is now located in 1858. In 1873 this building was turned over to the Presbyterians and the Baptists had no building until the early nineties, when quite a nice building was erected on the lot where the Nichols residence is now situated. This building was sold to Mr. Nichols and the present church erected.

The Presbyterians organized a church here in 1873 and used the old building originally used by the Baptists. Twenty odd years ago they erected the handsome building now situated on the lot where the old building stood. The old building was rolled away and converted into a dwelling house.

JACKSON IN 1923

Jackson is indeed a city set upon an hill. It is situated on a beautiful plateau, a half-mile east of the Tombigbee river, and half a mile north of the Southern Railroad. The town proper is two hundred and twenty-five feet above the low-water mark on the Tombigbee.

The town of Jackson shook off its Van Winkle slumber and began to step forward with the coming of the railroad in 1886-87, and it has made great progress since that day. It has grown from a town with one store in 1875, to a town of about twenty business houses; from a town of less than one hundred and fifty inhabitants to one of nearly two thousand inhabitants, including white and colored in both instances. Jackson is one of the leading towns of southwest Alabama. It is up to date in nearly all respects. It has telephone and telegraph service, electric lights, ice plant, waterworks on the way, up-to-date bank, two schools, three churches, three saw-mills, one veneer plant, one stave mill, and several small industries. The town has three barber shops, a shoe shop, several garages and repair shops, one up-to-date bakery. There are five medical doctors located in the town, one dentist, and three ministers of the Gospel. Each denomination — Methodist, Baptist and Presbyterian — owns a home for its pastor.

There are several saw-mills being operated near the town, which swell the pay-roll of the town. Every dwelling and business house in town is occupied.

Our churches, our schools and our enterprises will receive special mention under appropriate captions.

From the standpoint of healthfulness Jackson has an unsurpassed record. This is due chiefly to natural advantages, such as are possessed by few other spots. The high altitude, combined with an abundance of pure water, the ideal climate, and natural drainage, are making it sought more and more as a health resort.

C. L. WARNER RESIDENCE

The Warner residence is situated where the James Fitts stood more than a hundred years ago. James Fitts, familiarly known as Jim Fitts, was a prominent, well-to-do man, but was evidently not a very pious man, judging from the following story told in connection with him:

On one occasion a Methodist preacher named Honeymon (the first to visit Jackson) was on his way to the town on horseback. While traveling along a public road leading to the town he was overtaken by a gentleman mounted on a handsome steed. It was in the afternoon; they passed

RESIDENCE OF C. L. WARNER AND OTHERS

the accustomed greetings and rode on, conversing on the topics of the day. After they had traveled some distance the stranger ventured to ask the preacher where he was going. "I am going down to Jackson to fight the devil and Jim Fitts," said the preacher. A smile played over the countenance of the stranger, unseen by the divine, and there were no further questions asked along that line. About dusk they rode up to the front gate of a handsome home on the east side of the town of Jackson. The stranger halted and said to the man of God: "This is my home. Won't you get down, come in and spend the night?" "Who are you?" said the preacher. "This is Jim Fitts," said the man. "Well, I believe I will," said the preacher, and he did. It is said that when the two men went in, Mrs. Fitts, who had evidently been expecting Mr. Honeymon, met them at the door. Mr. Fitts said to her, "Here is your Methodist preacher; I hope you are satisfied."

It is said that Mrs. Fitts was a very pious woman, but whether or not she and the preacher were successful in persuading Mr. Fitts to "depart from the error of his way" tradition does not say.

It is said that Lorenzo Dowe, a pioneer preacher, who made his appearance in Washington County about the year 1804, had had some experience with Jim Fitts prior to the visit of Mr. Honeymon. Tradition has it that Mr. Dowe had been preaching in Jackson for several days, but finding his efforts of no avail, decided to leave town. On his way out of town he met an acquaintance, who inquired if he was leaving town, and Mr. Dowe answered, "Yes, I am leaving Jackson to the devil and Jim Fitts." This is perhaps what

TYPICAL BUSINESS HOUSES

led Mr. Honeymon to say that he was going to Jackson to fight the devil and Jim Fitts.

Lorenzo Dowe was well known to the pioneers of this country. He is said to have been the preacher who went to Old St. Stephens on one occasion to preach, and upon being asked to leave town, did so, but not until he had prayed the Almighty to send a curse upon the place, and predicted that the town would soon perish and the spot where it stood would become the roosting place for bats and owls. Whether or not God did send a curse upon the town we are not able to say, but it is a fact that the town did wither and decay, and the spot where this flourishing town was situated there is now a dense forest. The fall may have been from natural causes, but it makes one feel creepy to stand near that spot at night and hear the hoot of the hooting owl and the cry of the lone whip-poor-will.

JACKSON PHYSICIANS

The following is a list of physicians who have practiced medicine in Jackson during the last fifty years:

L. O. Hicks (now dead)   Jim Curtis
F. L. Sewell (now dead) J. R. Armistead
G. H. Moore   Isham Kimbell
G. S. Chapman   J. G. Bedsole
Bryan Boroughs   Kimbell Hicks
T. C. Kirven   G. C. McCrary
W. A. Kimbrough

Dr. Hicks located in Jackson in 1873, and was actively engaged in the practice of his profession until his death, which occurred on July 18, 1921. Dr. McCrary moved to Jackson in January, 1923, fifty years after the coming of Dr. Hicks. Dr. McCrary was reared in Mobile County.

DRUG STORE

Jackson's first drug store was established in 1897 by D. Adams, of Pine Apple, Ala. By uniform courtesy and close attention to business he has been very successful.

TOWN OFFICIALS

Since the town of Jackson was incorporated in 1896 the following-named persons have served the town in the capacity of mayor: S. T. Woodard, Sr., J. A. Savage, Sr., C. W. Boyles, J. B. Williams, L. E. McLeod, W. P. Cannady, A. E. Chunn, W. W. McCorqudale and W. A. Calhoun.

The present town officials are: W. A. Calhoun, mayor; Mrs. W. A. Calhoun, clerk; Thomas Kirven, treasurer; J. W. Bedwell, sheriff or marshal; J. C. Stewart, Jr., J. D. Guy, A. H. Rodgers, J. C. Skipper and W. W. McCorquodale.

MINISTERS

Methodist

Ministers born in Clarke County: C. W. Calhoun, J. S. Frazier, D. W. Haskew, B. C. Glen, Jr., Archie Coleman, Eugene Coleman, J. O. Lawrence, O. J. Goodman, D. B. Dismukes, George Fontaine, L. C. Calhoun, S. T. Woodard, Norman McLeod, Fletcher McLeod, Grady Cowan.

Ministers who have traveled in Clarke County: D. S. McDonald, Anthony Dickinson, —— Roper, W. A. Sampy, C. H. Carter, J. K. Tansey, J. P. Jones, A. M. Jones, Elisha Phillips, Henry Urquhart, J. F. Evans, W. S. Wade, B. C.

Glen, W. H. Morris, J. W. McCann, J. H. James (born in Ireland), J. W. Hamner, J. F. Feagan, C. W. Gavin, J. A. Greene, —— Truitt, O. V. Calhoun.

Local preachers born in Clarke County: Malcolm Calhoun, Hugh Calhoun, P. L. Martin, Stephen Gilmore, —— Windbush, W. O. Calhoun, Matthew Cox.

Baptist Preachers

—— Parker, Warren Whatley, Martin Whatley, Hiram Chreiton, Alex. Stringer, Jim Stringer, Jamie Chapman, D. D. (born and reared in Clarke), A. S. Adams, Frank McGill (born and reared in Clarke), Samuel A. Cowan.

SCHOOL BUILDINGS

On the opposite page will be seen pictures of the State Secondary Agricultural School and Farm, and the Graded School. No. 1 is the farm; No. 2 the high school, No. 3 the graded school building.

JACKSON'S SCHOOLS

The First District Agricutlural School, now called the State Secondary Agricultural School, was established in 1896, its first president being Rev. T. C. Klyce, of Kentucky.

FACULTY FOR 1923-24

Principal and Science	Mr. C. L. Smith
Athletics and Math.	Mr. Francis B. Pratt
English and History	Miss Helen Deal
Home Economics	Miss Annie C. Broughton
Agriculture	Mr. Paul Fisher

SCHOOL BUILDINGS

FACULTY FOR 1922-23

Principal and Math. - - -	Mr. R. D. Powell
Athletics and Science - -	Mr. T. H. Williams
English and History - - -	-Miss Ella Spurlin
Home Economics - - -	Miss Annie C. Broughton
Agriculture - - - - -	Mr. Paul Fisher

FACULTY FOR 1921-22

Principal, Math. and Athletics	Mr. R. D. Powell
History and English - - -	Miss Johnny W. Cooper
Home Economics - - -	Miss Annie C. Broughton
Agriculture - - - - -	Mr. Paul Fisher

(After February, 1922, Mr. Charles Tipton took classes in Math. and Science.)

FACULTY FOR 1920-21

Principal, Math. and Athletics	Mr. R. D. Powell
History and English - - -	Miss Johnny Cooper
Science and Home Economics	Miss Elizabeth Herring
Science and Agriculture - -	Mr. Paul Fisher

FACULTY FOR 1919-20

Principal and Agriculture	Mr. F. N. Nelson
Athletics and Science - - -	Mr. Charles Bush
English and History - - -	
Home Economics and English	Miss Bernice P. Jackson

FACULTY FOR 1918-19

Principal and Agriculture - -	Mr. Fred N. Nelson

In 1918 the State Department of Vocational Education recommended and installed a department of vocational agriculture in the State Secondary Agriculture at Jackson. A large sum of money was raised locally to equip this department, as is necessary under the state and federal laws governing schools giving this work.

The first year seemed fairly successful, but the following year the results were so far below expectation that the state department withdrew its support of this department. The following year a part-time teacher of vocational work made good, and as the year passed built up a class that met the requirements, and a full-time program was again put on. At the present time there are two departments of vocational education in operation at the State Secondary Agricultural School — one in Agriculture and the other in Home Economics.

Miss Annie Celeste Broughton — Daughter of Mr. and Mrs. J. C. Broughton, was born at Fries, Va., on June 27, 1902. She attended grammar and high school at Camp Hill, Ala., and was graduated from the Alabama Technical Institute and College for Women in Vocational Home Economics at Montevallo, Ala., in 1921. She has had charge of that department of Vocational Home Economisc in Jackson, Ala., for three years.

Miss Helen Margaret Deal — Daughter of A. J. Deal, of Knoxville, Tenn. Attended Farragut High School, Concord, Tenn., 1914-18. Entered Maryville College, Maryville, Tenn., in 1918; graduated with B. A. degree in 1922. Attended University of Tennessee summer of 1923. Was teacher of English in Marion County High School, Guin, Ala., 1922-23; teacher of English and History, State Secondary Agricultural School, Jackson, Ala., 1923-24.

JACKSON GRADED SCHOOL

Founded in 1909

Board of Education: John S. Graham, president; James Pritchett, secretary; George W. Powe, C. W. Boyles, Dr. George H. Moore.

Town officials: J. B. Williams, mayor; Councilmen: A. E. Chinn (treasurer), S. H. Andrews, W. B. Cannady, W. G. Bevill, S. T. Woodard, Sr.

W. R. Biggers, Mobile, Ala., architect.

Jett Bros. Construction Company, Mobile, Ala., contractor.

(The above was taken from a marble tablet placed in the hall of said building.)

TEACHERS OF JACKSON GRADED SCHOOL

Mrs. John Reinhardt - - First Grade
Mrs. Mary English - - - Second Grade
Miss Zell Chunn - - - Third Grade
Miss Tooma Stewart, succeeded by
Mrs. Claude McCrary - - Fourth Grade
Miss Thelma Rodgers - - Fifth Grade
Miss Lilian Pugh - - - Sixth Grade
Miss Rosa Lee Wilson, Seventh Grade—Prin.
Mrs. S. A. Stewart - - - Music Teacher

JACKSON SCHOOL BOARD

Following is a list of the members of the Town School Board; H. M. McLeod, chairman; C. L. Warner, J. B. Williams, G. G. Warren, Skipwith Coale.

COUNTY OFFICERS

Holding office in Clarke County during the last fifty years:

CIRCUIT CLERK

F. M. Moyler
W. W. Daffin
J. W. Cuninghame
Coma Garrett, Jr.
Chester McCorqudale
A. L. Paynne

SHERIFF

1. H. W. Burge
2. Dave Dalton
3. Dave Carter
4. George Allen
5. R. G. Allen
6. W. J. Taylor
7. W. W. Wade
8. C. A. Coates
9. Coma Garrett, Sr.
10. C. E. Cox
11. Charles Finch

TAX ASSESSOR

1. James C. Savage
2. H. P. Barge, Jr.
3. Dan Curry
4. J. B. Doyle
5. R. L. Dickerson

REGISTER IN CHANCERY

1. T. J. Ford
2. J. C. Savage
3. J. F. Gillis
4. W. D. Dunn
5. C. A. Coate

TREASURER

1. W. F. Woodard
2. J. M. Agee
3. Jesse Chapman

TAX COLLECTOR

S. J. Parker
R. H. Flinn
W. F. Woodard
Enoch Cobb
Mal. Cobb
S. R. Cobb

CIRCUIT JUDGES

The following is a list of the Circuit Judges presiding in Clarke County since the early seventies:

—— Elliott
Harry Toulmin
W. E. Clarke
James Taylor Jones
John C. Anderson
J. T. Lackland
Ben D. Turner

Lackland was the only one who lived in Clarke County. All of these men are dead except John C. Anderson and Ben D. Turner.

SOLICITORS

The following is a list of Circuit Solicitors:

John R. Tompkins
George W. Taylor
Benjamin F. Elmore
—— Harrison
O. L. Gray
John McDuffee

SUPERINTENDENT OF EDUCATION

J. W. Cunningham was appointed superintendent of education and assumed office on November 16, 1889. He was elected by a popular vote in 1890, and took office October 16, 1890, and served for two years.

L. L. McLeod was elected in 1892 and took his office on August 10th of that year for a term of two years.

Clayton Foscue was elected in 1894 and assumed office in August of that year for a term of two years.

R. C. Heard was elected in 1896, and served for several successive terms, or until October 1, 1909. During his service as superintendent the state began to wake up educationally, and the legislature passed several educational laws that put Alabama far toward the front in school progress.

T. L. Head was elected and assumed office October 1,

1909. He was re-elected in 1913 for a term of four years. During his second term of office the legislature passed a law taking the election of county superintendent out of the hands of the people and placing it in the hands of a county board composed of five members.

J. F. Gillis was elected by the County Board of Education for a term of four years, and assumed the office January 8, 1917, and served until January 4, 1922.

Under the law that divided the county into school districts there were originally created ninety-four distinct districts, but by the moving away of citizens, the growing up of the children, and consolidation, this number has been reduced to about seventy-five. There were originally thirty-six negro schools, but as they are so irregular in attendance and as negro teachers are so scarce, they never had over thirty-three schools taught in any one year, and even then one teacher has been known to teach as many as three schools of three-month terms in one year.

The last census showed a few more negro children than white, and there were less than six thousand each of school age. Dave C. Mathews is present superintendent.

J. R. Brewer was at one time superintendent, but we do not remember the date of his service.

COUNTY BOARD OF EDUCATION

Following is the personnel of the Clarke County Board of Education: Preston R. Bush, chairman, Gosport; J. W. Tucker, Thomasville; H. M. McLeod, Jackson; James P. Pugh, Grove Hill; John L. Scruggs, Sr., Coffeeville.

HISTORY OF PUBLIC EDUCATION IN ALABAMA

Early Backgrounds.—A study of the development of the Alabama school system is at once disappointing and reassuring — disappointing because of the numerous failures that might have been averted and the many promising beginnings that attained little success; reassuring because of the high points here and there reached, the absence generally of any considerable retrograde movement, and the presence in every period of at least a small coterie of able and far-seeing friends of public education.

Like other Southern states, Alabama followed the theory of Thomas Jefferson and developed its educational system from the top downward. The system was developed from the top downward, in fact, in a double sense, for not only was the State University established more than two decades before there was any general system of public schools, but the scheme of public school support likewise had its origin at the top — in federal grants and state appropriations or subsidies — and for many years local taxation, either county or district, played little part in the provision of the school revenues.

The first school in what is now Alabama was established in 1779 at the boat yard on Lake Tensas, not far north of Mobile.* Thirty-two years later, in 1811, an academy in Washington County, then a part of Mississippi Territory, was chartered by that young commonwealth, and in 1816 St. Stephens Academy was incorporated at the old town of St. Stephens in the same county; these appear to have been the same institution. In 1812 Green Academy made its ap-

---

*Pickett's Alabama, Owen's ed., p. 469.

pearance at Huntsville, in the Tennessee river valley. Such were the beginnings of education in the territory, which on December 14, 1819, became the State of Alabama.

On its admission to the Union Alabama received the usual federal grants of land for educational purposes. These comprised the sixteenth section in each township for the endowment of the common schools and two townships, or 46,080 acres, for a "seminary of learning." Two facts in connection with the grant for the common schools are of special interest. In the early years of the state's history the funds derived from these lands constituted the only public source of revenue for the schools; no intrastate public funds were provided until after the establishment of the Mobile school system, in 1826. The variation of value of these lands and their failure to produce anything like adequate school revenue for the state as a whole, added to an improvident habit of thinking which they begot in the popular mind, gave rise to difficulties that were still to be seen or easily traced many years after the grant was made. The second notable fact is that, like other federal grants for common-school purposes prior to the admission of Michigan, in 1837, the grant to Alabama was made, not to the state for the use alike of all the schools within its borders, but to the several townships within the state. Granted in this way, the sixteenth section became in each case the property of the township in which it was situated, though the state was made the trustee. Obviously the government's policy pursued after 1837 was preferable to that of giving land to the township, as was done in Alabama. For naturally the best lands were the first to be settled and soon became the homes of the wealthiest part of the population, and in consequence the more valuable school endowments were in the wealthier communities. The government's gift was therefore most bountiful where least needed and most niggardly where the needs were greatest. This condition, which only added to the self-sufficiency of the well-to-do communities, particularly in the Black Belt, and its companion evil, the aversion of the well-to-do to the free school, which was thought of only as an institution for "indigent persons," were bulky obstacles in the way of the public-school movement in the state.

It seems safe to assume that such schools as existed in Virginia, the Carolinas, Georgia and Tennessee, from which emigrants removed to Alabama, were carried by these emigrants to their new homes, though the Alabama school may have taken somewhat different form. Writing of life as it flourished in the town of Montgomery in the early twenties, Prof. Petrie says:

"A wholesome respect, at least, was shown for learning in the prompt establishment of schools and in the advertised arrival of such sturdy books as Murray's Grammar, Webster's Speller, Watts' Psalms and Hymns, and (for lighter use) song and dream books.___*

But there were not free public schools, nor yet were they public schools in any present-day sense. They were, in a word, subscription schools. A teacher who was thought qualified was permitted to organize a school, or interested citizens of the community would make the preliminary arrangements, and the teacher was paid by means of tuition fees, usually in a manner guaranteed in advance by a form

---

*George Petrie, "Montgomery the Cradle of the Confederacy." In Powell's "Historic Towns of the Southern States."

of subscription. These schools, though of the nature of private institutions, soon began to be subsidized with the income of the township school lands or of the endowment derived therefrom. But in all probability there were many communities of the state in which not even this primitive type of school was organized.

Beginnings in Mobile.—By act of January 19, 1826, the legisuature of Alabama passed the first law in the state that saw in the provision of schools a public responsibility. This act applied to Mobile County and created a board of school commissioners whose function was to "establish and regulate schools," and otherwise to promote the education of the youth of the county. Public funds were provided from such sources as land grants, certain fines and penalties, taxes on auction sales and shows, small fees on suits in court, and twenty-five per cent of the "ordinary county tax." From this auspicious beginning one might expect to find that the county school commissioners organized public schools and conducted them in some degree of accord with present-day practice; but such was not the case. As a matter of fact, Alabama, even in one of its most advanced communities, was not yet ready to provide public schools.

For a quarter of a century the schools of Mobile struggled, sometimes for existence, and at other times to hold a bit of ground that had been gained, but always there was want of adequate public support and proper administration as a public enterprise. The money derived from the sources of revenue provided in the law were generally used to subsidize private institutions, the school commissioners being little more than agents for the receipt and distribution of these moneys; and Barton Academy, a public-school building erected in 1835-36, was rented to private schools and for other private purposes. There was even a proposal in 1852 to sell this academy, but the time had come now for the public school. The people, thoroughly aroused, voted overwhelmingly against the proposal to sell, and thus marked the beginning of a public-school system in fact. The schools were reorganized under a new law, and on a public basis, and the system thus inaugurated has, with improvements from time to time, continued to the present day.

The State System.—While the Mobile schools were coming through their struggle from 1826 to 1852, those of the state at large were running a somewhat parallel but even more laggard course. A law of 1819 did little more than direct that the proceeds of the sixteenth section of land be used for educational purposes, but in 1823 a somewhat clearer conception emerged in an act which provided for district trustees and the organization of schools. These schools, however, were to be supported by subscription or tuition fees in the case of parents or guardians able to pay, and the income of school lands and funds was applied to payment for the tuition of poor children. Here is seen in clear outline the old idea that a free school was for "indigent persons" only. Such as there was of public school was hybrid public and private.

No very important change in the school law was made prior to 1839. In that year the State Bank and its branches were directed to pay out of their net profits $150,000 annually to the schools, and in 1840 this amount was increased to $200,000. Thus the state, in 1839, began to participate in the support of schools within its borders, but, as has too often been the case, a mere makeshift was mistaken for a sound system of support of public institutions. In 1843 the State Bank, owing to its mismanagement and the long period of financial depression then prevalent, was unable longer to survive the strain, and this source of school support went out of existence. The schools now settled back to the tuition-fee basis; even the permanent funds, which included the surplus revenue fund of 1836 and were in large measure invested in the stock of the State Bank or otherwise involved with its assets, were lost with the fall of that institution, though the state's resultant indebtedness to the school fund was subsequently recognized and honestly assumed. To the mistaken policy of the federal government in granting school lands as it did at the time Alabama was admitted, to the misconception of the people of the state regarding these grants as practically all that was needed in financing education, and to the aversion of the well-to-do dominant class to free schools, there was now added for a time another retarding element, the discouragement that always attends the loss of money or property. And moreover, the dominant political forces now had additional excuse for doing little or nothing to promote public education.

Another cause of loss from the resources of the schools was the failure in early years of some purchasers of sixteenth-section lands to pay all of the purchase price, and the failure in some cases to sell the lands at the highest market value. The low estimate which was placed on public-school resources in that day and the tendency toward neglect and mismanagement of the school lands were conducive to dishonest practice on the part of those who were willing to take much value for little or nothing paid. Nor was the legislature always blameless, for not only did it fail to enact constructive legal measures for husbanding the school endowments, but it also fell into the practice of extending by special acts the time of payments on land purchased and otherwise encouraging delinquency on the part of debtors to the school fund. It is the old story of mismanagement and tendency to dishonesty in connection with that which came as a gift and without outlay of effort by the recipient.

Through the long period of vicissitudes and difficulties which beset the schools prior to the enactment of the public-school law of 1854 there was probably no time when public education was without many friends in the state. If the educational profession is thought of, there was no state in the South which had an abler group of men. Among these were Dr. Basil Manly, president of the University of Alabama from 1837 to 1855, and one of the best-known Southern educators in ante-bellum times. Associated with him at the university was a group of faithful and scholarly professors, among whom were Dr. Frederick A. P. Barnard, afterward president of Columbia College, New York; Prof. Michael Tuomey, who made a geological survey of the state; and Prof. J. W. Mallet, F. R. S., afterward of the University of Virginia. In the field of secondary education was Dr. Henry Tutwiler, for many years head of the Greene Springs Academy, in Greene County, and father of Julia S. Tutwiler, a distinguished Alabama educator and social worker of post-bellum times and principal of the State Normal School at Livingston from 1883 to 1913.

Nor was education without friends in other vocations, for it counted among its advocates many ministers and no inconsiderable number of leading men. The legislature early had a "committee on education," and an old chronicle* tells us that this committee in several years submitted "able reports," but an able report seems to have been thought sufficient by the dominant element in the legislatures of the thirties and forties. In 1837 Daniel P. Bestor, a Baptist minister, entered the legislature from Greene County. He was thoroughly imbued with the educational spirit and determined, if possible, to improve the school law. Through his efforts a special committee on education was created, and he became its chairman, but another "able report" was all that he ever had to show for his pains. He retired from the legislature in disappointment, and perhaps in disgust. The Rev. Mr. Bestor was in the field too soon for positive accomplishment, but such efforts as his would presently bear fruit.

It should be said, in mitigation of the neglect of the common school by the political leaders, that there was much else to engross their attention. Between 1820 and 1850 the white population of the state increased from 85,451 to 426,514, or 499 per cent; and the number of slaves mounted up from 41,870 to 342,844, an eight-fold increase. To keep legislation abreast with the state's material growth was no small task.

The Coming of the Public School.—In the school of experience, as Dr. Weeks suggests,† Alabama was learning to keep school. By a process of empiricism the state was developing its own type of public-school system, there be-

---
*Garrett, Public Men in Alabama.
†Stephen B. Weeks, History of Public School Education in Alabama, p. 43.

ing little of the best educational practice to learn from nearby states.

It was in the decade immediately preceding the Civil War that public schools in fact came into existence throughout the state. By act of February 15, 1854, the legislature provided for a state distributive school fund including a direct appropriation, a county school tax, a state superintendent of education, boards of county school commissioners, township trustees, and for the examination and certification of teachers.

The first state superintendent was William F. Perry, afterward a general in the Confederate army. He immediately set about the organization of the smaller administrative units, the enumeration of the children, and the general supervisory work of getting the system in motion. The legislature in 1856 amended the school law at several minor points and in one important particular. The latter embodied a provision for county superintendents of schools.

Perhaps a better understanding of the occasion of the establishment of the public-school system of Alabama may be had if the reader will turn aside for brief notice of the men, three in number, who are generally credited with the leading part in putting through the legislature the school law of 1854 In the senate the man who wielded most influence in this respect was Robert M. Patton, of Lauderdale County, and afterward governor of the state, who was born in Russell County, Southwestern Virginia, in 1809, and whose parents had removed with him to Alabama when he was still a child. His father was a native of Ireland and belonged to that sturdy stock known in this country as Scotch-Irish Presbyterian. When this fact is considered it is not hard to understand how young Patton came to be a friend of education. There were many of the Scotch-Irish stock among the settlers of North Alabama.

The chairman of the committee on education in the lower house and the man who drafted the educational bill was Alexander B. Meek, who was born in Columbia, S. C., but who, like young Patton, was brought by his parents to Alabama in his early childhood. He was graduated from the university and became a lawyer. In the administration of President Polk he resided about two years in Washington as a legal adviser in the Treasury Department. Returning to Alabama, he became United States attorney for the southern district of the state, and soon thereafter established his residence in Mobile. Being a man of literary attainments and an able lawyer, and having had a period of residence at the National Capital, he was eminently fitted to assume the chairmanship of the important committee to which he was assigned and to obtain for his committee a respectful hearing.

It will be noted that Mr. Patton represented the extreme northwest part of the state, and Mr. Meek the southern end. From Talladega County, in the north-central part, there came a young representative not yet thirty years old, who was also placed on the house committee, and who soon showed himself an able lieutenant of the chairman. This young man was Jabez Lamar Monroe Curry. Born in Georgia in 1825, he had been brought by his father to Alabama when about twelve years of age, but returned to Georgia for his college education and studied law at Harvard University. Thus, like his able chief on the committee, young Mr. Curry had come under strong extrastate influences which had no doubt given him a broader view of the meaning and function of the public school. The state was fortunate in having three such men as Patton, Meek and Curry; it was doubly fortunate in having them in the legislature at the same time and at the same task. Before them opposition hitherto effective must now crumble.

A brief survey of the Alabama school system as it existed in the half decade immediately preceding the outbreak of the Civil War must suffice here. Writing of the establishment of the system many years after his incumbency as the first state superintendent of education, General William F. Perry said: "Alabama was the first of the cotton states, and one of the first of the slave-holding states, to enter upon such an undertaking."* But some allowance should probably be made for General Perry's father-like enthusiasm over the school system the beginning of which had taken form under his care. What is probably nearer a correct statement is that between 1856 and the outbreak of the war Alabama had one of the most effective school systems in the whole South, and apparently the most effective in the lower South. In his last published report,† before the schools of the state entered the twilight of the Civil War period, State Superintendent G. B. Duval reported 180,160 children in the state between six and twenty-one years of age, and 98,274, or 54.5 per cent, enrolled in school. The total expenditure given for that year was $564,210.46. In that period the state school funds were apportioned on the basis of the school census, but the state superintendent was instructed

---
*W. F. Perry, The Genesis of Public Education in Alabama, In Transactions of Alabama Hist. Soc., vol. 1, 1897-98.

†For the year ending Nov. 30, 1858.

to eliminate, as far as possible, the inequalities due to the fact that some townships possessed large endowments while others had little or none.

The Instruction of Slaves.—Historical writers have given little or no concern to negro education in slave times. Presumably this want of concern has been due to the assumption that there was no such thing as the instruction of slaves, but as a matter of fact there was.‡ No inconsiderable number of negroes in Alabama came out of slavery with the ability to read and write. At least three causes operated to give to a small proportion of the slave population a modicum of text-book instruction. These were (1) the clandestine efforts of anti-slavery enthusiasts; (2) the profits accruing to some masters by reason of the ability of their slaves to read, write, and otherwise transact business; and (3) the kindness of young masters and mistresses in instructing their servants. There was, moreover, a more or less general feeling that negroes might be permitted to learn to read their Bibles, and what is known as "vocational training" was widespread. But the fear of insurrectionary influence and the spread of abolitionist propaganda led to the legal regulation of slave assemblies and to the creation of the patrol system;* and, as the abolitionists became more insistent, the education of slaves, in the case of individuals as well as in assemblies, was prohibited by law. In making this prohibition, Alabama was neither first nor last among the slave states, but occupied a middle ground; its law was enacted in 1832.† These laws generally had the effect of

---

‡See C. G. Woodson, The Education of the Negro Prior to 1861.
*The occasion of the negro's fear of the "patteroller."
†Clay, Digest of the Laws of Alabama, p. 543.

preventing organized effort to instruct the slaves, so that such literacy as negroes possessed when emancipated was of the sort that young masters and mistresses had chosen to give, in disregard of the law, to their favorite servants.

Private Academies.—Before the ante-bellum period of public education is passed, it is well to note briefly the private academy, which sprang up and flourished in that period. From the admission of the state to the enactment of the public-school law of 1854, one of the principal forms which educational measures in the legislature took was the incorporation of academies, numerous such measures being considered by each legislature. In 1850 there were in Alabama 166 such institutions with 380 teachers, 8,290 pupils, and an estimated income of $224,279.‡ Academies throughout the country were in general of two classes: (1) Those whose function was to meet the local school needs, elementary as well as secondary; and (2) those designed to serve a wider clientele and organized with grammar and secondary grades with a view to drawing boarding pupils. The academies of Alabama were largely of the former type. State Superintendent Duval, in his report of 1858, noted the beginning of the decline of the academy in that state.

Higher Education.—Alabama has no great number of institutions of higher learning, but in the opinion of many it has enough, if those that have been established were only more generously supported and their usefulness consequently more widely extended. The State University was the first of these institutions to be founded. It was provided for by legislative act of December 13, 1821, but not until April 17, 1831, was it formally opened. Its chief source

‡American Journal of Education, vol. 1, p. 368.

of support has been throughout its history the grants of lands made by congress. The proceeds of the first of these grants, on the failure of the State Bank, ceased to have actual existence and have since constituted only a paper fund, or an indebtedness of the state to the university. The present constitution guarantees to the university $36,000 annually as interest on its funds. In 1865 a body of federal cavalry destroyed nearly all of the university buildings, but in 1884 congress made somewhat tardy but generous restitution in the form of an additional land grant of two townships, or 46,080 acres. Much of this has proved to be mineral land.

The Dawn of Better Things.—By the year 1898 it was clear that a new day was at the dawning. From the time of its adoption, the educational article of the constitution of 1875 had been unsatisfactory to many of the friends of education. The want of authority to provide local public funds was the chief point of attack, and a number of cities and towns even went to the extremity of seeking to stretch the constitutional limitation and make a local school levy. But the supreme court of the state, true to the high standard which it has long maintained, refused to read into the constitution what had not been put there by the framers, and local taxation specifically for school purposes was declared unconstitutional. The "Hundley amendment," a proposal to provide for a district tax of two and one-half mills on the dollar, was submitted to the voters in 1894, but the state was at that time stirred to its depths by a bitter political contest between the Democratic and Populist parties, and the period of financial depression was then at its worst; so the amendment was lost. But the outlook was widening, and the time was at hand for a forward movement. Many of the northern counties, and some of those in the south, were undergoing great industrial development; cities and towns either took new life or sprang up from the beginning to be considerable centers of population; and the people were more and more recognizing the need of increased intelligence.

In 1898 John W. Abercrombie, a man who knew to its remotest limits the educational system of the state, came to the superintendency of education. The times were changing, and with them the quality of the state superintendency. Mr. Abercrombie saw, as few if any of his predecessors had seen, the fundamental needs of the schools and dared to tell the whole truth with regard to them. With the question as to how much the new superintendent contributed to the changed viewpoint of the people we shall not concern ourselves; questions of the influence of personality have always perplexed the historian. But the fact is of great concern that in the last years of the century the people began fast to become forward looking and showed a growing desire to know precisely what their educational status was. "With the administration of Mr. Abercrombie begins the modern era of public education in Alabama," says Dr. Weeks.

Mr. Abercrombie was superintendent from October, 1898, to July 1, 1902, when he resigned to accept the presidency of the State University. His recommendations to the legislature were in accord with the best educational practice of the time, and some of them were embodied in law before he left the superintendency. They comprehended local taxation, adjustment of the poll-tax law, apportionment of funds within the counties on the basis of average attendance, qualified county superintendents to devote all their time to school work, state certification of teachers, improved school buildings, employment and payment of teachers according to grade of certificate held, absolutely free schools for five months each year, compulsory school attendance, a single board of control for the congressional district agricultural schools, regulation of degree-conferring institutions, and appropriations for summer normal schools. In the incumbency of Mr. Abercrombie the legislature provided for a system of state certification of teachers, state uniformity of textbooks, a five-month term of free school, and for a convention to frame and submit to the people a new state constitution.

Education and the New Constitution.—The constitution proposed by the convention organized to frame it was ratified by vote of the people and went into effect in November, 1901. Under its provisions, the superintendent of education remained the chief administrative and supervisory officer of the schools, but, with other state officers, was made ineligible as his own successor. The administration of the common schools and of the higher institutions remained, in fact, substantially as before. It was in the matter of school support that the most noteworthy changes were made, but even here there was no radical change in policy. The state remained the chief source of support, and the local district was still denied the right to tax itself. A substantial increase in the aggregate school funds, however, was provided. An obligatory school tax of 30 cents on the hundred dollars was provided for, and a ten-cent county tax was authorized. Only in the case of a few specified cities was a district tax permissible, but the older practice of levying a local tax for general municipal purposes and appropriating to the schools from the fund thus provided was still valid. Again Mobile County was permitted to retain its separate system.

From these constitutional provisions the schools received decided impetus, but those who had hoped for much from the convention must have felt keen disappointment. True, the state as such was now contributing generously to the support of public education, but the much-needed local self-help, far from being encouraged, was positively denied.

Under the new constitution two adverse conditions continued as they obtained prior to its adoption. First, the schools in rural communities suffered more than those of the cities for want of funds, for the cities had recourse to appropriations from their general municipal revenues and were able by this means to maintain reasonably good schools, while the rural community had to rely on the state and county taxes alone; and these were insufficient in the great part of the state. The second adverse condition was the provision from state funds for the schools for whites of the Black Belt to the detriment of the schools for the negroes of that part of the state. State funds are apportioned under the constitution to counties on the basis of the number of persons between seven and twenty-one years of age, and these funds are distributed within the countries in the discretion of the county school authorities. As a result, in the Black Belt section of the state, the white schools are provided for from state funds alone and without the provision of local taxation, and the Negro schools receive less than their proper share. Thus the people of the Black Belt, feeling no need of local school funds and being therefore indifferent, if not positively opposed to local taxation, have continued one of the retarding elements in the educational development of the state.

Some of the laws enacted in years immediately following the adoption of the new constitution have already been mentioned. Further legislation enacted in succeeding years included the revision of the certification and textbook laws, the substitution of the county school district for the older township organization and community district except in the case of incorporated municipalities of 2,000 population or more, the establishment of county high schools, the provision for schools for dependent and delinquent children, the placement of the normal schools for whites under a central state board, the reorganization of the district agricultural schools, the appropriation of money for rural school-houses and for the development of rural-school libraries, and in 1915 a compulsory-attendance law.

The Progressive School Legislation of 1915.—The most important recent change in the state's school law was embodied in the constitutional amendment submitted by the legislature of 1915 and ratified by the people in November, 1916. This added to the taxes already authorized a three-mill county tax when voted by a majority of the electors and a three-mill district tax when likewise voted after the county's decision to levy a county tax of three mills. The machinery was now provided for supporting a system of free public schools in fact, machinery which, from the birth of the state, the framers of constitutional provisions had seemed loath to see pass to the hands of the people. Two things of prime importance remained to be done. First, the permissible taxes remained to be voted in the several counties and districts, and, secondly, the property valuation of the state needed to be raised to a point where it would produce adequate revenue for the support of the schools and other public enterprises. The first of these has already been in large measure accomplished.

As the educational leaders become more aggressive and forward-looking in the closing years of the past century, so they have continued in more recent years. The recommendations and efforts of all recent state superintendents have generally been in accord with the best educational thought of the country, and whatever shortcomings may be charged to their administrations have probably been due more to the circumstances than to the personal element.

The principal fault of the Alabama educational system has been the century-old disposition of the people, particularly the molders of policies, to look too much upon education as something to be bought in the market by the well-to-do or to be provided by the state at an irksome personal sacrifice on the part of the individual taxpayer. If now the people will clearly see a public responsibility in the provision of schools and will wisely put ample public money in them as an investment paying large dividends, the state may soon take educational rank suited to its great material advantages.

The above was taken from Bulletin, 1919, No. 41, sent out by the Department of the Interior, Bureau of Education.

SCHOOLS OF CLARKE COUNTY

There are sixty-five public schools in Clarke County, forty white and twenty-five colored. There are 140 teachers, 100 white and forty colored.

There are 9,833 children of school age in the county, 4,715 white and 5,118 colored.

KING INSTITUTE

King Institute was situated three and a half miles west of Grove Hill, in a community of intelligent farmers, among whom the spirit of education was strong. They had for patrons such men as Isaac Grant, Stephen Pugh, J. Pickens Pugh, E. M. Chapman, and many others who have crossed over the "Great Divide" with their teacher. The school ranked high and did preparatory work. Students who left or finished King Institute entered or were ready for entrance at the State University at Tuscaloosa.

The school continued under the control of W. A. McLeod for about four years. The school was established and began its sessions in September, 1882. Prof. McLeod taught school for several years at Grove Hill, then, together with his family, moved to Jackson, having purchased a lot and built a home. He taught school here several years in the early nineties, in what was then called the Jackson Academy, a one-room building which is now situated and annexed to the west side of the Agricultural College building. Prof. McLeod went from here to Demopolis and taught school there for several years. He was killed in Mobile by a Louisville and Nashville Railroad train some years ago. Prof. McLeod was a good man and a successful teacher. His only living son is a member of the firm of Stephens, McCorvey, Rogers & Goode, of Mobile.

REPRESENTATIVES IN STATE LEGISLATURE FROM CLARKE COUNTY

William Murrell, Girard W. Creagh, 1819; William Murrell, Girard W. Creagh, 1820; James Magoffin, Edward Kennedy, 1821; James Fitts, Edward Kennedy, 1822; James Fitts, John G. Creagh, 1823; Richard Dickinson, John G. Creagh, 1824; John G. Creagh, 1825; Elias H. DuBose, 1826; Neal Smith, 1827; William Mobley, 1828, 1829, 1830; Samuel Wilkinson, 1831; John G. Creagh, 1832, 1833; Abel DuBose, 1834; Neal Smith, 1835; Thomas Saunders, 1836; R. P. Carney, 1837; G. W. Creagh, 1838; Samuel Forwood, 1839; W. F. Jones, 1840; Lorenzo James, 1841; Peter Du Bose, 1842; John W. Portis, 1843, 1844; Morgan Carleton, 1845; Thomas B. Rivers, 1848; Lorenzo James, 1849; A. L. Henshaw, 1851; E. S. Thornton, 1853; James J. Goode, 1855, 1857; W. J. Hearin, 1859, 1861; John Y. Kilpatrick, 1863; Thomas B. Savage, 1865 (no election in 1867); H. C. Grayson, 1870; John C. Chapman, 1872; F. W. Baker, 1874.

(The above list is taken from Ball's History, and Ball says that Mr. Brewer is his authority.)

Samuel Forwood, 1876, 1877; Frank Winn, 1878, 1879; Stephen B. Cleveland, 1880, 1881; Isaac Grant, 1882, 1883, 1884, 1885; J. R. Cowan, 1886, 1887; A. L. McLeod, 1888, 1889; J. W. Armistead, 1890, 1891; E. O. Calhoun, G. E. Jones, 1892, 1893; E. O. Calhoun, Isaac Grant, 1894, 1895; T. A. Long, J. S. Hinson, 1896, 1897; T. A. Long, J. W. Mathews, 1898, 1899; F. E. Poole, Massey Wilson, 1900, 1901; F. E. Poole, Isaac Pugh, 1903, 1904, 1905, 1906; Isaac Pugh, J. D. Doyle, 1907, 1908, 1909, 1910; J. W. Mathews, A. S. Johnson, 1911, 1812, 1913, 1914; J. D. Doyle, Isaac

Pugh, 1915, 1916, 1917, 1918; John S. Graham, David Mathews, 1919, 1920, 1921, 1922; Hadley Tyson, J. F. Boykin, 1923, and will serve for 1924, 1925 and 1926.

Clarke County was entitled to but one representative until and including the year 1891. The county having increased in population, it has since that time had two representatives. Up to the election of 1902 representatives were elected every two years. At the election of 1910 and since that time they have been elected every four years.

SENATORS

From the nineteenth senatorial district, elected in Clarke County, are as follows: Joseph B. Chambers, 1819; Neal Smith, 1822; George S. Gaines, 1825; Joseph B, Earle, 1827; Neal Smith, 1828, 1831; Samuel Wilkinson, 1834; Neal Smith, 1836; G. W. Creagh, 1847; Cade M. Godbold, 1849; Lorenzo James, 1851; James S. Dickinson, 1853; James S. Jenkins, 1855; Noah A. Agee, 1857; Stephen B. Cleveland, 1859; O. S. Jewett, 1861; Robert Brodnax, 1862; John Y. Kilpatrick, 1865; John W. Foster, 1868; Simeon Walton, 1872; Eli S. Thornton, 1876.

(The above list was taken from Ball's History.)

J. R. Cowan, 1888, 1889, 1890, 1891; Isaac Grant, 1896, 1897, 1898, 1899; W. D. Dunn, 1900, 1901, 1902, 1903; Norman Gunn, 1907, 1908, 1909, 1910; T. J. Bedsole, 1919, 1920, 1921, 1922.

The nineteenth senatorial district is composed of Washington, Clarke and Choctaw Counties. We have not mentioned the names of senators from Choctaw and Washington.

Up to 1903 the legislature met in December following election. Since that time the legislature convenes in January following election. Representatives are elected in even-numbered years, but the legislature does not convene until January of the next year.

PROBATE JUDGES OF CLARKE COUNTY SINCE 1821

1. John G. Creagh, from September, 1821, to January, 1823.
2. Robert Lee, from January, 1823, to January, 1824.
3. Edward Kennedy, from February, 1824, to January, 1824.
4. Samuel Wilkinson, from April, 1827, to November, 1833.
5. William R. Hamilton, from January, 1834, to 1838.
6. William T. Jones, from January, 1838, to December, 1838.
7. Joseph P. Portis, from January, 1839, to December, 1844.
8. Terrell Powers, from January, 1845, to May, 1850.
9. H. M. Coate, from May, 1850, to May, 1856.
10. Z. L. Bettis, from May, 1856, to February, 1866.
11. Isaac Grant, from February, 1866, to May, 1866.
12. R. J. Woodard, from May, 1866, to August, 1868.
13. J. R. Wilson, from August, 1868, to November, 1880.
14. John M. Wilson, from 1880 to 1904.
15. Clayton Foscue, from 1904 to 1910.
16. Coma Garrett, from 1910 to 1923.

17. J. G. Cunninghame is present Probate Judge, having taken office January 1, 1923.

DOCTORS

Following is a list of the names of the medical doctors who were born in Clarke County and practiced more or less in the county, and with whom the writer was personally acquainted:

Henry G. Davis, Gainestown (dead).
B. S. Barnes, Suggsville (dead).
L. O. Hicks, Jackson (dead).
Bryan Boroughs, Jackson.
G. S. Chapman, Jackson.
T. C. Kirven, Jackson.
Kimbell Hicks, Jacksonville, Fla.
Cobb Nichols, Rockville.
J. W. Fleming, Salitpa.
Leon McVay, Mobile, Ala.
J. R. Armistead, Pritchard, Ala.
J. W. Armistead, Grove Hill.
Clem Pugh, Grove Hill.
Albert Pugh, Grove Hill.
J. M. Cobb, Grove Hill.
C. C. Pugh, Mobile, Ala.
T. J. Pugh, Grove Hill.
Jesse Chapman, Birmingham, Ala.
Leiland Chapman, Sheffield, Ala.
Isham Kimbell, Pascagoula, Miss.
A. N. Robinson, Coffeeville.

ATTORNEYS

Following is a list of attorneys who lived in Clarke County and practiced in its courts since 1875:

Colonel J. S. Dickinson (deceased).
Colonel H. W. Portis (deceased).
Rivers Portis (deceased).
Ira Portis (deceased).
W. J. Johnson (deceased).
Harris Barefield (deceased).
W. D. Dunn (deceased).
J. T. Lackland (deceased).
Thomas W. Davis (deceased).
Massey Wilson, removed to St. Louis, Mo.
E. P. Wilson, removed to St. Louis, Mo.
A. L. McLeod, removed to Selma, Ala., and died there.
Benjamin F. Elmore, removed to Demopolis, Ala.
J. F. Aldridge, removed to Eutaw, Ala.
Harwell Davis, attorney-general of Alabama.
Frank E. Poole.
Q. W. Tucker.
T. J. Bedsole.
John Adams.
Vaughan Chapman.
A. S. Johnson.
Norman Gunn, removed to Jasper, Ala.
J. Carney Hicks, removed to Washington, D. C.
John S. Graham, Jackson.
There may be a few who have escaped our memory.

BANKS

The first bank established in Clarke County was the First National Bank, established in 1901, B. H. Warren, president; S. T. Woodard, cashier. Later on the Planters Bank and Trust Company was established in Jackson, with T. M. Phillips as president and C. C. Pritchett as cashier. In a few years these two banks were consolidated under the style of Jackson Bank and Trust Company. The present officers of this bank are: S. H. Andrews, president; G. G. Warren, cashier, and J. D. Guy, assistant cashier.

Some years after the First National Bank was established here the Farmers Bank and Trust Company was established at Thomasville, and a little later on the Grove Hill Bank was established. All of these banks are doing a profitable business.

OLD MEN OF CLARKE COUNTY

Following are the names of men who were living in Clarke when the writer came to the county forty-eight years ago: Captain J. R. Cowan, T. J. Cowan, Dave Cowan, James Armistead, Eli S. Thornton, William Scruggs, J. Foscue, Tom Bratton, S. B. Nobles, Rial Nobles, W. E. Johnson, S. J. Johnson, Charles Poole, James Foster, —— Tyson, Terrel Fountain, Dr. —— Bush, S. P. Chapman, Steve Chapman, Caleb Fleming, Jack R. Wilson, George Allen, Isaac Grant, George Nettles, J. M. Agee, Judge J. R. Woodard, Frank W. Woodard, Captain S. T. Woodard, Enoch Cobb, Mal. Cobb, J. J. Tompkins, John Calhoun, Neal Calhoun, Matthew Cox, Joe Cox, Ab. Payne, Dan

Payne, J. D. Payne, S. E. Thomas, John Collins, John Bumpers, Henry Dawson, Sam Atchison, Dr. T. J. Prim, Billy Benson, Charles Day, Tom Bolen, Dan H. Howell, J. V. Stringer, Rev. Alex. Stringer, O. H. DuBose, Jack DuBose, George W. Walker, Jack Daffin, S. J. Parker, S. W. Parker, Joe McVay, Fayette McVay, Joe T. Singleton, William Sanders, Colonel J. S. Dickinson, Isham Kimbell, Captain T. I. Kimbell, A. S. Smoot, Seth P. Stringer, John R. L. Stringer, Walter Taylor, John C. Chapman, Frank Baker, Captain Luck Wainright, A. M. Wing, Dr. F. I. Sewell, Dr. L. O. Hicks, Robert Dolbear, E. J. Doty, L. W. Fleming, John S. Moore, Tom Moore, Elias Dykes, Sr., Elias Dykes, Jr., Josh McDonald, L. E. Sewell, Sr., John Bradley, Frank Bradley, Charles Bradley, Robert Bradley, Josiah Jones, Peter Gwin, Josh Gwin, Jack Gill, Wash Gill, William A. Myrick, A. M. Myrick, J. F. Murphy, N. E. Drew, Colonel John W. Portis, Dr. Thomas Rivers, Dr. Krouse, Major S. B. Cleveland, Edmond Portis, Dr. Thomas Rivers, Dr. Krouse, Dr. Theo. Krouse, Dr. S. B. Barnes, Milton Barnes, Alfred Barnes, Dr. Henry G. Davis, J. S. Lambard, Reese Norris, Dr. Files, Samuel Forward, Captain Lea, R. H. Flinn, J. M. Howard, Frank Payne, W. H. Cherry, James Mobley, Durr Bryant, A. S. Bryant, Cy Allen and A. H. Howell.

The above list shows the names of men who lived in Clarke when the writer came to the county in 1875, and with whom he became acquainted, intimately so with a majority of them, often meeting them in social, business and political circles. The majority of these men were born in Clarke County, and all of them were born in the first half of the nineteenth century — and a few in the early part

They have all passed away. Some lived four-score years, and some four-score years and ten.

Following are the names of men who made their appearance on the stage of life a little later, some coming from other parts, and with whom the writer was closely associated, and are also dead: W. M. Mobley, Robert Mobley, Ora Jewett, John E. Hoven, James Sykes, W. D. Dunn, J. T. Lackland, Clayton Foscue, John M. Wilson, Leonard Chapman, Allen McLeod, A. L. McLeod, C. W. Boyles, Jim Bryant, Joe Powell, Jack Baker, Sol Baker, Garrett Dykes, J. S. Deas, Will Rivers, L. A. Porter, Ernest Corquodale, Charles Corquodale, Cage York, Oscar York, J. D. Cunningham, S. J. Taylor and Robert Wilson.

VOTING PLACES

Clarke County has twenty-one voting precincts and twenty-two voting places, as follows: Saltworks, Gainestown, Gosport, Suggsville, Walker Springs, Jackson, McLeods, Good Springs, River Hill (Salitpa), New Prospect, Coffeeville, Grove Hill (and Whatley voting place), Thomasville, Cane Creek, Andersons, Pleasant Hill, Tallahatta Springs, Morvin, Bashi, Campbell and Cunningham.

CRIMINAL COURT OF CLARKE COUNTY

A criminal court of Clarke County was established by an act approved March 13, 1907. This court had jurisdiction of all misdemeanors committed in the county. Judge Davis was appointed judge of this court by Governor B. B. Comer, and held office under this appointment until the

November election in 1910, when he was elected for a four-year term.

A. S. Johnson, of Thomasville, was elected judge of this court during the year 1914, and was commissioned judge of the County Court November 14, and served as judge of said court until it was consolidated with the Circuit Court in January, 1917.

HIGH WATER OF 1874

In the winter of 1874 the waters of the Tombigbee reached the highest point in the history of that stream, before or since. It was several miles wide at this place, and the waters swept past the west bank of the river at a rapid speed. They seemed to be in a hurry to get out to sea and were taking all the near-cuts. At this time the old Grand Trunk was bringing freight to the west bank of the river. Freight was delivered from a high dump in times of high water. Mr. F. W. Dahlberg, now a very old man, perhaps over ninety years, living at Suggsville, was lessee of the ferry at this place at that time. His ferryman was a colored man named Jeff Daffin.

When the water was at its highest point, Mr. Dahlberg, his ferryman, and Mr. Archibald S. Smoot, who was the warehouse-keeper, took the ferry flat and went across the river after a load of freight. They crossed over and got the freight on board and started back. After going up the west bank of the river for some distance, before branching out for the east bank, the ferryman lost control of the boat and it turned broadside across the river, struck a tree and turned bottom side up, and dumped men and freight into the angry, surging waters. The ferryman, who was said to be an expert swimmer, immediately went out of sight and drowned. Mr. Dahlberg climbed a tree and held onto it until rescued. Mr. Smoot, who was about seventy-five years old, swam to an old house some distance below, the comb of which was just above the water. He was rescued by Steve Tate, a colored man, using a small boat or skiff. Steve was a genuine African, a fisherman and a good swimmer, but he was claimed by the cruel waters of the Tombigbee. He went down when no human eye was looking that way. He was putting out a trot line, and it was surmised that he became entangled in the line, and was drawn down by the weight attached to it.

Old Steve was a familiar character about Jackson. He was a great pedestrian. He would walk to Mobile Creek every week or two, shopping. Sometimes he would buy a sack of flour or meal, put it on his shoulder and step back home with it. He never rode on the old Grand Trunk. He said that it was too slow for him. He had a little old dog that followed him everywhere he went, but Steve finally walked him to death.

CLARKE COUNTY POSTOFFICES

On railroad: Jackson, Walker Springs, Allen, Whatley, Dickerson, Fulton, Rural, Thomasville, Atkinson.

Off railroad: Choctaw Bluff, Carlton, Rockville, Alma, Manila, Gainestown, Barlow Bend, Gosport, Suggsville, Chance, Nettleboro, Scyrene, Morvin, Tallahatta Springs, Campbell, Woods Bluff, Cunningham, Coffeeville, Salitpa,

McVay, Winn, Grove Hill, Bashi, Failetown, Forestdale, Glover, Opine, Peacock, Symer.

THOMASVILLE NEWSPAPERS

We are indebted to Mrs. Flossie Bickell Kerridge for the following information concerning the newspapers of Thomasville:

"When Thomasville was first planned the members of the Thomasville Real Estate Company bought a printing outfit and installed a newspaper here. There were several editors, eight in number, until in December, 1896, Mr. Henderson recommended to the stockholders W. E. Bickell, of Chicago, Ill., while the latter was in Mobile on a sojourn. He came to Thomasville and started the Thomasville Argus. He met with success, and brought his family, consisting of a brother, Rev. E. J. Bickell, his wife and four children, to Thomasville.

"The Argus was a five-column four-page paper, and was enlarged into an eight-page paper later on. The plant was well taken care of and several cases of type, purchased from the Mobile Register after the latter had installed its linotypes, were added to the original plant. The Argus and job outfit were swept away in the awful fire which visited Thomasville in the night of November 1, 1899.

"In September, 1900, Dr. J. S. Davidson bought a modern newspaper plant, and with C. C. DuBose, of Columbiana, began publishing the Thomasville Echo. The paper was prospering, but one day C. C. DuBose failed to show up for duty, and the doctor called on W. E. Bickell to take charge, and so he became manager and remained so until stricken with paralysis, from which he never fully recovered.

"O. H. Hill was then pressed into service by the doctor and was editor for almost a year. L. A. Grayson then assumed charge, and was business manager until in November, 1902, A. B. Tucker purchased the plant from Dr. J. S. Davidson.

"First issue of the Thomasville Times on December 8, 1921, O. A. Shepard, editor, and E. K. Campbell, business manager."

NEWSPAPERS OF GROVE HILL

We are indebted to George A. Carlton, present editor of the Clarke County Democrat, for the following data concerning the newspapers published at Grove Hill:

"The Macon Banner was the first paper established here. We have on hand Vol V, No. 5 of this paper, dated January 10, 1846. As I figure it, this would mean that the paper was established in December, 1840. The Macon Banner was edited by G. W. Megginson and was 'published every Saturday by W. T. Megginson & Co.'

"The Southern Recorder, edited and published by Gideon B. Massey, was the next newspaper established at Grove Hill. We hold Vol. I, No. 2, of this paper, dated January 20, 1847, and so can say definitely that its first issue was dated January 13, 1847.

"The Grove Hill Herald was published by Daffin & Figures (Derusha Daffin and James T. Figures). We have in our possession Vol. III, No. 43, of this paper, dated October 27, 1852. From this it seems that the Herald was established in January, 1849. Derusha Daffin was the father of our esteemed fellow-townsman, W. W. Daffin, while James T. Figures was the man who refused to leave town with the majority when yellow fever broke out here in 1853, heroically caring for and nursing those who were ill until he took the fever and died with it. He is buried in the cemetery back of the old Methodist church at this place.

"The Clarke County Democrat was established by Isaac Grant in January, 1856, and edited continuously by him until a few months before his death on December 4, 1907. Since that time it has been edited by me, his grandson.

"In looking over the old papers mentioned above I find also that the name of the town was changed from Macon to Grove Hill in 1846. The Macon Banner of 1846 carries the date line of Macon, while in the Southern Recorder of January, 1847, we find that it is Grove Hill."

THE SOUTH ALABAMIAN

The South Alabamian was established in Jackson, Ala., in September, 1887. Its first editor was Archie L. McLeod. The paper was owned by the Jackson Publishing Company, a corporation. Early in the nineties Mr. McLeod removed to Selma and entered the practice of law. John S. Graham assumed the editorship of this paper about 1892 and continued to edit it until 1904, at which time he leased the paper to Page Bros., subsequently selling it to them. Page Bros. operated the paper for a short while and sold to E. L. Colley. After Colley had operated the paper for several years John S. Graham repurchased it and edited it for several years, and sold to R. E. Sutton, who edited the paper for several years, and sold to W. A. Calhoun, the present editor and proprietor.

TOLBERT SPRING

Tolbert Spring is situated about seven miles northeast of Jackson. This spring was once known as the Singleton Spring. In 1875 old Mr. Joe T. Singleton lived close to this spring — had lived there many years, and lived there until he died, in the latter part of the seventies or in the early part of the eighties.

This is, perhaps, the largest spring in the county, and is, perhaps, the spring mentioned in connection with the following story:

According to tradition, a pioneer well-digger was digging a well a short distance above a large spring. After he had reached quite a depth, suddenly the bottom of the well "dropped out" and the well-digger was dropped into a swift runing stream, and he was carried head forward down this underground stream. Of course, the man naturally thought his career on this mundane sphere was about to come to an end. Just as he had finished his petition to the Almighty for help, he was suddenly shot out into the open, the force of the water shooting him out like a ball out of a cannon. The man received no bodily injuries, but the community lost a well-digger.

AUTUMN TIME

This is a beautiful autumn day, Sunday, November 18, 1923. The day is ideal. Old Jack Frost was much in evidence early in the morning, but when the sun came out, sending its bright, warm rays down on mother earth, the frost quickly disappeared. The autumn season is fast drawing to a close. The woods have laid aside the mantle of green and donned the mantle of brown. The nut-trees are dropping their rich, brown nuts, and the grape-vine is weighted down with clusters of delicious grapes; the black haw and the persimmon are fully ripe; the birds are having their annual feast; the wise squirrel is storing away his winter's supply of food; the opossum is getting fat and the sweet potato is ready for the bake-pan. The farmer is ginning his fleecy staple, housing his corn, hauling the yellow pumpkin for his Christmas pie, grinding his cane, digging his potatoes and pinders, and storing his velvet beans. Wood is being stacked in the back yard and coal put in the bin, so that when the chilly winds of winter come all can "eat, drink (water), and be merry."

Our winters are short and not severe. Spring will soon come again and the forests will be "wearing of the green" again. The dogwood and the honey-suckle will be in bloom, the violets and the blue-bells will be peeping up everywhere. The song-birds will be filling the woods with their sweet music. The humming-bird and butterfly will sip the nectar from the rose, and the "busy bee" will be busy making honey from the sweets extracted from the many flowers. The man who does not enjoy the sweet "blossom-time" has no love for nature.

A FOOTPRINT

Upon a high ridge about seven miles east of Jackson is situated a huge sand-rock, six or eight feet in length, two feet wide, and not quite so thick. This rock lies on the surface of the earth and looks as if it had been placed there for some specific purpose. On the top side of this rock is a track made by someone wearing a number four or five shoe, presumably a woman. The track is perfectly distinct, showing the full length of the shoe from heel to toe. This rock was evidently soft when this track was made, and was, perhaps, even with the surface of the ground.

It is known that this rock has been there for at least seventy-five years, and perhaps very much longer. The track was evidently made by a white person, and could have been made as far back as the first of the nineteenth century, when the whites first came into this territory. It is a mystery that will never be solved. From the appearance of the track, the person making it was moving swiftly, whether chasing some animal or being chased by one we do not know.

PROHIBITION IN CLARKE

The legislature of 1880 passed an act prohibiting the sale of intoxicating liquors in Clarke County. Major Steve B. Cleveland was in the lower house from Clarke at that time. Cleveland was not a total abstainer, but he supported the bill because he believed that it was for the best interest of the county that the open saloon be closed. In spite of this law, whiskey was shipped in here from Mobile and other wet districts, and much whiskey was used in the county until we got statewide prohibition. Footprints of the "blind tiger" are still found in some parts of the county, and more or less "shinny" is made on the sly.

WOMEN VOTE

For the first time in the history of the state the women voted in the primary and general elections of 1922. We do not know how they turned out in other counties, but they polled a large vote in Clarke County.

WATERSHED OF CLARKE

The Choctaw boundary line in this county is the dividing line of the watershed of the county. This line is the crest of a high ridge, and it crosses no running stream. All streams and all water falling east of this line empty into the Alabama river, and all on the west side empty into the Tombigbee river. The town of Thomasville is situated on this ridge. We are told that the Methodist parsonage at that place is situated on the dividing line, and that the rainfall on the east side of the roof of that building finds its way to the Alabama river, and on the west side finds its way to the Tombigbee river.

PROTESTANTS

Almost the entire population of Clarke County believe in the Protestant religion. There has never been a Catholic church in the county, and but few Catholics have ever resided there. A great majority of the people are Methodists and Missionary Baptist. There are quite a number of Presbyterians in the towns of the county. There are, scattered over the county, a few Primitive Baptists, a few Campbellites, a few Universalists, and a very few Seventh-

Day Adventists. There may be a few infidels and atheists in the county, but if there are they keep quiet. If it were possible for Lorenzo Dowe and Mr. Honeymon, who preached in this county more than a hundred years ago, to take a bird's-eye view of this county today and see a church building in every town and village, at every crossroads, and on every hilltop in the county, they would doubtless envy the preachers of today. In the days when they preached in the county there were no church buildings. They preached in the open, in school-houses, or in the humble cabins of the God-loving settlers. And they, perhaps, walked from one preaching place to another. There were no automobiles in those days, no buggies, and but few horses.

COMA GARRETT, JR.

Born near Thomaston, Ala., July 24, 1886. Graduated from South Alabama Institute, Thomasville, Ala., May, 1904. Entered University of Alabama, sophomore class, September, 1904; president Philomathic Literary Society one term; member Athletic Executive Committee, 1906-07; class baseball team, 1906; varsity football team, 1906-07; graduated from university May 29, 1907. Principal Grove Hill Academy, 1907-09. Clerk Circuit and County Courts, 1911 to 1917; Judge of Probate, 1917 to January 1, 1923.

C. W. BOYLES

C. W. Boyles was born in Monroe County on the 8th day of March, 1862, and lived in that county until 1898, when he removed to Jackson, where he embarked in the mercantile business, becoming a member of the firm of Savage &

Boyles. He later engaged in the livery stable business, which business he remained in until his death, which occurred September 11, 1917. He was married to Miss Evie Kimbell on the 28th of March, 1899, who is still living. Mr. Boyles was mayor of Jackson several terms. He was very popular, especially with the traveling men. He left surviving him four children by his last wife and five by his first wife. Children by his last wife were Thomas, Kimbell, Douglas, Bruce and Alice, the girl being the wife of Edward C. Graham.

AUSTICO BUSBEE TUCKER

Born at Shiloh, Marengo County, Alabama, December 27, 1873; son of Rev. J. Lee and Mrs. Lizzie W. (Busbee) Tucker; reared on farm; attended country schools (only few months); moved to Thomasville in Clarke County, September 1, 1898; engaged as salesman and partner in mercantile establishment prior to assuming charge of the Thomasville Echo November 8, 1902.

First political activity in 1909 as county committeeman in campaign against ratification of constitutional amendment to prohibit manufacture and sale of alcoholic beverages in Alabama, carrying county against proposition by majority of 159. First and only political office held in county was on the County Board of Commissioners to which he was appointed by Governor Emmet O'Neal in December, 1912, as successor to John S. Henson. Served four years, during which the first permanent improved highways of the county were constructed. The chief road in this program was from the Wilcox County line through Thomasville, Fulton Grove Hill and to the Tombigbee River at Jackson. Twice aspired to the office of State Senator, being defeated in 1914 by T. J. Hollis of Choctaw County and in 1918 by T. J. Bedsole of Clarke County. Defeated for re-election as county commissioner in 1916 by J. E. Williams.

Suspended publication of the Thomasville Echo in September, 1918, to accept a position with the Montgomery Advertiser, serving in various capacities, chief of which was assistant managing editor and state news editor.

(Still maintains home at Thomasville.)

Personal

Married Miss Lula Hall of Thomasville early in 1902; father of three sons, the oldest of whom graduated at age of 20 in the class of electrical engineers at Auburn in May, 1923; is a member of the Baptist church, also member of the Knights of Pythias and Woodmen of the World; named member of Grand Tribunal in the order of Knights of Pythias in May, 1923; is captain on brigade staff in the uniform rank, Woodmen of the World.

JOHN McDUFFIE

Mr. McDuffie is not a citizen of Clarke County, but he represents the First congressional district (of which Clarke is a part) in the Congress of the United States, and we deem it proper to give him a place in this book.

Mr. McDuffie was born September 25, 1883, at River Ridge, Ala., on a cotton plantation; attended Southern University at Greensboro, Ala., one session; graduated at Auburn, 1904, taking B.Sc.; graduated at University of Alabama law school 1908; in 1907 represented Monroe County in Alabama legislature; began the practice of law in Monroeville, June 1, 1908; elected solicitor First judicial circuit of Alabama in 1910, and served until January, 1919; married Miss Cornelia Hixon of Hixon, Ala., on October 18, 1915, and they have one child. He is now serving his second term in Congress; captain and adjutant, Second Infantry, Alabama National Guard, 1908 to January, 1915.

JACK R. WILSON

Judge Jack R. Wilson, who died in 1898, was a prominent citizen of Clarke County for many years. He was elected probate judge of the county in 1868 and served as such until 1880, when he was succeeded by his son, John M. Wilson, who held the office for 24 years. He has three sons living, Massey, Ed and Albert. Massey Wilson was at one time attorney general of the state of Alabama. He now resides in St. Louis, Mo., and is president of a prominent insurance company. Massey Wilson is one of the ablest attorneys ever produced in the state of Alabama. Ed Wilson is also an able attorney and resides in St. Louis.

Albert Wilson is a prominent citizen and business man of Montgomery, Ala. Miss Sallie Wilson of Mobile is perhaps Judge Wilson's only living daughter. She is an estimable lady. It has been the good fortune of the writer to know all of these people personally.

J. C. STEWART

Mr. J. C. Stewart, who died at his home in Jackson the 1st day of November, 1923, was one of the most widely known business men in the county of Clarke. He was a farmer and merchant. He embarked in the mercantile business at Clarkesville, this county, about fifty years ago. He started out with limited capital, but by strict economy and close application to business he made rapid strides and soon became one of the biggest taxpayers in the county. He came to Jackson in 1893 and purchased the Walter Taylor home on Commerce Street, moved into it the same year and lived there until his death. He soon, after moving here, purchased the lot on which the bank is situated and erected a store house and commenced a general mercantile business, associating with him Mr. George W. Powe, Sr. He and Mr. Powe subsequently dissolved co-partnership and Mr. Stewart purchased a lot and erected the house now occupied by J. C. Stewart & Co., conducted by his sons. Mr. Stewart was a good man and will be greatly missed by his friends and acquaintances. He left a widow and six children, four sons and two daughters. His sons are S. A., J. C., W. C. and Bob H. His daughters are Tooma and Velma. His daughters are single, but his sons are married. W. V. is engaged in the drug business, the other three are in the general mercantile business.

Mr. Stewart was born near old Clarkesville in January, 1853. He was the son of J. C. Stewart, Sr., and Nancy Stewart. J. C. Stewart, Sr., came from South Carolina and settled in Clarke County many years ago. He had two sons and eleven daughters. An explanation is here necessary. J. C. Stewart, the subject of this sketch, married Nancy McVay, so it will be seen that both his wife and his mother were named Nancy. There are two more J. C. Stewarts, namely, Carley Stewart and his little son.

Mr. Stewart was married to Nancy McVay on May 11, 1876. His only brother, Doog Stewart, was in the Confederate army, and died in prison. His living sisters are as follows: Mrs. E. M. McLeod, Mrs. Elijah Chapman, Mrs. G. W. McVay, Mrs. Andrew Calhoun, Mrs. J. T. Wilson and Mrs. John Calhoun.

GOVERNOR MURPHY

Clarke County, as such has never had the distinction of furnishing to the State of Alabama a governor, but the territory now embraced in the county did. As has already been mentioned, the territory east of the Choctaw boundary line, which runs through the county from south to north, was once a part of Monroe County. John Murphy, who in the early part of the nineteenth century resided near present Gosport, then in Monroe County, was elected the fourth governor of Alabama.

Governor Murphy was the grandfather of John F. Murphy, once a merchant at Walker Springs, and of Mrs. B. O. Boykin, now of Jackson (who was a daughter of Robert Murphy, of Perdue Hill), and great granddaughter of John F. Boykin, present representative in the legislature from Clarke County. Ball has the following to say about Governor Murphy:

"In the latter part of the eighteenth century there came from Scotland Murdock Murphy and his son, Neil Murphy, who settled in North Carolina. Neil Murphy married Miss Downing, and about 1785 John Murphy, their son, was born. They removed to South Carolina and the son became a teacher to secure funds for completing his course at the South Carolina College.

"Fellow-students with him there were James Dellet and John Gayle. Of the three, one was Scotch, one was Irish and the other probably of English descent. England, Scotland, Wales and Ireland have been well represented in this region. Graduating in 1808, clerk of the South Carolina senate for eight years, in 1818 John Murphy became a citizen of Monroe County, was admitted to the bar, became a planter, represented the county in the legislature, and in 1825 was elected governor. He occupied this position for two terms, and afterward served one term as a representative in congress. He was master for a time of the Alabama Grand Lodge of Masons. He was married twice. His second wife was Mrs. Carter, a sister of Colonel John Barrington. He died in 1840 on his plantation near Pigeon Creek, once Monroe, but now Clarke County, and his remains lie near Gosport in a little burial ground of Clarke."

BEN D. TURNER

Judge Turner was born near Healing Springs, November 6, 1886. His father was Benjamin D. Turner, who resided for many years at Bladon Springs, in Choctaw County, Ala., and later at St. Stephens, and who married in early life Miss Mary Binton Cocke, of Marion, Ala., who is the judge's mother, and who is still living at St. Stephens. His grandfather on his father's side was Benjamin Dickerson Turner, who resided in Washington and Choctaw Counties many years. His mother was the daughter of Colonel Jack Freming Cocks, of Marion, Perry County, Ala.

The judge's early days were spent in Washington County at St. Stephens. From the Mobile District High School, a school which was operated there for many years, he went to the Marion Military Institute for two years, after which he took his law degree at the University of Alabama. He began the practice of law at St. Stephens, and from there moved to Chatom when the court-house of Washington County was moved. For four years he was a member of the State Democratic Committee. He was appointed to the position of circuit judge of the First Judicial Circuit on January 1, 1915, by Governor Emmett O'Neal, then governor of Alabama. He has been elected twice consecutively to that office. He now resides at Chatom, Washington County, Alabama. He married Miss Florida Garner Powell, daughter of Daniel T. Powell and Sallie Bowling Powell, of Carson, Ala., and has four children by that marriage.

Judge Turner is, perhaps, the youngest circuit judge in the state of Alabama, and one among the ablest judges. Comparatively few of his decisions have been reversed by the Supreme Court.

BENJAMIN SHIELDS BARNES

Dr. B. S. Barnes, who was a son of Samuel T. Barnes, one of the pioneer settlers of east Clarke, was born in Suggsville, in 1839, and died in 1911.

He was a gentleman of the old school in the truest sense. The writer knew him well. He graduated in medicine at Philadelphia when quite a young man and served in the Confederate army for four years as surgeon. At the close of the war he returned to Suggsville, where he continued the practice of medicine until declining years prevented his ministering to the afflicted. He was for many years a regular contributor to the columns of the South Alabamian (edited by the writer), under the pen name of "Chippendale," and his articles were always read with deep interest. He possessed a rare skill in wood-carving, and many of his friends and relatives possess beautiful specimens of his work, which they will prize only the more highly now that the giver is no more. The writer has a specimen of his work, in the shape of a pipe, which he prizes very highly, although he does not smoke. He prizes it because of its uniqueness and because it was presented to him by one whom he counted among his friends.

Dr. Barnes was loved and admired by all who knew him. We reproduce below a memorial written by one who knew and admired him. These lines were written shortly after his death, which, as stated above, occurred on March 9, 1911.

IN MEMORY OF DR. B. S. BARNES

"Died, at Jackson, Ala., at the home of his daughter, Mrs. J. M. Chapman, on Thursday, March 9th, Dr. Benjamin S. Barnes, in the seventy-third year of his age. And he, too, has passed from the material into the celestial, and many hearts are sad that no more will we meet him in our daily walk of life. Though having been spared more than the allotted life of man, in his manner and feelings he never grew old, and while so many of his contemporaries had passed away, he adapted himself to those who considered it a treat and a privilege to listen to his words of wisdom and his storehouse of knowledge. Born and reared in Suggsville, he was the last of the old links that bind the present to the past. To us who have loved him, and lived with him for over a quarter of a century, it almost seems impossible to think of Suggsville without Dr. Barnes, and with him, this, the native village, was a hallowed spot. By nature he was endowed with a fine intellectual mind, and he had enlarged it both by omnivorous reading and the wielding of his facile pen, and nothing came from his pen that was not for good and the unlifting of mankind.

"After a preparatory education, when quite a young man, he graduated from the University of Pennsylvania, in Philadelphia, in the study of medicine, his chosen profession, and was a successful practitioner for many years. And not only as a physician, but as a skillful surgeon, he took a prominent place with the first M. D.'s of this and adjoining states. He kept up with current events in his life work, and many serious cases were saved, by God's grace, through his instrumentality.

"He was gifted in many ways; he was a fine musician; his soul was attuned to melody. His was the wizard's touch on the violin, and many a weary hour he has beguiled by this same magic touch. He also was an artist of ability and made a specialty of wood-carving. In the last years of his life, with a pen-knife he carved a beautiful violin and completed the instrument in every particular, and the writer of this sketch never enjoyed a musical number more than the one he produced after completion of the instrument.

"We feel that we cannot say enough in praise of this gifted man, a gentleman of the old school, kind and courteous to all, and especially to the gentler sex.

"When the last great change had taken place and he passed from mortality into immortality, in a last look at the dear face that for the first time had no responsive greeting, we feel it can be truly said of him:

"'It is not all of life to live,
Nor all of death to die.'

"He cultivated his talents and gave his best to suffering humanity, almost to the very last.

"'When he went home to dwell with the angels forever,
   In that home beyond the sun,
On that day when his heart forgot to beat
   And his life work was done.'

"He was borne by loving hands from Jackson to be interred in the family lot in the Suggsville cemetery, by the side of his wife, the love of his youth, and his life companion for over forty years. Many there were to do him honor at the last sad rites, which were held in the Methodist church, where he always was a regular attendant, and he was laid to rest among a bank of beautiful flowers. From far and near came the floral tributes as a slight testimonial of how he was regarded by his fellow-men. In the grounds outside of the House of God a large number of the colored fraternity had assembled to do him honor, for to so many of them he had been the good, kind doctor, adviser and friend. His children can truly rise up and call him blessed.

"He is survived by six sons and two daughters — C. E. and W. M. Barnes, of Suggsville; R. E. Barnes, of Mobile; S. T. Barnes, of Jackson; B. S. and J. E. Barnes, of Montgomery; Mrs. J. M. Chapman, of Jackson, and Miss Annie Mae Barnes, of Suggsville; one sister, Mrs. R. H. Flinn, of Barlow Bend, and one brother, R. E. Barnes, Sr., of Selma, of his immediate family, and a number of nephews and nieces and other relatives, and many friends to mourn his loss. A FRIEND."

HOME OF DR. NICHOLS

On the opposite page will be seen a picture of the home, built on the foundation of the old Rock Castle, which was erected long before the Civil War.

HOME OF DR. NICHOLS

DR. COBB NICHOLS

Dr. Cobb Nichols was born September 4, 1869, and was educated in the schools of Clarke County. He was clerk of the Probate Court in the county about four years. During Cleveland's administration he was in the customs service in Mobile, Ala. He attended the Alabama Medical College in Mobile and graduated in the class of 1899. He served during enlistment in the Spanish-American War, in the Hospital Corps, with the rank of sergeant-major. He was mustered out in Montgomery, Ala., and went to Mexico as assistant surgeon of the Mexican Central Railway; was in charge of the hospital at Tampico about two years. On his return to the United States he practiced medicine in Jackson, Ala.

Dr. Nichols married Miss Pearl Lee Wilson, daughter of Judge John M. Wilson, in Mobile, June 21, 1910, and resided there until he returned to Clarke County, where he erected a modern house of the airplane-bungalow type on the site of the old Rock Castle, built during ante-bellum days by Dr. H. G. Davis.

Besides doing a lucrative practice, the doctor farms extensively. His home is situated in section 35, township 5 north, range 2 east.

JOHN W. NICHOLS

John W. Nichols, son of William Nichols, was born February 17, 1865. He moved to Clarke County in 1887 and engaged in the mill business. He married Miss Kate

Jones, daughter of C. B. Jones, in 1889. He was a successful mill man for a number of years, a prominent member of the Baptist church, and moderator of that association. He reared two fine sons, Earle and John Coma, and has one daughter, who will soon be as fine as her parents.

C. B. JONES

C. B. Jones, son of G. E. Jones, was born and reared in Clarke County. He graduated from the University of Alabama. He married Miss Lon May early in life. To them were born eight children, five of whom are still living. He numbered his friends by all with whom he was associated.

J. W. TUCKER — THE PIONEER BANKER

Among the early comers to Thomasville was one James Wilson Tucker, who was born in Marengo County August 20, 1866.

Mr. Tucker is not only prominent as a business man, but holds high positions in church, fraternal, municipal and county affairs. He is president of the Farmers Bank and Trust Company, an institution with resources valued at million dollars. He is a member of the Board of Stewards of the Methodist church. He is a trustee of Thomasville public schools, is treasurer of the county school funds, a member of the County Board of Education, and is a Mason of high rank. Mr. Tucker is recognized one of Clarke County's foremost citizens.

HARWELL G. DAVIS

Harwell Goodwin Davis, son of Judge Thomas W. Davis (Mollie Goodwin), was born in Marengo County, near Hoboken, and reared in Thomasville, Ala. He graduated at the South Alabama Institute, and from the law department of the University of Alabama.

He served two years as assistant attorney-general of the state, which place he resigned when war was declared to attend a training camp. Although without previous military training, he completed the course and was commissioned a captain, in command of Company B, 327th Infantry.

During the St. Mihiel drive Captain Davis acted as regimental operation and intelligence officer. After this he was placed in command of the third battalion, 327th Infantry, which he commanded while in the Argonne forest fight. The day that he was wounded by machine-gun fire, October 11, 1918, he was promoted to major. General John J. Pershing awarded an official citation to Major Harwell Davis for distinguished and exceptional bravery in action.

He was discarged from the army May 29, 1919. He was appointed assistant attorney-general the early part of 1920, and served in that position until February 8, 1921, when he was appointed by Governor Thomas E. Kilby to fill the unexpired term of Attorney-General J. Q. Smith, who resigned to accept appointment as circuit judge in Jefferson County. He became a candidate for the Democratic nomination for attorney-general to succeed himself, and was given the Democratic nomination without opposition. He was elected in November, 1922, as attorney-general of the state, and began his present term of office January 15, 1923. In 1921 he was elected outer guard of the Grand Lodge, Knights of Pythias of Alabama, and was elected inner guard in 1922, and grand master-at-arms in 1923. He was elected by the Alabama department of the American Legion on the national executive committee to represent this state.

As attorney-general of the state he has been required to serve in several ex-officio positions of importance. One of these positions is a member of the Budget Commission, which prepares the financial program of the state. He served also as a member of the Bond Commission, which determines the time of issue and the character of the highway bonds authorized by what is commonly known as the highway amendment to the constitution.

He served as a member of the State Board of Compromise, which has power to adjust doubtful claims due the state. He is chairman of the State Board of Pardons, which makes recommendations as to applications for pardons and paroles, and determines the expiration of sentences under the indeterminate sentence law. He also serves as a member of several other commissions.

JOHN AUSTIN KIMBROUGH, M. D.

John Austin Kimbrough, M. D., one of the most eminent physicians and surgeons of Clarke County, was born in Wilcox County February 22, 1872. He is a son of William T. and Relevia Kimbrough. His scholastic training was secured at the neighborhood schools. He entered the medical college at Louisville, Ky., in 1895, where he received his professional degrees. Later he took a post-graduate course at New Orleans. He was among the early comers to Thomasville, where he has practiced his profession with a pronounced degree of success. He was married November 1, 1899, to Miss Stella Oakley, of Marengo County. He has served as town and county health officer, serving also as railroad surgeon for the Southern Railway. He was for a number of years counsellor of the Alabama State Medical Association. Dr. Kimbrough is widely known as a sportsman, is a good marksman and fond of the chase. He is no politician, but gives strong support to his party. He is prominent in fraternal circles, is a Mason of advanced rank. He is quiet and unassuming in his manner, never seeking publicity, but is progressive and generously contributes to the interest and advancement of his community.

G. A. CARLETON

George A. Carleton was born in Grove Hill February 27, 1889. His education was limited to the public and high schools of that town. He commenced work in the Democrat office in January, 1907, and purchased it in the spring of 1908. Mr. Carleton is a Democrat and a forceful writer. His paper compares favorably with any weekly newspaper published in any of the small towns of the state.

JOHN CRAWFORD ANDERSON

Born in Greene County, Ala., August 5, 1863, son of Dr. John Crawford Anderson, formerly of Spartanburg, S. C., and Elizabeth McAlpin Anderson, a native of Greene County, educated in the schools of Greene County and the University of Alabama (LL.B., 1883). Practiced law in Marengo County for ten years at Linden and Demopolis. Appointed by Governor Oates judge of the First Judicial Circuit in 1895, nominated and elected without opposition in 1898 for a full term of six years. Elected associate justice of the Supreme Court in 1904, re-elected in 1910 for a period of six years. Appointed chief justice in 1914, elected for the unexpired term during said year, re-elected chief justice in 1916 for a term of six years, and re-elected in 1922. Judge Anderson married Miss Mary Bird Martin, a native of San Marcos, Texas, at Tuscaloosa, in February, 1897. Have two children, Julia and Elizabeth. He is a Presbyterian and a Democrat. Business address, Montgomery; home, Demopolis, Ala.

DR. WILLIAM M'GOWAN

Dr. McGowan, who practiced medicine in Jackson from about 1860 to 1868, when he died, was greatly loved by the people of Jackson and vicinity, as is evidenced by the following memorial, written by Dr. Benjamin S. Barnes, of Suggsville:

"In Memoriam: Dr. William McGowan, died at Jackson, Ala., A. D. 1868, after a long and laborious practice devoted mainly to the distresses of the poor. Dr. McGowan was a native of South Carolina and a graduate of Charleston College of Medicine, succeeding Dr. W. M. Buroughs in the practice of medicine at Jackson just prior to the war, and remained steadfastly at his post of duty, loved by a host of patrons, while his death was a source of unsinister sorrow to a multitude of friends who silently and in tears followed his remains to his last resting place, and as the relentless clods fell with a mournful thud upon his coffin, friends mute with grief stood around the cold charnel house of death. When all was said that should have been said in truthful praise of his many virtues of mind and his immeasurable generosities of soul, while the preacher in deep grief repeated the 'dust to dust,' loving friends cast immortelles upon his remains yet cold in death, inaudibly praying, God rest the soul of our friend, our physician, our counsellor. Today it is a tribute of love and grateful esteem as we pass his grave to drop thereon the silent tear in grateful memory of the man who had no enemies, but whom everybody loved."

JOHN MARSHALL WILSON

John Marshall Wilson, son of Jack Roper Wilson and Sallie Marshall; born March 19, 1852, at Turnbull, Monroe County, Ala. Educated in schools of Clarke County, University of Alabama, 1869-1870. Cadet at United States Military Academy, West Point, N. Y., 1870-1872. Served as clerk in probate office, 1873-1880, during which time he studied law and was admitted to the bar. On October 31, 1877, married to Miss Fannie Mayer, of Lower Peach Tree, Ala.

Was elected probate judge in 1880, and served continuously until 1904, when he retired. In December, 1904, moved to Mobile, Ala., and engaged in the cotton business as a commission merchant, and was a partner in the firm of Davis, Wilson, Gaillard Commission Company, in which business he remained active until his death, February 15, 1910. He was buried in Mobile, Ala.

He was the father of six children, two sons and four daughters. His first son, John M. Wilson, is a prominent physician and surgeon of Mobile. His second son, Lewis Wilson, is a successful dentist at Mobile. His daughter, Annie Marshall, married Quincy W. Tucker, of Grove Hill; she is now dead. His daughter Pearlee married Dr. Cobb Nichols of this county. Kossie married Richard J. Chapman, now dead. His daughter Helen married K. C. Winter, of Mobile. The wife of Judge Wilson, mother of these children, died some years ago.

The writer was intimately associated with Judge Wilson for about thirty-five years and found in him a true friend, always courteous and accommodating. His long experience in the probate office made him the most efficient officer in the history of the county.

ISAAC GRANT

Isaac Grant was born September 17, 1828, and died December 4, 1907. He was editor of the Clarke County Democrat from 1856 until his death. He was one of the best known and greatly admired men of Clarke County. He held many important positions. He was at one time probate judge of the county, and was also one time superintendent of education of the county, and represented the county several times in both the lower and upper house of the legislature of Alabama.

ISAAC GRANT

"The Notable Men of Alabama" says of him as follows: "To play 'Hamlet' with Hamlet left out would be as proper as to write of the prominent men of Alabama and not mention the name of Isaac Grant, the veneral editor of the Clarke County Democrat, published at Grove Hill. For over fifty years Mr. Grant has been more or less prominently identified with the history of the state. He has been editor and publisher of the Clarke County Democrat most of the time, and has frequently been connected both in an official and unofficial way with the stirring scenes encompassed within that period. He is now seventy-six years old, having been born September 17, 1828. He is a native of the County of Onslow, North Carolina, and is the son of Isaac and Elizabeth Helen (New bold) Grant. The father was also a native of North Carolina, from which state he removed in the early thirties. He died while Isaac, Jr., was still a mere youth, so that the family history of the Grants is somewhat abbreviated on account of the lack of information. The Newbolds are said to come from the state of Maryland. Mr. Grant was reared in Marengo County, but at maturity had acquired a good common school education. At twenty he entered upon the business which he has followed for a lifetime, accepting a position in the office of the Jeffersonian, at Linden, in July, 1853."

The above was written in 1904, three years before the death of Mr. Grant. The author of this book was well acquainted with Mr. Grant, having known him from the year 1875 up to his death in 1907. He was a good man and a Jeffersonian Democrat, and his friends were legion.

JAMES ADDISON NEWMAN

(By William B. Newman)

About the year 1810 Ransom Kimbell, of Warren County, North Carolina, moved with his family to the vicinity of the present village of Whatley. He and most of his family perished at the Fort Sinquefield massacre in the Creek War. His son, Isham Kimbell, for many years county clerk, and an eminent citizen of Jackson, escaped the massacre, and Isham's son, Captain Thomas Isham Kimbell, who married his cousin, Martha Jane Boroughs, was for many years one of the Nestors of Jackson.

In 1817 John Morriss, Jr., of Randolph County, North Carolina, who had married Elizabeth Lee Armistead, a niece of Ransom Kimbell, came to Alabama, and bought land in Marengo County. He returned in 1818, buying land in Wilcox and Clarke Counties, but was murdered in Washington County by a murderous gang known as the Murrell clan.

In 1819 William Armistead, born in Elizabeth City County Virginia, in 1762, moved to Alabama, with his children and grandchildren. In 1790 he had married in Warren County, North Carolina, Rebecca Kimbell, daughter of Benjamin Kimbell, Sr., and his wife, Mary Ransom. By her he had (1) Westwood, born 1791, married Elizabeth Boroughs, sister of Thomas Boroughs, hereinafter named, (2) John Kimbell, born 1792, married Julia Gaines, (3) Elizabeth Lee, born 1794, married John Morriss, Jr., and (4) Martha, born 1796, married Edmund Waddell, an uncle of Thomas Boroughs. William Armistead married in Halifax County, North Carolina, secondly, Elizabeth Morriss (nee Lewis), widow of John Morriss, Sr., by whom he had (5) Robert Starkey, born 1800, married Ann Carney, a sister of Isham Kimbell's wife, and (6) Jane Westmoreland, born 1802, who married Dr. Neal Smith. As stated, his stepson, John Morriss, Jr., married his daughter, Elibabeth Lee.

Westwood and Elizabeth (Boroughs) Armistead had several children, William Westwood, Bryan, Robert, James W., ———, who married her cousin, John Kimbell, and Emma, who married ——— Cunninghame. Judge Cuninghame is her son. The Clarke County Armisteads of this time are descendants of Westwood.

John Kimbell Armistead moved to Mississippi in 1845. One of his sons, Charles, became a general in the Confederate service.

Elizabeth Lee (Armistead) Morriss had four children by her husband John, namely, Rebecca Kimbell, who married Thomas Boroughs, who was born in Moore County, North Carolina; William Armistead, who married Ann Hearin; Washington, who married ———, and Martha Jane, who married Samuel Forwood.

Martha (Armistead) Waddell's children moved to Louisiana, as did her nephew, William Westwood Armistead.

Robert Starkey Armistead moved to Washington County, Texas, and died there without issue.

Jane Westmoreland (Armistead) Smith had many children, among others (1) Kate, who married Dr. Henry G. Davis; (2) ———, who married, first David White, second

James M. Jackson; (3) Mazie, who married her cousin, Thomas Boroughs, Jr.; (4) ——, who married first Starkey Jones, second —— Rixey; (5) Margaret, who married first —— Harrison, second —— Lewis; (6) ——, who married —— Savage; (7) Robert, (8) Neal, and others not remembered.

William Armistead, the patriarch of our family, is buried at Amity. He died in 1842 and was a Revolutionary soldier.

My father, James Addison Newman, was born July 24, 1836, at Gum Spring, near Orange, Va. He and mother (Ann Elizabeth, daughter of Thomas Boroughs and Rebecca Kimbell Morriss) were married in November, 1863. Her first husband, Henley Washington Coate, born at Newberry, S. C., in 1815, was the first probate judge of Clarke County. He had previously been county clerk. To him and mother were born (1) Richard Smith, born May 9, 1849, died May 28, 1866; (2) Martha Elizabeth, born March, 1853, married her cousin, Samuel Forwood, Jr., in March, 1873; (3) Mazie Rebecca, born August, 1855, married June, 1876; Arthur Paul Jones, of Texas, died —, 1914; (4) James Buchanan, born 1857, died 1859.

My father and mother's children were: William Boroughs, born May 30, 1866; Thomas Reuben, born April 24, 1868; James Bryan, born December 19, 1870.

Father enlisted in a Virginia artillery company commanded by William D. Leake, brother of Shelton F. Leake, an eminent Virginia politician. The Leakes were connected with father through the Quisenberrys and with the

Dickinsons through the Sheltons. He served with Leake in a campaign on Seabrooke's plantation, near Povotaglio Inlet, S. C., and was ordered back to Virginia just in time to participate in the seven days' battles around Richmond. He had been detached from Leake's command and attached to the King William Artillery, then commanded by Captain Thomas H. Carter, a cousin of General Lee. In this were three of his bosom friends and schoolmates, Charles, William and Argyle Turner. He was in the seven days' battles, Cedar Mountain, second Bull Run, Antietam, Fredericksburg, Chancellorsville, Gettysburg, Wilderness and Spottsylvania C. H. battles. He was captured and his battery destroyed on May 12, 1864, at the bloody angle at Spottsylvania. He was in prison at Fort Delaware until July 1865, when, having refused to take the oath of allegiance, he was sent on a gunboat to New Orleans, where he was paroled as a prisoner of war. He died March 21, 1891.

WILLIAM BOROUGHS NEWMAN

W. B. Newman was born in Clarke County, Alabama, in the town of Grove Hill, May 30, 1866. He was graduated at Howard College with the degree of master of arts in 1884, thence matriculating at Washington and Lee University in Virginia, where he graduated from the law department in 1886. For the two following years he practiced at Franklin, Texas. He then moved to Talladega, Ala., where he practiced law until the year 1895. He then removed to Washington, D. C., where he now resides, and where he holds an important position in the government service.

JOHN A. BOLEN, SR.

J. A. Bolen is the son of Tom Bolen, who moved from South Carolina to Wilcox County in 1826, where John A. was born on April 30, 1837. From there he moved to Marengo County in 1840. From Marengo County John A.

Bolen moved to Clarke County in the fall of 1860, and in the same year married T. P. Kelly's daughter, who died in the fall of 1861.

Mr. Bolen, speaking of his war record, says: "I enlisted in the Confederate army in 1861 and left Jackson, Ala., April 2, 1862. I was mustered into the Thirty-second Alabama Regiment, McKinstry, colonel, and Harry Morry, colonel. We left Mobile, Ala., July 1, 1862. We went to Chattanooga, thence back into North Alabama. There we had one or two little skirmishes at Stevenson and Bridgeport, Ala. We then went to Tullahoma, Tenn. Then we went from there to a little place called Luverne, Tenn. There our regiment and about 800 dismounted cavalry had a battle and we lost 400, killed and captured. We then went back to Murfresboro, Tenn. Then on January 1, 1863, we were mustered into Dan Adams' Louisiana brigade. On January 4 our brigade made a charge on the battery and railroad cut. After the battle we retreated to Tullahoma, Tenn. Then we went from Tullahoma, Tenn., some time in June, to Jackson, Miss., cutting our way into Vicksburg, Miss. We left there on July 5, and on the morning of the 7th we got word from some men that were paroled that Vicksburg had surrendered on the 4th. We then came back to Jackson, Miss. On Sunday morning, afterward, the Yankees made a charge on our part of the line, where we killed 320 and not a one of our men was hurt. We fell back into Mississippi, near Morton's Station; left there and went back into Georgia in September, 1863. Then the Chicamauga battle came off, and we drove the Yankees back into Chattanooga, Tenn. We camped on Missionary Ridge two months, and on November 20th I was transferred to Clayton's brigade, Stewart's division, Breckenridge's corps. On November 23, at the battle of Missionary Ridge, I was captured and carried to the Rock Island prison, Rock Island, Ill. I was there nineteen months."

Mr. Bolen says the number of prisoners received at the Rock Island prison was 12,215; number died, 1,881; number that joined the U. S. N. I., 19; number that joined the army, 1,797; number released, 136; number escaped, 45; number transferred to other prisons, 11; number exchanged, 119; number present, 5,629; number unwilling to be exchanged, 1,175; number to be exchanged, 4,454.

Mr. Bolen left Rock Island June 2, 1865, and reached home on July 6, and in October, 1865, he married Mary

Jane Thompson, to which union eleven children were born, eight of whom are living, two girls and six boys.

Mrs. Bolen died June 12, 1912. Mr. Bolen is now eighty-six years and six months old, and has forty-one grandchildren and five great-grandchildren. His children now living are: Mrs. Hugh L. McVay, Mrs. Eugene Wilson, E. J. Bolen, H. H. Bolen, J. A. Bolen, Jr., Horace Bolen, Sid Bolen, all of this county, and Archie Bolen, of Birmingham.

Mr. Bolen lives with his children the greater portion of the time being spent with Mrs. McVay in Jackson. He has lived in Clarke County for sixty-three years, has done a noble part by his family, and we venture to say that he hasn't an enemy in the county. The writer has known him for more than forty years and has found him to be honorable and upright in all his dealings with his fellow-men.

Tom Bolen, father of J. A. Bolen, was born in 1794, and was a soldier in the War of 1812. He died in Marengo County January 6, 1856.

DAVID CHAPMAN MATHEWS

David Chapman Mathews, of Allen, Clarke County, representative in the legislature, 1919, from Clarke County,

was born June 10, 1866, near Jackson, Clarke County; is the son of James Waldrum and Frances Isabella (McLeod) Mathews; the grandson of David and Rebecca (Waldrum) Mathews, and of John and Christine (Calhoun) McLeod. The Mathews family came to Alabama from Edgefield district, S. C. David Mathews was in the Confederate army, Thirty-second Alabama Infantry Regiment, and was captured at Lookout Mountain. John McLeod was also in the C. S. A., and was killed at the battle of Franklin, Tenn. Representative Mathews received his education in the public schools of Clarke County and at the First District Agricultural School, Jackson. He is a teacher and a farmer; has taught for twelve years in the Counties of Clarke and Washington. He is a

Democrat and a Baptist. He married, April 24, 1910, at Jackson, Emma Lee, daughter of R. S. and Mima Bumpers, of Allen, Ala. Mr. Mathews was elected superintendent of education for Clarke County and took office January 1, 1923.

REV. JOHN STANLEY FRAZER, D. D.

Rev. John Stanley Frazer, D. D., was born in Clarke County, Alabama, January 24, 1849. He is the son of William Emsley Frazer and Satira (Cassity). He was educated at Summerfield Institute, Summerfield, Ala. The degree of doctor of divinity was conferred on him by the Southern University, Greensboro, Ala., in 1900. He married Mary Ella Chapman, of Clarke County, on February 10, 1874. He was licensed to preach in the M. E. Church, South, in 1870. He served the following circuits in the order given: Jackson circuit, 1873; Rembert Hill circuit, 1874; Forkland circuit, 1875-76; Citronelle, 1877; Evergreen, 1878-81. While only thirty-two years old he was appointed presiding elder of Marianna district, in 1882. He was presiding elder of Pensacola district in 1883-85, of Union Springs district in 1886, of Montgomery district in 1887-89, of Selma district in 1890-93, of Mobile district in 1894-97; pastor of First Methodist church, Eufaula, Ala., 1898; presiding elder of Pensacola district, 1899-1900; of Montgomery district, 1901-04; of Mobile district, 1905-08; Pensacola district, 1909. Conference missionary secretary, 1910; conference commissioner of education, 1911-12; presiding elder of Mobile district, 1913-15; commissioner of Emory University, 1915-20; secretary of Christian education movement for Alabama conference, 1920-22. Is now presiding elder of Selma district since November, 1922. Five times a member of the general conference of the M. E. Church, South — Dallas conference, Birmingham conference, Asheville conference, Oklahoma City conference, Hot Springs conference; member of the Ecumenical conference which met in London in 1901; member of Federal Council of Churches of Christ in America, 1906-14; member of book committee of M. E. Church, South; chairman of board of trustess of Southern University; appointed by Governor B. B. Comer member of board of trustees of Alabama Polytechnic Institute, Auburn, Ala. Has traveled in the interest of the M. E. Church, South, in Cuba, Mexico, England, France, Scotland and Belgium. Is a Democrat, Methodist, Mason. His children are: Mrs. W. F. Betts, Evergreen, Ala.; Mrs. W. F. Washington, Selma, Ala.; Mrs. D. H. McNeal, Enterprise, Ala.; Rev. J. W. Frazer, Pensacola, Fla.; Mrs. L. L. Shertzer, Demopolis, Ala.; Dr. G. Stanley Frazer, Macon, Ga.; Prof. Keener Chapman Frazer, Johns Hopkins University, Baltimore, Md.; Mrs. Hubert Baughn, Atlanta, Ga.—From "Who's Who in America," page 1170.

REV. S. A. ADAMS

The subject of this sketch resides in Mobile, and has resided there for the last ten years, but he was partly reared and educated in Clarke County, highly respected and esteemed by his peoeple, and we feel that he is entitled to special mention in this book.

Mr. Adams was born in Pine Hill, Ala., on August 5, 1855, and lived there with his step-mother, who was a Miss Nettles, who, it is said, was one of the best women in the world. He says his literary training was in the old-fashioned log school-house when a boy, and at the age of twenty-one entered a private school taught by Prof. M. B. Du Bose, and remained there for three sessions. Soon after this he was married to Miss Connor, the oldest daughter of Dr. Ephriam Conner, of Magnolia, Ala. Together they began teaching school on the old school-master system. While teaching at Coffeeville he entered the ministry in 1886. He was ordained a Baptist minister by the Ulcarnush Baptist church. During these thirty-seven or thirty-eight years he has been in the pastorate he covered a territory in Alabama, most of which was in Clarke County. He was pastor of the Baptist church in Jackson for twenty-five consecutive years. He recessed for two years and then served the church for two years more. Mr. Adams has the distinction of baptizing 1,800 persons and marrying 200 couples. It was his sad duty to perform burial services on about 300 occasions. By his first marriage there were two children, Nellie Louise and Robert Gayle. His daughter married Mr. William Chambers, of Catherine, Ala. After becoming the mother of Mary Louise, now in Judson College, her health broke down and she died in New Mexico. Gayle, his son by his first marriage, finished at Auburn in electrical and mechanical engineering. After a few years of successful work he broke down in health and died. About thirty-three years ago he married Miss Corally Gessie Richardson. By this marriage they have three sons—John Clausel, a surgeon in the United States navy; William Eugene, an accountant with the United States Steel Corporation; Orlando Chambers, an engineer on merchantman Chattanooga City. According to his statement, Mr. Adams has been quite a builder. He has erected and sold ten splendid dwelling houses and assisted in the building of two or three school-houses, and was instrumental in having ten handsome churches erected. Mr. Adams moved to Mobile in order to educate his boys, but says he has never shaken the dust of Clarke County from his shoes, especially the red dust in and around Jackson.

Mr. Adams is now in his sixty-eighth year, but judging from his appearance he is good for many more years. He is jovial, full of humor, and has a heart full of the milk of human kindness.

T. J. BEDSOLE

Travis Jesse Bedsole, of Grove Hill, Clarke County, state senator from the nineteenth district, 1919, was born May 27, 1885, at Tallahatta Springs, Clarke County; is the son of Travis Linyer and Martha (Goodman) Bedsole; the grandson of Edward and Susie (Blackwell) Bedsole, and of Matthew and Mary Ann (Sheffield) Goodman. Senator Bedsole received his early education in the public schools of Tallahatta Springs and the high school of Thomasville, Ala. He graduated from the University of Alabama in 1907 with an A. B. degree. He taught school at Geneva, Ala., 1907-08; returned to the university, entered the law department, graduating in 1909 with a LL. B. degree; has been practicing law at Grove Hill since June 8, 1909. He was elected county solicitor of Clarke County, 1914, and served until court was abolished; member of State Democratic executive committee, served four years; elected member of state senate, 1918. He is a Democrat, a Baptist, a Mason, K. of P.,

Woodman of the World, and a member of the Kappa Sigma fraternity. He married, June 20, 1913, Mary Ellis, daughter of John Duncan and Leona (Ellis) Carmichael, and granddaughter, on mother's side, of George and Martha (Currie) Ellis, who lived at Greensboro, Ala. Mr. Bedsole is the only senator now living who was elected from Clarke County to represent the nineteenth senatorial district in the legislature of Alabama.

ISAAC PUGH

A member of the Pugh family furnished the author with the following information:

The first of the large Pugh family to enter Clarke County was Isaac Pugh, who came from North Carolina in 1807. He lived for a year with the Choctaw Indians, who at that time occupied all of Clarke County west of the Tombigbee and Alabama river watershed.

He became a friend of Pushmattah, who was a young man, but had not yet become Chief. He presented Pushmattah with a rifle which he had made himself, and which was inlaid in silver with figures of deer, bear, etc.

He returned to North Carolina and married and remained until 1811, when he returned to Clarke County with his wife and baby, accompanied by his father, Thomas Pugh, and family. They brought their effects in water-tight rolling barrels or hogsheads, drawn by horses and floated over the rivers. This was necessary, as the Creek Indians had heard of cannon on wheels, and would not allow any wheeled vehicle to enter their territory. When they reached Clarke County they found the site, southwest of

Grove Hill, which they had selected for their settlement, no longer occupied by the friendly Choctaws. An old dispute about the western watershed of Clarke County between the Creeks and Choctaws had been determined by agreement by a ball game played at old Choctaw Corner. The Creeks won, and Bashi Creek was made the dividing line. Bashi means boundary. The Creeks were found to be very hostile, due to the English influence at Mobile and Pensacola. The English were allied with the Spanish at that time in the war against the French under Napoleon. The United States was very friendly to the French on account of the aid given us against the British in the Revolution.

Isaac Pugh soon after his return to Clarke County joined a party of settlers under Colonel Callar and attacked a party of Creeks at Burnt Corn, returning from Pensacola, where they had been outfitted by the British with arms and ammunition. The Creeks soon retaliated by the massacre at Fort Mims and the attack on Fort Sinquefield, near Whatley. The Pughs placed their women and children in Fort Madison (near Suggsville) and joined the settlers. Isaac Pugh, being a gun-maker, was selected by Pushmattah, who had become Chief, to assistant Chief, in training the 3,000 Choctaws. Pushmattah had brought to the aid of the settlers in the war against the Creeks in the use of firearms. He was made a member of the Choctaw tribe by the ceremony of mixing blood. While the Creeks under Weatherford were chasing "Old Hickory" Jackson and his troops back toward Tennessee, Pushmattah's Choctaws, aided by the settlers and the Georgia troops under Claiborne, devastated with fire and sword all the Creek county south of Montgomery, and later joined Jackson's reinforced army in wiping out the Creeks at Horse-Shoe Bend, near Montgomery. Jackson with his united forces came south through Clarke County, crossing the river at Jackson, to Mobile, ran the English out of Pensacola, and then went to his great victory at New Orleans. The Pughs, Isaac and Thomas, were with the Choctaws in all these battles.

Isaac Pugh was enlisted in the Seminole Indian War a number of years later, volunteering in place of a younger brother, Ransom Pugh, who was drafted. He did no fighting in the war.

Many descendants of Isaac Pugh are now citizens of Clarke County. Hundreds are in other parts. Among them are the following medical men: Dr. Jesse Pugh, who died in Texas; Dr. Alfred B. Pugh, who was murdered at Bladon Springs; Dr. J. L. Pugh and Dr. Albert S. Pugh, now living at Grove Hill, and Dr. Sidney Pugh, of Mobile, dentist; Dr. Woodie S. Pugh, of Mobile; Prof. E. S. Pugh, of Opelika; Dr. C. C. Pugh, Baptist minister, of Kentucky, and a great many others.

Mr. J. Pickens, a centenarian, who has lost his eyesight, but is physically and mentally yet young, is the youngest son of Isaac Pugh, and lives near the site of the original settlement.

Jesse Pugh, a brother of Isaac Pugh, left Clarke County one hundred years ago and settled, with his eleven sons, in Western Louisiana. The Pughs, who are numerous and wealthy in Louisiana, are his descendants.

DR. SIDNEY S. PUGH

Dr. Sidney S. Pugh is a grandson of Isaac Pugh, is the son of E. Stuart Pugh and Amelia Chapman, and was born near Grove Hill February 26, 1863. After graduating at the University of Alabama with A. B. and A. M. degrees, he graduated in medicine at Tulane University in 1889. After taking a course in surgery in Berlin, Germany, he practiced surgery in Mobile until the Spanish war. He served as major and surgeon in the Second Alabama Volunteer Infantry through the war with Spain. He contracted yellow fever and appendicitis in the tropics during this war. This brought on rheumatism, affecting his hands to such an extent that he had to abandon his favorite work, surgery. He has continued to do office practice and consultations. He volunteered for service in the World War the day war was declared, but was rejected for physical disabilities. He then became a member of the district draft board for the southern district of Alabama, giving two years' full service to the government as supervisor of county boards.

He married Miss Sallie Harrington, of Monroe County. They have three children—Kathleen, who is Mrs. Dr. Dowling, of Mobile; Miss Margaret, who is an art student of Tulane University, and Jessie Stuart, a law student of the University of Alabama.

He has been very successful in a business way as well as in his chosen profession. He still loves old Clarke County, which he still frequently visits.

JESSE V. BOYLES

Hon. Jesse V. Boyles, a distinguished jurist, was born in Monroe County in 1884. He was the son of N. B. and Lucy (Adams) Boyles. He came to Clarke County in his early childhood, the family settling in Thomasville, where he received a high school education. Later he attended the University of Alabama for a term of five years, winning honors with an A. B. degree. He graduated in law from that institution in 1905. He was a born athlete, took part in all college activities, played varsity football for three years, won two medals, the Bryan and the Mary Fern. He was admitted to the bar and practiced his profession in Mobile for two years, after which he returned to Clarke County and was thoroughly identified with the affairs of the county, and was county solicitor at the time of his death, which sad event occurred in October, 1920. As a citizen Mr. Boyles was held in the highest esteem, was progressive and enterprising, and took an active interest in the moral and material prosperity of the county. He was prominent in fraternal circles and was a staunch supporter of the Democratic party. He was married to Miss Janie May Clarke, of Lower Peach Tree. She with their son Jesse, Jr., still lives in Thomasville.

ALBERT SIDNEY JOHNSON

Albert Sidney Johnson, of Thomasville, Clarke County, Ala., was born July 29, 1888, at Choctaw Corner, Clarke County; is the son of William James and Susan Emma (Evans) Johnson, the former of Bashi, Clarke County, and the latter of Linden, Marengo County, Ala.; and grandson of William England and Louisa (Davis) Johnson) of Bashi, Ala., and of Louis G. and Harriet E. (Grayson) Evans, of Linden, Marengo County, Ala. The father of A. S. Johnson was a merchant at Choctaw Corner and at Thomasville, and became a lawyer in 1888; the great-great-grandfather, William Johnson, was a general in the War of the Revolution; the great-grandfather, William Johnson, was a captain in the War of 1812; and William England Johnson served in the War of Secession. Albert Sidney Johnson was educated at South Alabama Institute, Thomasville, Ala., and graduated at the University of Alabama with degree of LL. B. in 1907; he is a lawyer and has been city attorney; is a Democrat, a member of the M. E. Church, South, is a Mason, a K. of P., and a W. of W., and prepared a code of ordinances for Thomasville, Ala., which was adopted September 12, 1910. He is not married. In addition to having held the office of county judge, he has for several years been county solicitor for Clarke County.

DAVID TAYLOR

David Taylor had eight sons and three daughters. Columbus Taylor, the eldest son, by the first wife, died in Georgia; another son died in infancy; Ann Taylor, a daughter by the first wife, married Mr. William Jones, of Suggsville; there was one child who preceded her mother to the grave. Four of David Taylor's sons were in the Confederate army. Walter Taylor was rendered physically unfit for army service from an accident, he having suffered two broken ribs and other injuries when thrown from a buggy by a runaway horse. John B. Taylor, the next son, was a prisoner on Ship Island when the Civil War ended. Robert, the next son, was killed at the battle of Chicamauga; David, the next, was killed in the Shenandoah Valley, Virginia; W. Jesse Taylor, the youngest son, was badly wounded at the battle of Shiloh, and never fully recovered from the wound in his knee. Jesse married Miss Minnie Cole, now Mrs. T. J. Cowan, at present a resident of Jackson. One of the daughters of David Taylor, Aurulia Taylor, married Archibald Smoot. Of this marriage there were two daughters, the youngest of whom married Henry Hall, of Mobile, the other dying when a young girl. Amelia Eugenie Taylor, youngest daughter of David and Judith Taylor, married Augustus Rufus Lankford, a brother of Amanda Caroline Lankford Taylor, wife of Walter Taylor. There was one son of this union, Henry, who died in infancy. A. R. Lankford (colonel in the Confederate army) was a prisoner on Johnson Island when the war closed. To Walter Taylor and Amanda C. Lankford Taylor were born ten daughters and one son, all of whom have passed away except three daughters, now living in Jackson, Ala.

TAYLORS OF JACKSON, ALA.

David Taylor, born in Augusta, Ga., July 7, 1780; moved to Jackson, Ala., in 1812. Married Judith Carr Parker, and they brought up seven children: Walter Taylor, John Taylor, S. Parker Taylor, David Taylor, Robert H. Taylor, William Jesse Taylor, and Miss Amelia Eugenia Taylor, who married Colonel A. R. Lankford. David Taylor merchandised in Jackson, and also owned the ferry landing, a saw-mill and a wheat-mill. He died October 15, 1839. His wife, Judith C. Taylor, was born October 25, 1792, and died June 1, 1851.

Walter Taylor, son of David Taylor, was born in Jackson September 14, 1817, died March 24, 1886. He married Amanda Caroline Lankford, of Coffeeville, Ala., January 5, 1841. She died September 19, 1898, in Jackson. They had eleven children: Fredonia A. Taylor, Florence A. Taylor, Aurulia A. Taylor, Mary Estelle Taylor, Eva Carr Taylor, Teresa Halo Taylor, Caroline Holt Taylor, Amelia Eugenia Taylor, Walter Taylor, Jr., Josephine Lankford Taylor, and Sarah Smoot Taylor.

S. Parker Taylor married Miss Sarah J. Parker. They had one child, Leland Taylor, who died when a small boy.

John Taylor died unmarried. David Taylor died unmarried. Also Robert H. Taylor never married, as he was killed at the battle of Chicamauga during the Civil War.

William Jesse Taylor married Miss M. E. Cole, of Gosport, Ala. Two children born of this marriage lived to be grown—Skipwith C. Taylor, now in Calvert, Ala., and W. Jesse Taylor, living in Dallas, Texas. Both have several children.

Walter Taylor graduated at a college in Augusta, Ky., then studied law and won his diploma at Transylvania University, but became a merchant in Jackson after his marriage.

S. Parker Taylor also merchandised in Jackson for some years, then moved to Florida, where he died.

JAMES A. LANKFORD, OF COFFEEVILLE, ALA.

Thomas Lankford moved from Scotland to Tennessee in the early part of 1700. Had eight children. One of them, James A. Lankford, moved to Coffeeville, Ala., bringing with him his four living children — Fredonia Adeline and Amanda Caroline, twins, born September 12, 1821; Augustus Rufus, who was also a twin, but his twin brother died quite young. James A. Lankford's wife was Miss Jean Rutherford, whose parents moved from Scotland to Randalsburg, Tenn. She died in Tennessee, and after he moved with his children to Coffeeville he married a Mrs. Murray. They had one daughter, Victoria Laulette, who died when an infant. He died October 6, 1841.

A. Rufus Lankford married Miss Amelia Eugenia Taylor, sister of Walter Taylor. They had one boy, Henry Hugh Lankford. A Rufus Lankford was a soldier in the Mexican War, and when the Civil War came on was one of the first to volunteer. He was made first lieutenant of the Suggsville Grays. Was rapidly promoted, and the close of the war found him colonel of the Thirty-eighth Alabama Regiment. He is better remembered in Clarke as the gallant captain of the Suggsville Grays.

Miss Fredonia A. Lankford married Mr. William K. Barnes, of Suggsville, Ala. They had several children who died young.

Miss Josephine Angerene Lankford married Mr. William M. Weibling, of New Orleans, La. He operated steamboats on the Mississippi river until the Civil War, when he was stricken with death at Meridian, Miss., in 1863. His wife died in Taylor, Texas, at the home of her youngest son, Lankford Weibling.

J. F. GILLIS

J. F. Gillis was born in Lowndes County on February 21, 1866. His father was Rev. Neil Gillis, a Methodist minister, and his mother was Margaret Josephine Miles, the daughter of Aquilla Miles. She was also the granddaughter of Club-Ax Davis, the great old Irish pioneer Baptist preacher and Indian fighter of early Alabama history. J. F. Gillis was educated in the grammar school of Troy, the Ozark High School, and the Southern University. From this college he was graduated in June, 1887, with the degree of A. B. He taught school for ten years under an Alabama first-grade certificate. He served from October, 1887, to October, 1894, as a member of the county board of education of Clarke County, and when the new county board was created by law in 1904 he was elected one of its members and served continuously thereon until he was made superintendent of education in 1917. He was made register in chancery in August, 1899, and served until January 15, 1917.

ARCHIBALD LONZO M'LEOD

Of the gentlemen prominent in legal circles throughout the state, Hon. A. L. McLeod, of Selma, stands well to the front. Beginning practice at Jackson, Ala., in 1889, he settled in Selma the followinig year. He has done a general law business and has a large and constantly growing clientele. Mr. McLeod is a Democrat in politics, and has been a leader in the councils of the party for a number of years. He served in the legislature from Clarke County during the sessions of 1888 and 1889, and after his removal to Selma still continued to interest himself in public affairs. He was mayor of the city from May, 1899, to May, 1903, and has served in various semi-public positions in social, lodge and religious circles. He is an earnest worker in the Methodist church. In fraternal circles he is affiliated with the Masons (Santa Fe Lodge, of Jackson) and the Odd Fellows. He is also a member of the Elks. In the social life of the community both Mr. McLeod and his wife take an active part. Mrs. McLeod is of a family well known throughout the state, being a daughter of George W. Hails, the present tax collector of Montgomery County. Her marriage to Mr. McLeod occurred February 6, 1901. Mr. McLeod's first wife, Mary A. Jordan, of Selma, died November 1, 1891. There is a daughter to the second marriage named Elizabeth Furniss McLeod. Mr. McLeod was born in Jackson, Clarke County, December 27, 1859. He is the son of John and Christian (Calhoun) McLeod. John McLeod was a native of Clarke County, his wife being the daughter of Duncan Calhoun, who came to Alabama from North Carolina. Our subject's father was a man of intensely patriotic mold, and during the Civil War offered himself a willing sacrifice on the altar of his beloved Southland. He became a member of Company C, Thirty-second Alabama Infantry, and served with faithfulness and devotion until the bloody battle of Franklin, where he was one of the many brave heroes who paid the full price of their devotion to duty. He was wounded and died in hospital. Mr. McLeod is a graduate of the University of Alabama, of the class of 1885. After his graduation he taught in the public schools of Selma two years. After that he organized a newspaper in Jackson, Ala., known as the South Alabamian. Soon thereafter he removed to Selma, where he has ever since engaged in the practice of law. As heretofore stated, he was mayor of Selma from 1899 to 1901, and was re-elected without opposition for the term ending May 1, 1903.

The above was taken from the "Notable Men of Alabama," published about twenty years ago. He died April 11, 1910.

DR. BRYAN BOROUGHS

Thirty-five years in storm and sunshine, at any time of the day or night, without an hour's sickness. A good refutation of the old claim concerning the "shoemaker's children always being without shoes," when taken in connection with the life of the gentleman here mentioned, for that is the record of this physician. Dr. Boroughs lives in Jackson, Ala. He was born May 14, 1847, in Clarke County, Ala. He was carefully trained in the common schools of the day, and finished his literary education at the University of Alabama. The profession of medicine appealcine appealing to him as the one most likely to suit his tastes, he repaired to New Orleans, where he pursued studies in the medical department of Tulane University, and finished his course at Louisville Medical College, taking his degree in 1869. He at once commenced the practice at Grove Hill, Ala., thence removing to Vashti, where he remained until 1897, the date of his settlement in Jackson. Here Dr. Boroughs has built up a practice and stands among the first in his profession. He has served a number of years as health officer of the county, and also of the town of Jackson. He has been a member of the American Medical Association fifteen years. Dr. Boroughs is of a social and genial nature, in common political parlance "a good mixer." He is a Free and Accepted Mason, and he and his family are members of the Baptist church. The doctor takes an active interest in public affairs, which every good citizen owes his government, serving his party on the different committees when called upon, attending the different county, state and congressional conventions to nominate good men to office. He is proud to be called a Jeffersonian Democrat. Colonel James S. Dickinson, of Grove Hill, gave him his daughter, Mary Elizabeth, for his wife, the event occurring in October, 1871. Colonel Dickinson had long been a prominent and respected resident of that community, having served as state senator for Clarke, Monroe and Baldwin Counties, 1853-55, as a Breckenridge elector, 1860, and as a member of the Confederate congress, 1863-65. To the marriage of Dr. and Mrs. Boroughs have been born seven children, whose names are in order as follows: Imogene, James

Dickinson, Bryan Morris, Bessie (deceased), Edwin Armistead, Lillian and Frederick. Bryan Boroughs, grandfather of our subject, lived and died in the state of North Carolina. His son Thomas came to Alabama when a young man and settled in Clarke County. He married Rebecca M. Morris and continued to reside in Clarke County until his death in 1866. Rebecca Morris came of a family closely related to the great financier and philanthropist, Robert Morris, of Revolutionary fame. Her father came to Alabama about the year 1818 and purchased land in the four counties of Dallas, Marengo, Clarke and Montgomery. These were the days of bad Indians and worse white men, and his sudden disappearance while on a trip to St. Stephens, then the territorial capital, was attributed to foul play on the part of one or both of these elements. Certain it is that he never was heard of after he left his own domicile.

The above was taken from the "Notable Men of Alabama," published about twenty years ago.

Dr. Boroughs is still living. His two daughters are married. The older daughter, Imogene, married Dr. T. C. Kirven. They have one son, B. E. Kirven, who was married to Miss Tinnie McDonald. They have one daughter, whose name is Tinnie Imogene. His younger daughter, Lillian, was married some years ago to Fred Lett, who resides in Mobile. They have no children. His four sons are not married.

A. M. WING

A. M. Wing was a resident citizen of Jackson, Ala., for sixty-four years, or from July, 1859, until his death on June

30, 1910. Mr. Wing was born in Baldwin County, Ala., at Montgomery Hill, or Tensas, on the 9th day of December, 1837. He came to Jackson in July, 1859, and clerked for James O'Gywn, who had opened up a general mercantile business in the building on the northeast corner of Broad and Commerce streets, now owned and occupied by Charles Howard. Later he secured a clerkship with Mr. Peter DuBose, who was doing a mercantile business on the northwest corner of Carroll and Monoroe streets, where Smith's bakery is now situated.

When the Civil War was declared and volunteers were called for he enlisted in Company G, Thirty-second Alabama Infantry Regiment, in 1861. He was in many important battles and was taken prisoner at the battle of Missionary Ridge on the 25th day of November, 1863, and carried to Johnson Island and kept there until June, 1865, when he was released and came back to Jackson.

After the war he clerked a while for Captain Wainright, who was doing a general mercantile business in the old DuBose storehouse, where he was clerking before he went to the war. He worked there for a short while, then went to farming on what was afterward known as the Wing plantation. In a few years he opened up a mercantile business in the storehouse on the southwest corner of Broad and Commerce streets, now known as the Bolen storehouse. He later purchased and moved into the house in which Charles Howard does business. He was engaged in the mercantile business off and on until a short while before his death. He farmed extensively, having one plantation north of Jackson and one south, and these were in operation at his death. He did a large advancing business, and in that way helped many a poor farmer to keep the wolf from his door. Mr. Wing was a public-spirited man and contributed liberally to every worthy cause. He was a Presbyterian, the Presbyterian church at this place being organized in his home on the south side of Carroll street, where Horace Frisbie now lives, in 1873. He contributed liberally to the support of his church as long as he lived.

Mr. Wing was first lieutenant of his company at the time of his capture at Missionary Ridge, and his sword was taken from him by a Federal officer. This sword was returned to him forty-one years afterward. The following correspondence will tell the story connected with the sword:

"East Liverpool, O., January 15, 1904.
"A. M. Wing,
"Jackson, Ala.
"Dear Sir:

"At a joint meeting of Gen. Lyon Post, G. A. R., and Gen. Garfield Camp, S. of V., held in this city two or three weeks ago, in the course of telling and relating of experiences in the war of '61 to '65 there was a comrade who got up and told of taking a man prisoner at the battle of Missionary Ridge on November 25, 1863, and that he had the man's sword yet and that he would only be too glad to return it to him if he could find him, and also that it would be the greatest pleasure of his life to meet the man and return his sword to him, 'for,' said he, 'boys, if that man's revolver had not missed I would not have been here to tell the tale.' 'Now,' he said, 'if any of you want to try to find the man for me, do so.' I said, 'Are there any marks on the sword?' He said, 'Yes, the man's name only.' I said, 'What is the name?' 'A. M. Wing, C. S. A.,' said he.

I told him that I would undertake to find the owner of that sword. With the help of the War Department and the commander of Camp Lomax of Montgomery, Ala., John B. Fuller referred me to L. A. Callear of Fort Deposit, Ala., and he gave me your address.

"Now I feel greatly pleased with my success so far and it only remains for you to complete it by paying us a visit and get your sword if it is possible for you to do so. We will try to entertain you as best we can, I am sure. Now I will say that the man that has your sword is a very great friend of mine, a man that holds a government position and stands high in social circles, yet one of the most common of men and the most friendly, too. Now he does not know that I have located you, and if you could make it possible to come I would like to spring a surprise on him. Try and come if possible. Of course, I suppose you know this is the City of Potteries, and if you come will try to show you all the pottery business that we can. We are the pottery center of the world.

"I would say that I am not one of the soldiers of '61 to '65, only one of the sons of Veteran. My father was a member of Company F, 46th Pennsylvania, and died in the hospital at Nashville, Tenn., and is buried there.

"Now I will close. Hoping to hear from you soon, I remain,

"Your friend,
"ARCHIE SEARIGHT,
"No. 126 Station A, East Liverpool, Ohio.
"P. S.—I am anxiously awaiting a reply. Of course, if

it is impossible for you to come, will try to make some other arrangement by which you get the sword."

Whereas, Col. Archie Searight, commander of Garfield Camp, Sons of Veterans, of East Liverpool, O., had in his possession a sword captured at the battle of Missionary Ridge November 25, 1863, and having the name of Lieut. A. M. Wing engraved upon it—no company or regiment. Col. Searight, after months of correspondence with Confederate camps and the War Department at Washington, found that Lieutenant Wing belonged to Company G, 32nd Alabama Infantry, was captured at the battle of Missionary Ridge November 25, 1863, and taken to Johnson's Island, where he was kept until the close of the war. He is now living at Jackson, Clarke County, Alabama.

The precious sword will be restored to him after forty years. Such action on the part of the sons of our former foes calls for recognition upon our part. Therefore be it,

Resolved, That this camp as a body of Confederate Veterans show our appreciation of the patriotic and fraternal act of Col. Searight by extending to him our sincere thanks for his indefatigable efforts and final success in locating Lieutenant Wing and restoring to him his sword.

Resolved, That these resolutions be spread upon our minutes and a copy be sent to Col. Searight and also to Lieut. Wing.

Mr. Wing was married three times. His last wife, who was Miss Cora R. DuBose, now resides in Jackson. She has three children, A. M. Wing of Mobile, Mrs. W. E. Johnson and Nelson Clayton Wing of Jackson.

Mr. Wing had two children by his second wife, being Lieut. Glover Wing, who died in the Philippines, and Mrs.

Lula Bedwell, wife of James W. Bedwell of Jackson. Her first husband was John D. Cunningham, who died years ago.

Mr. Wing was a Mason and an elder in the Presbyterian Church.

JOHN SIMPSON GRAHAM

A prominent citizen of Jackson, Ala., and for many years the fearless and able editor of the South Alabamian; is a Mississippian by birth, born in Tishomingo County on the present site of Corinth, January 24, 1848. The unsettled conditions consequent upon the war made it impossible for him to secure much schooling, but he managed to get enough to serve for a basis, and the activities of life have transformed him into a well-informed man. He had a varied career, and has been successful in several different lines. When but sixteen years of age he entered the army, becoming a private in Company A of the Thirty-sixth Alabama Infantry. His service was at points

in the extreme south, and he was at a Spanish fort when it fell into the hands of the Federals. He waded out across the swamps and made his way to Blakely and from there to Mobile. He was discharged soon afterward at Meridian, Miss. He was engaged in the mercantile business at Warsaw, Ala., in 1869, 1870 and 1871; removed from there to Birmingham in 1871, and in 1872 went to Mobile, at which place he remained until 1875 when he settled at Jackson and was engaged in the mercantile business until 1880. He then went to Texas, thence to Louisiana, returning to Jackson in 1885, and soon afterward entered the office of the South Alabamian, of which he later became editor and proprietor. He leased the paper in January, 1904, and now devotes his time to the practice of law, having been admitted to the bar in Clarke County in 1895. He is a member of the Methodist Church, and unbending in his advocacy of the principles of the Democratic party, leaning toward Clevelandism at present. During the past twelve years his paper has been fearless and aggressive in its efforts to expose the fallacies of the populists. On December 21, 1868, he married Ophelia J. Houston of Warsaw, Ala. After becoming the mother of three children, all of whom died quite young, this lady died August 21, 1872. On March 21, 1877, in Jackson, Ala., Mr. Graham married Teresa H., daughter of Walter and Amanda Taylor. Four children were born to this wife, her death occurring in July, 1889. He married December 24, 1895, to Sara Belle Pittman, daughter of E. D. Pittman of Waynesboro, Miss. She has borne two children, John Pittman and Edward Carr. Only two of the other children are now living, Rufus L., late a soldier in the Philippines, and now residing at Jackson, and Eva Pearle, who married Samuel A. Cooper and now living in Houston, Tex.

Mr. Graham is the son of Willis Williford and Amanda Wales Graham, the former a native of South Carolina, and the latter a native of Tennessee and a daughter of Col. T. C. Clark of the Creek Indian war. She died in 1868 and her husband in 1879. They passed the early part of their married life in Corinth, Miss., and were living at that place when the war broke out. They refugeed to different points, finally settling at Warsaw, Ala. His mother died near Warsaw, after which his father purchased a plantation near West Point, Miss., and moved to it about the year 1869 or 1870, and there spent the remainder of his days. Willis W. Graham was a farmer by occupation and a man of intensely democratic proclivities. He favored the idea of secession and furnished four sons for the service, all of whom did their duty manfully and were spared to do their part in the resuscitation of their beloved Southland.—From Notable Men of Alabama.

The above was published about nineteen years ago. Many things have transpired since that time. Mr. Graham sold the South Alabamian shortly after this and in a few years bought it back again. He edited it for several years and then sold it again, in the meantime keeping up his practice of law. He was elected in 1918 as a member of the lower house of the legislature of Alabama and served during the years 1919-20-21-22. He is now the grandfather of eight children.

Mrs. Eva P. Cooper, daughter of John S. Graham, was born in Jackson, Ala., February 5, 1881. She graduated at the Alabama Conference Female College at Tuskegee under Prof. John Massey. She is now living with her second husband, Homer Snyder, at Tampa, Fla. She has two children by her first husband, Samuel A. Cooper, whose names and ages are as follows: Graham, born May 20, 1902, and Laura Teresa, born September 15, 1905. Graham Cooper is now a member of the United States Marines. Laura Teresa is with her mother.

JOHN P. GRAHAM

John P. Graham, son of John S. Graham, was born May 23, 1897, in Jackson, Ala. He enlisted in the United States army and was on his way to France when the war was suddenly terminated. He was married on January 30, 1920, to Miss Ruby Champion, daughter of H. J. Champion of Clarke County. Two children have been born of this union, a girl and a boy. Sarah Margaret was born November 11, 1920, and John Champion was born November 14, 1921. For the first eighteen months of his married life, Mr. Graham was employed in the drug business, most of the time in Crowley, La. For the last ten months he has been engaged in saw milling, but is now merchandising.

EDWARD C. GRAHAM

Edward C. Graham, son of John S. Graham, was born September 3, 1901, in Jackson, Ala. He was married on June 20, 1922, to Miss Alice Grace Boyles, daughter of C. W. Boyles of Jackson, Ala. Charles Edward was born to them on August 10, 1923. They reside in Jackson. Mr.

Graham owns and operates the Steam Clothing Pressing business.

RUFUS L. GRAHAM

Rufus L. Graham, son of John S. Graham, was born in Jackson, Ala., May 22, 1878. He attended the schools of Jackson. He was working in the office of his father, and when he became 21 years of age he enlisted in the army and was sent to the Philippines, where he was in actual service for about eighteen months. After this he traveled much, not only in the United States but visited many foreign countries. He was in the World War from start to finish. He enlisted at Sidney, Australia, in August, 1914, in the Australian division of the English army, and was immediately sent to Egypt, camping at the foot of the Pyramids near Cairo. From there his command went into actual service. He was in many battles and was wounded seven times. When he was not in a hospital being treated for his wounds, he was on the battlefield. On July 10, 1916, he received a wound on the Verdun front which came near ending his service. His left arm and shoulder was crushed by a shell, and it was many months before he was able to perform further service. However, he finally recovered and was sent to northwest Russia, at Archangel, where he remained until December, 1918, when he returned to London. When he was wounded at Verdun, he was sent to a hospital in Manchester, England. In September, 1916, he was married to a lady who was born and reared in Manchester. After the war was over, he with his family went to Sidney, Australia, the government requiring him to return to the place where he enlisted before receiving his discharge. He now has three children, two boys and a girl, and will perhaps make Australia his permanent home.

He was decorated several times by the English government for bravery on the battlefields.

Bobbie Graham, David Graham and Teresa Graham, children of Rufus L. Graham, were born August 4, 1918, June 26, 1920, and January 10, 1922, respectively.

The following letter was written by Rufus L. Graham to his father, John S. Graham, after the close of the war:

"From Durban and Capetown I went up through the Natal and did some pioneering with the N. M. P., and then came out to Durban again. I stayed at Durban a few days and decided to go to Sydney. After leaving Durban we were notified by wireless that England had declared war on Germany. So when we reached Sydney, found everything in a great state of excitement, troops were being mustered in and so on. I and a few others went out to the barrack grounds at Victoria and watched the proceedings one morning for a few minutes, and I said to a mate, 'Let's have a cut-in.' He said, 'Right.' So we went to the recruiting officer and he said, 'Yes, fill in this sheet for enlistment.' I was enlisted in the Third battalion of Australia Infantry on August 19, 1914, and assigned to duty with Company E as acting sergeant instructor of ordnance. On account of my ability to drill troops and general knowledge of most everything pertaining to military affairs, I was sent to brigade headquarters as temporary captain on precedent work. Later on I was obliged to step down for permanent trainers. Returned to the battalion and was attached to the intelligence department and have been employed in the intelligence department ever since up to date of my discharge September 29, 1919. Went away from Australia with the first expedition on October 20, 1914, and was at the scene of the naval battle at Cocas Island when the Sydney sank the Emden. It was on Sunday morning, November, 1914, about 10 a. m. Landed at Alexandria, Egypt, November 23, 1914. Was at both fights on the Suez, December 28, 1914, and February 8, 1915, and at the landing at Lemnas, April 18, 1915. Was at the famous and terrible landing at Anzac Cove on Gallipoli, Turkey, April 25, 1915 (you will notice that all these dates are on Sunday).

"After the landing I was sent to Malta with a bullet through my leg, joined up the 5 French Chasseures and went back to Turkey with them. Stayed with them a short time; was returned to my own regiment. Organized Graham's detachment of scouts and intelligence bureau on Gallipoli; acted as chief scout and spy while there and got into a mix-up December 13, 1915, in which I got four bullets slipped into me; came very near doing the job for me. However, was sent to No. 5 General Hospital, Alexandria, Egypt, for treatment; remained there until February, 1916. The tribesmen broke out and I stole a uniform from one of the hospital men; put it on over my pajamas and walked 32 miles to join the advance column against the Nashuds and Bedonins; had a yard of gauze packed away in some holes in my body, but managed to get to the firing line. My colonel found me in the lines one morning and was for sending me back to the hospital, but I begged him to let me stay. He finally consented. I stayed and had rather a bad time, as my wounds got bad from the constant moving about and not being able to keep them clean. However, I kept going. Then we were ordered to France and on the boat the trip quite healed me up.

"We landed in France and then started straightaway. I used to get on a German uniform and go in Fritz' lines. Then I took charge of the raiders, as well as the scouts: managed to get two or three holes drilled in me, but came through, all right.

"Went to Russia on secret service work in 1918. It was a rough stunt. Was staff captain and adjutant for A2 Column with the Cossacks and Czeck-o-Slavs. Then went to spy work again. Got captured at Moscow and sentenced to be shot; killed the sentry and got away. Got a bayonet through my arm at Berenitskya and made my way to Archangel and got back to Lewrick, Shetland Islands, and then to Dundee and back to London to see baby, whom I had not yet seen. No one knew I was coming home. I walked in the door unannounced. My little wife nearly fainted.

"I am back in Aussy now safe and sound. I am a fatalist.

"Five times wounded.

"Once covered by a shell.

"Twice mentioned by the commanding general for merit.

"Three times mentioned in dispatches for gallantry (whatever that means).

"Granted the French Medal National and French Croix de Guerre by the French government for bravery.

"Granted the Distinguished Conduct Medal and the

Military Medal for bravery in the field by the King of England.

"And last, but not least, got a wife to boot and she is one of the best.

"The government owes me some money yet and I am going to stop here until I get it. When I get it I am coming to America to spend a while. But I like Australia. It is a fine country. It is always fine and lots of sunshine and flowers. Everything is much cheaper here than in America. We get better wages and only have to work five days in the week."

DR. THOMAS RIVERS

Dr. Thomas Rivers, father of our townsman, J. C. Rivers, practiced medicine in Jackson in 1832, ninety-one years ago. He removed to Suggsville in 1836, where he continued the practice of medicine and also engaged in farming. He died in 1890. He has two boys and six girls. His boys were Blount and Joseph, and his daughters were Sarah C., Ellen (who became Mrs. Rush of Marion), Pauline, Virginia, Emma Lena and May (now Mrs. Krouse).

CAPT. THOMAS I. KIMBELL

Capt. T. I. Kimbell was born in Jackson in the house now occupied by Horace Frisbie on May 10, 1829, and died January 19, 1914. Therefore, he would have been 85 years of age at his next birthday. He was a man of genial nature, true to his fellow-man, and always lent aid to any movement that tended toward the uplift of humanity. He was married, back in the fifties, to Miss Martha Boroughs, an estimable lady, who passed "over the river" some years ago. When the Civil War was declared between the states, Captain Kimbell, the patriot he was, at once fell into line. He joined the army in October, 1861, and served to the end. He was captain of Company E, Twenty-fourth Alabama Regiment, which regiment he on several occasions commanded. He was well liked by all his men. He was at one time captured by the enemy and afterwards paroled, but just when and where, the writer does not recall. After the war he resided at Pineville, Monroe County, this state, and engaged in farming. After the death of his father, Isham Kimbell, one of the few who escaped the massacre at Fort Sinquefield, he removed to Jackson about forty years ago and took charge of his father's farm, warehouse and so forth about the year 1885. He was for many years a member of the firm of Prim & Kimbell doing business at this place. He was a Mason and was buried in Pine Crest Cemetery at this place with Masonic honors. He left surviving him two sons and three daughters. His sons are Dr. Isham and Morris Kimbell of Pascagoula, Miss. His daughters are Mrs. Evie Boyles of Jackson, Ala.; Mrs. Albert Prim of Jackson, Ala., and Mrs. O. H. P. Wright of Selma, Ala.

DR. GROSS SCRUGGS CHAPMAN

Among the physicians of Clarke County who have served their communities for nearly half a century is Dr. G. S. Chapman. Though only a student in the medical college at the time the epidemic of local diseases in the summer of 1878, made his entrance into the practice of medicine in that year necessary. With the exception of a residence of two years in another county, there has been since that date an uninterrupted service in Clarke County.

Gross Scruggs Chapman was born July 2, 1856, near Grove Hill, Clarke County, Alabama. He is the oldest child of Jesse P. and Mary Frances (Fluker) Chapman, the grandson of Giles and Achsah (Pugh) Chapman, great-grandson of Elijah and Elizabeth (Martin) Chapman, great-great-grandson of Giles and Mary (Summer) Chapman, great-great-great-grandson of Giles and Sarah (Jackson) Chapman. The family is of English origin, with one line of Welsh descent. They came to Alabama from Newberry and Edgefield District, South Carolina.

The education of Dr. Chapman was had in the neighborhood schools, Grove Hill Academy, and Mobile Medical College. The earliest school was one built by his father on his plantation, for which teachers were employed by the whole community. Professor ("Bill") Nunnally was regarded as a superior teacher, and a promotion to his school was later made. The best school in the county was Grove Hill Academy. Here the youth was so instructed that he became fitted for teaching, and Mt. Nebo school was offered him and he accepted. At the Mobile Medical College a professional course was taken, ending with the conferring of the medical degree on March 26, 1879.

The practice of medicine was begun near Grove Hill, Dr. Chapman living at his father's home till January 1, 1881. On that date he opened an office in Grove Hill. In 1883 he moved to Evergreen, where he became a member of the firm of Drs. Jay & Chapman. In 1885, through an invitation from Capt. T. I. Kimball, he established himself at Jackson, where death had recently removed the physician. For two score years he has made this his home.

On coming to Jackson, Dr. Chapman secured the office formerly occupied by Dr. A. Denny, who came to Clarke County from Boston, and Dr. T. B. Savage, his immediate predecessor, whose death had occasioned the invitation to Jackson. In this office was and has remained among other things an office chair that is a full century of age. On it has been carved "A. Denny." A book of date 1778 was also inherited.

During these years the subject of this sketch has served several terms as health officer, both city and county. He has held a vital relation to the County Medical Society, of which he has been president, secretary, critic and long-time supporter. His relation to the Alabama Medical Society has been as active as time and opportunity would permit.

Dr. Chapman is a democrat, and a member of the Baptist Church. Following the tradition in his family he is a member of the Masonic order and of the Knights of Pythias. On coming to Jackson he found diversion in the Jackson Infant Order of Mystics, a social society of the town.

On November 26, 1879, Gross Scruggs Chapman and Eugenie Horton Woodard, daughter of Judge Richard J. and Elizabeth H. (Ball) Woodard, were united in marriage. Their children are (1) James Horton, (2) Leiland Woodard, (3) Jesse Pugh, (4) Helen Adelaide, (5) Frances Elizabeth, 6) Jeanette Ball, and (7) Eugenie Ayrault.

MISS ALICE CALLER

Miss Alice Caller, who was reared in Clarke County, was a grand-daughter of Col. James Caller (prominent in History of Alabama), and one of the pioneers of Clarke County. The following mention of her is found in "Who's Who in America:" "Mary Alice Caller was the teacher and author of 'Literary Guide for Home and School.'"

The author made the acquaintance of Miss Caller in the latter part of the seventies, having met her in Jackson. She was a teacher of note, and was with Dr. Massey at Tuskegee for several years. She has a brother and sister living in this county, John Caller and Miss Mariah Caller.

REV. T. H. BALL

Rev. T. H. Ball, author of "Ball's History of Clarke County and Surroundings," came to Clarke County in 1851 from Crown Point, Ind., to be the principal of a large boys' and girls' school at Grove Hill. He had graduated from Franklin College and came highly recommended, intellectually, morally and religiously, to mould character, and his work was proof of his capabilities. With him came his sister, Miss Elizabeth Ball, as assistant, with fine recommendations from New York city schools. These two teachers did a great work in Clarke County moulding and improving the young, many of whom made excellent citizens of Grove Hill, West Bend, Jackson and Coffeeville. He was president of the schools at West Bend and Rockcastle. Mr. Ball married a southern girl and moved to Boston, Mass., to teach. His sister married Judge R. J. Woodard of Grove Hill, Ala., in 1853, and lived a long useful life in this county. During the four years of war between the states she was a great help in writing addresses, making flags and sewing and knitting for the soldiers. Mr. Ball worked untiringly to get up the first history of Clarke, and he gathered much interesting material for the preservation of our splendid families and business occupations which now are valued by our citizens. He wrote the history in 1876. He also wrote a large history of his home county of Lake, Ind., it being the first and only history of that rich county adjacent to Chicago. He organized, built and managed the Crown Point Institute, where many boys and girls were educated. He organized boarding schools of high order; organized several literary societies in Lake County. His was a life devoted to mankind. He was devoted to Clarke County from his early coming to his last days on earth. Through love for his southern wife he was buried by her side in Clarke County. As a minister of the gospel here, as a teacher, as a citizen doing his duty as he conceived it, and as an historian to record the events of his day that the future citizens might gather inspiration from the lives of those who laid the foundation of our modern civilization, the purpose of his life is here expressed by his own quotation of words at the close of his history of Lake County:

> "I live for those who love me,
> For those who know me true,
> For the Heaven that soars above me,
> And awaits my spirit, too."

"For the wrong that needs resistance,
For the cause that lacks assistance,
For the future in the distance,
And the good that I can do."

At the last meeting of the Lake County Historical and Old Settlers, the unveiling of the "Ball Marker" attracted a large crowd from various places. A large granite boulder set in concrete, bearing the names of an old pioneer family and placed at their old dooryard. The tablet bears the following inscription:

1799—Judge Hervey Ball—1868
Early Probate Judge in
Lake County

His Wife
1804—Jane Ayrault Ball—1879
First School Teacher in
Lake County

Their Son
1826—Rev. T. H. Ball—1913
Lake County Historian

Through the influence of these people, the community remained one of the most prominent in religious, educational and literary achievements during pioneer days.

The dedication address was delivered by Prof. H. C. Belman of Hammond at Cedar Lake, Ind., at the Ball's old home, August, 1923.

DR. L. O. HICKS

Dr. L. O. Hicks was born in Lower Peach Tree in 1849 and died July 18, 1921. He located at Jackson in the early seventies and practiced his profession continuously until his death. He was married to Miss Mamie Chapman late in the seventies, to which union there were born eleven children, four of whom are still living. They are Attorney J. C. Hicks and Dr. Kimbell Hicks of New Orleans, Dewey Hicks of Washington, D. C., and Mrs. Richard C. Kirk of Mobile, Ala. His widow is still living and is with her daughter in Mobile. Dr. Hicks was a Mason and an elder in the Presbyterian Church. He was prominent in church circles and was devoted to the cause of education. As a physician, he enjoyed the confidence of the public and of his fellow-practitioners.

J. A. SAVAGE

John A. Savage was born at Claiborn, Ala., in 1855, a son of H. J. Savage and Anna Savage. He was educated in the schools of the neighborhood and graduated from the Eastman Business College. Mr. Savage moved to Jackson in 1894, where he was engaged in the sawmill business. Later he built a large brick store at Jackson, where he engaged in the mercantile business for several years.

Mr. Savage married Miss Minnie Locklin of Perdue Hill, who survives him. To them were born nine children, two of them who died in infancy. Seven children survive him. Andrew Savage, the eldest son, is the owner of the largest department store in Tuscaloosa. Charles Savage, who volunteered in the navy when the war began, has been promoted to captain surgeon and is stationed at Jersey City. Pomeroy is in the United States navy stationed at Washington. Lawrence is the youngest son and is with his mother in Jackson. His oldest daughter, Barbara, married Rev. Pearson Hassel, a Presbyterian minister. They went to Japan as missionaries and have been engaged there for the past sixteen years. Carrie married Rev. Fisher Bell, a Presbyterian minister, who has charge of a church in Charlotte, N. C. His youngest daughter, Mary, married Leroy Wilson of Mobile, Ala.

DEATHS IN THE WORLD WAR

Deaths from Clarke County, Alabama, in the European war as reported in the official United States Bulletin, January 1, 1918, to March 29, 1919. The records cover deaths from all causes and are presented exactly as they appeared in the Bulletin (compiled by Alabama State Department of Archives and History, Dr. Thomas M. Owen, Director, Montgomery, Ala.):

Clarke County, Alabama,

Joseph W. Coleman, Allen; James Gibby, Barlow Bend; Ozie B. Downey, Campbell; George H. Tyre, Carlton; Elmer Kidd, Chance; James W. Dease, Coffeeville; Henry Reed, Dickinson; John Moss, Glendon; Lonnie Bettis, Gosport; Claude Chapman, Grove Hill; Robert Coates, Grove Hill; John R. Lavender, Grove Hill; John W. Oliver, Jackson; Henry Skinner, Jackson; Hance F. Stokes, Jackson; Thomas G. Beck, Saltips; Willie J. May, Saltips; James S.

Overstreet, Saltipa; Willie C. Overstreet, Saltipa; William F. Atchison, Thomasville; John E. Autry, Thomasville; Gus Coates, Thomasville; Alver Friddle, Thomasville; Raybourn Dowey, Thomasville (died on ship en route home, buried in Thomasville); Frank B. Brower, Walker Springs; Leonard, Whatley; John Chapman, Grove Hill; Harrison Welch, Winn.

This list includes both white and colored.

JOURNEY OF LIFE

When we first started out on the journey of life, all is sunshine and happiness; our hearts are full of joy and gladness; the world to us is a veritable paradise; we love everybody and everything; we love the songs of the songbirds, the field and flowers, the green woods and babbling brooks, and all of Nature's beauties. Our hearts are unacquainted with sorrow and disappointment; life to us is "one sweet dream." But the average man soon realizes that "man born of woman is but of a few days and full of trouble." Stormy clouds soon begin to rise and cast their dark shadows across his pathway, his pathway soon begin to grow rough, his feet are bruised upon the jagged rocks, and when he reaches out to pluck a few of life's roses his fingers are pricked by cruel thorns. He meets with sorrow and disappointment; his friends and loved ones wander far away, some sicken and die; he meets with reverses, fortune sometimes takes wings and flies away; he finds that the pathway of life is "a rocky road to travel," but he journeys on and day by day sees the sources of his joys wither and decay and fall one by one like leaves from the stem of the withered rose. When he reaches the evening of life, when life's sun is low in the West, he finds no joy left for him in this world, save that that he finds in trying to smooth out the rough places found along the pathway of his loved ones and in building budges for those who are to follow him.

An old man traveling a lone highway,
Came at evening, cold and gray,
To a chasm deep and wide;
The old man crossed in the twilight dim,
The sullen stream held no fear for him,
But he turned when he reached the other side,
And builded a bridge to span the tide.

"Old man," cried a fellow pilgrim near,
"You are wasting your strength with your building here,
"You never again will pass this way,
"Your journey will end with the ending day,
"You have crossed the chasm deep and wide,
"Why build this bridge at eventide?"

But the builder raised his old gray head,
"Good friend, in the path I have come," he said,
"There followeth after me today,
"A youth whose feet must pass this way,
"This stream which hath meant naught to me,
"May to that fair-haired boy a pitfall be,
"He, too, must cross in the twilight dim,
"Good friend, I am building the bridge for him."

WHAT THE AUTHOR STANDS FOR

The author of this book stands for white supremacy, for United States Americanism; for a government of the people, by the people, for the people; for a government economically administered; for the principles of old-time democracy. He stands for law enforcement, for Christianity, morality, honest and up-right dealings among men. He stands for strict observance of the provisions of our constitution, both state and federal. He stands especially for a strict observance of the provisions of Article 6 of the Constitution of the United States, which reads as follows:

"In all criminal prosecutions, the accused shall enjoy the right to a speedy and public trial by an impartial jury of the state and district wherein the crime shall have been committed, which district shall have been previously ascertained by law, and to be informed of the nature and cause of the accusation; to be confronted with the witnesses against him; to have compulsory process for obtaining witnesses in his favor, and to have the assistance of counsel for his defense."

He stands for a free press, for free speech, for free public schools and for the separation of the church and state.

He is opposed to bolshevism, socialism, and every other "ism" which holds itself out as being superior to this government, and demands allegiance to its members first before allegiance to this government. He is opposed to the liquor traffic, to the descration of the Sabbath, and all kinds of rowdyism.

BATTLE OF THE HORSESHOE—WEATHERFORD SURRENDERS HIMSELF AT FORT JACKSON

Leaving a guard at Fort Williams, General Jackson put his army, which consisted of two thousand men, upon the march. He opened a passage across the ridge which divides the Coosa and Tallapoosa, and, in three days, advanced to the immediate neighborhood of the enemy.

Cholocco Litabixee—the Horse-Shoe—where the Red Sticks had assembled to make a desperate defense, was admirably adapted by nature for security if well guarded, but equally for destruction if not well defended. About one hundred acres of land was bordered by the Tallapoosa River, forming a peninsula. Across the neck of the bend, the Sticks had a breastwork of logs, so arranged as to expose assailants to a cross-fire. The houses of the village stood upon some low grounds at the bottom of the bend, where hundreds of canoes were tied to the banks of the river. The warriors of Hillabee, Ocfuske, Oakchoie, Eufaulahatche, New-Yauca, Hickory Ground and Fish Pond towns had concentrated upon the remarkable peninsula. General Coffee, with a large body of mounted men, and the friendly Indians, forded the Tallapoosa two miles below the breastwork, and, having gained the eastern side, extended his lines for a great distance, so as to encompass the bend. As soon as Jackson saw, from signals which were made, that Coffee had taken his position, he marched the remainder of his force towards the breastwork, planted two pieces of artillery, eighty yards distant from the nearest part of the Indian defense, and, at ten o'clock in the morning, began to open them upon the enemy. These pieces, accompanied by occasional discharges from the muskets and rifles, effected but little. In the meanwhile, the Cherokees, under Coffee, swimming the river, took possession of the canoes, and returning with them to the opposite bank, they were presently filled with friendly Indians and Americans, the latter headed by Colonel Morgan and Captain Russell. They reached the town and wrapped it in flames. Jackson then ordered his troops to storm the breastwork, behind which all the warriors had posted themselves. A short contest was maintained at the port-holes, but presently the impetuous Americans mounted the breastwork, and, dyeing the huge logs with their blood and that of the enemy, they finally, after a most desperate struggle, became masters of the interior. The Red Sticks, now assailed in front by Jackson, who had taken possession of their breastwork, and attacked them from behind by a portion of Coffee's troops, who had just completed the conflagration of their village, fought under great disadvantages. However, none of them begged for quarter, but every one sold his life at the dearest rate. After a long fight, many of them fled and attempted to swim the river, but were killed on all sides by the unerring rifles of the Tennesseans. Others screened themselves behind tree-tops and thick piles of timber. Being desirous not to destroy this brave race, Jackson sent a messenger towards them, who assured them of the clemency of the general, provided they would surrender. They answered by discharges from their guns and shouts of defiance. The artillery was then ineffectually brought to bear upon them. The Americans then applied fire to their retreat, which soon forced them to fly, and, as they ran, they were killed by American guns. It was late in the evening before the dreadful battle ended. The Red Sticks numbered about one thousand warriors, and, out of that number, five hundred and fifty-seven were found dead on the peninsula. As many were killed in the river, by Coffee's troops, while they were endeavoring to swim over, it may be safely stated that not more than two hundred survived. Some of them long afterwards suffered with the most grievous wounds. Manowa, one of the bravest chiefs that ever lived, was literally shot to pieces. He fought into the river, where the water was four feet deep. He held to a root, and thus kept himself beneath the waves, breathing through the long joint of a cane, one end of which he held in his mouth, and while the other end came above the surface of the water. When night set in the brave Manowa rose from his watery bed, and made his way to the forest, bleeding from many wounds. Many years after the war, we conversed with this Chief, and learned from him the particulars of his remarkable escape. His face, limbs and body, at the time we conversed with him, were marked with the scars of many horrible wounds. Another Chief was shot down, among a number of slain warriors, and, with admirable presence of mind, saved his life by drawing over him the bodies of two of them, under which he lay, till the darkness of the night permitted him to leave the horrible place.

The loss of the Americans was thirty-two killed and ninety-nine wounded. The friendly Cherokees had eighteen killed and thirty-six wounded. The tory Creeks had five killed and eleven wounded. Among the slain were

Major L. P. Montgomery and Lieutenants Moulton and Somerville, who fell in the charge upon the breastworks.

Major Lemuel Purnell Montgomery was born in Wythe County, Virginia, in 1786. He was a relation, by consanguinity, of the gallant general of that name, who fell at the storming of Quebec. His grandfather, Hugh Montgomery, of North Carolina, a man of fortune and talents, commanded a whig company during the revolution, which he equipped and supported at his own expense. With this company he fought the British and tories with great success. He was a member of the convention which formed the constitution of the state of North Carolina, and not long afterwards one of the counties of that state was named in honor of him. The father of Major Montgomery, also named Hugh, was a man of talents, and, having removed to Virginia, was a member of the senate of that state. At Snow Hill, in Maryland, he married a lady, whose maiden name was Purnell, which was the middle name of her son, the brave major who fell at the Horse-Shoe. The father removed from Virginia to East Tennessee, near Knoxville.

Major Montgomery completed his education at Washington College, Tennessee, studied law with Judge Trimble of Knoxville, and established himself in that profession at Nashville, where, in four years, his attainments, eloquence, zeal, fearless independence and popular bearing rendered him a formidable rival of the able Felix Grundy. During this period, he was frequently placed at the head of parties of armed horsemen; and with them he scoured the dark gorges of the Cumberland mountains in pursuit of desperate banditti, who had long pillaged the people in the valleys.

At length he was appointed by Madison first major of the thirty-ninth regiment, which he gallantly led to the breast-works of the Indians at the Horse-Shoe. He was the first man that mounted the breast-work, and, while waving his sword and animating his men, a large ball, shot from the rifle of a Red Stick, entered his head and instantly killed him. When the battle was ended, Jackson stood over his body and wept. He exclaimed, "I have lost the flower of my army!"

At the time of his death, Major Montgomery was only twenty-eight years of age. His eyes were keen and black; his hair was of a dark auburn color; his weight was one hundred and seventy-five pounds; his height was six feet and two inches; his form was admirably proportioned, and he was altogether the finest looking man in the army.

A diversity of opinion prevails among the soldiers of this campaign as to the disposition of the body of Major Montgomery. Some contend that Jackson caused it to be sunk in the Tallapoosa River to protect it from Indian brutalities. We have in our possession the affidavit of two soldiers now living in Tennessee—John Lovelady and Samuel Gearing—which states that they assisted to bury the body of Montgomery, and bore off the surplus dirt which remained about the grave upon the skin of a beeve and threw it into the river. They then burnt brush over the grave to conceal it from the keen eyes of the savages. Since then, and only a few years ago, the people of Tallapoosa County took up these remains, conveyed them to their court house and deposited them in the ground with military honors. The county of Montgomery, Alabama, was named in honor of Major Montgomery, while the memory of his relation, who fell at Quebec, is preserved in the name of the city.

The day after the terrible battle of the Horse-Shoe, General Jackson assumed the line of march and reached Fort Williams on the second of April, 1814.

Upon an examination of the Coosa river, it was found impracticable to transport the stores from Fort Williams to the termination of the falls, by water, and the reduced condition of the horses and the roughness of the country rendered it impossible to transport them by land in any quantity. However, with such provisions as the men could carry upon their backs, Jackson marched towards the Hickory Ground, relying upon the eastern army, whose advance guard was then under Milton, for supplies. Heavy rains retarded his march, but he reached Fooshatchie, where he captured a few prisoners. The Red Sticks fled from Hoithlewaule and other towns across the Tallapoosa.

Colonel Milton, with troops from the two Carolinas, had been a month at Fort Decatur, situated upon a commanding bluff, on the eastern side of the Tallapoosa, but took no steps to co-operate with Jackson in preventing the escape of the Indians.

Prevented from pursuing the enemy by a flood in the river and the scarcity of provisions, Jackson marched to the head of the peninsula formed by the confluence of the Coosa and Tallapoosa, and planted his colors upon the spot where Governor Bienville, one hundred years before, had erected Fort Toulouse, so long garrisoned by French troops. Here the rivers approach within six hundred yards of each other, and diverging unite four miles below.

The battle of the Horse-Shoe had nearly put an end to the war, and the dispirited Red Sticks made but few efforts to rally. Many came in and surrendered, while the larger portion escaped towards Florida. The old French trenches were cleaned out, and an American stockade with block-houses was erected upon the site, which received the name of Fort Jackson.

Deputations of Chiefs continually arrived, and submitted, in behalf of themselves and their people, to such terms as General Jackson thought proper to impose. Among the most conspicuous of these was William Weatherford, who led the Indians at Fort Mims, and at the battles of Calebee and Holy Ground. Jackson had directed that he should be captured, if possible, and brought to him, confined, to receive such punishment as his crimes merited. Weatherford, a man without fear, boldly resolved to appear at the American camp voluntarily. Mounting the same splendid gray steed which had borne him over the bluff at the Holy Ground, he rode within a few miles of Fort Jackson, when a fine deer crossed his path and stopped within shooting distance, which he fired at and killed. Reloading his rifle, with two balls, for the purpose of shooting the Big Warrior, should he give him any cause at the fort, he placed the deer behind his saddle and advanced to the American outposts. Some soldiers, of whom he politely inquired for Jackson's whereabouts, gave him some unsatisfactory and rude replies, when a gray-headed man a few steps beyond pointed him to the marquee. Weatherford rode up to it, and checked his horse immediately at the entrance, where sat the Big Warrior, who exulting exclaimed:

"Ah! Bill Weatherford, have we got you at last!"

The fearless Chieftain cast his keen eye at the Big Warrior, and said in a determined tone:

"You d—d traitor, if you give me any insolence, I will blow a ball through your cowardly heart."

General Jackson now came running out of the marquee, with Colonel Hawkins, and, in a furious manner, exclaimed:

"How dare you, sir, to ride up to my tent, after having murdered the women and children at Fort Mims?"

Weatherford said:

"General Jackson, I am not afraid of you. I fear no man, for I am a Creek warrior. I have nothing to request in behalf of myself; you can kill me, if you desire. But I come to beg you to send for the women and children of the war party, who are now starving in the woods. Their fields and cribs have been destroyed by your people, who have driven them to the woods without an ear of corn. I hope that you will send out parties, who will safely conduct them here, in order that they may be fed. I exerted myself in vain to prevent the massacre of the women and children at Fort Mims. I am now done fighting. The Red Sticks are nearly all killed. If I could fight you any longer, I would most heartily do so. Send for the women and children. They never did you any harm. But kill me, if the white people want it done."

At the conclusion of these words, many persons, who had surrounded the marquee, exclaimed, "Kill him! Kill him! Kill him!" General Jackson commanded silence, and, in an emphatic manner, said:

"Any man who would kill as brave a man as this would rob the dead!"

He then invited Weatherford to alight, drank a glass of brandy with him, and entered into a cheerful conversation, under his hospitable marquee. Weatherford gave him the deer, and they were then good friends. He took no further part in the war, except to influence his warriors to surrender. He went to the place of his former residence, upon Little River, but soon had to leave it, as his life was in constant danger.

He then went to Fort Claiborne, and the commanding officer of that place saved him from being killed, by placing him in a tent by himself, which was pitched very near the marquee, and which was constantly guarded by a file of soldiers. After he had been kept there ten or fifteen days, the commanding officer became still more uneasy, for fear he would be killed by persons who had lost relations at Fort Mims, and who were bent on his destruction. He now resolved to send him beyond the lines, during a dark night. About midnight he sent his aid, followed by Weatherford, to the station of Major Laval, who was then a captain, and the officer on guard. He said, "Captain Laval, the commanding officer says you must take Weatherford to yonder tree, under which you will find a horse tied, and that he must mount the horse and make his escape." Captain Laval instantly told Weatherford to follow him. He passed by the guard, giving the countersign, and reached the tree. Weatherford eagerly seized the limb to which the horse was tied, threw the reins over the animal's head, shook Laval by the hand, and said, in earnest and grateful tones, "Good-bye! God bless you!" He then vaulted into the saddle and rode off rapidly. That was the last time he ever saw Weatherford. For the distance of one mile, at least, Laval heard the clattering of the horse's feet.

After the war was over, Weatherford became a permanent citizen of the lower part of the county of Monroe, where, upon a good farm, well supplied with negroes, he lived, maintained an excellent character, and was much respected by the American citizens for his bravery, honor and strong native sense. In 1826 he died from the effects of fatigue, produced by a desperate bear hunt.

Many persons yet living bear testimony to the bravery and honor of William Weatherford in private life, an instance of which we here take occasion to mention:

In 1820 many people assembled at the sale of the effects of the deceased Duncan Henderson, in the lower part of Monroe County, Alabama. An old man, named Bradberry —the father of the gallant lieutenant, who fought at Burnt Corn, and who was afterwards killed in another action— was cruelly murdered upon this occasion by one C——r, who plunged a long knife into the back of his neck. The murdered had an accomplice, one F——r, who was in pursuit of Bradberry at the same time, and who had, a few moments before, broken a pitcher over his head. These men were so desperate, and flourished their knives with such defiance, that Justice Henderson in vain called upon the bystanders to seize them, while the poor, unoffending old Bradberry lay weltering in his blood.

Shocked at the cowardly and brutal act, and provoked at the timidity of the bystanders, William Weatherford, who lived in that neighborhood, now advanced towards Henderson, and said in a loud voice: "These, I suppose, are white men's laws. You stand aside and see a man, an old man, killed, and not one of you will avenge his blood. If he had one drop of Indian blood mixed with that which runs upon the ground there, I would instantly kill his murderers, at the risk of my life." Justice Henderson implored him to take them, and, being assured that the white man's law would not hurt him, but that he would be commended for the act, Weatherford now drew forth his long, silver-handled butcher-knife and advanced towards the murderers, who stood forty paces off, threatening to kill the first man who should attempt to arrest them. He first advanced to C——r, who, trembling at his approach, let his knife drop by his side, and instantly surrendered. Seizing him by the throat, he said the bystanders, "Here, tie the d—d rascal." Then, going up to F——r, upon whom he flashed his tiger eyes, he also arrested him without the least opposition, F——r exclaiming, "I will not resist you, Billy Weatherford."

General Pinckney arriving at Fort Jackson, and being the senior officer of the Southern army, assumed the command and approved of all the acts of Jackson. Learning that the Indians were generally submitting, he ordered the West Tennessee troops to march home. Two hours after the order was issued they were in motion. Arriving at Camp Blount, near Fayetteville, Jackson discharged them, after gratifying them with a feeling address. He then repaired to the Hermitage, from which he had been absent eighteen months, in a hostile land, and, a portion of the time, almost alone.

Pinckney remained at Fort Jackson with the troops from the two Carolinas and those from East Tennessee. Four hundred of General Dougherty's brigade of East Tennessee were stationed at Fort Williams. General Johnson, at the head of five hundred men, had been dispatched to the Cahawba river, who proceeded to its source and joined Jackson before he reached the Tennessee river. Several detachments were sent forth from Fort Jackson, who scoured the country in all directions for the fugitive Red Sticks. Colonel Hawkins performed several trips to the Chattahoochie, and exerted himself to induce the wretched Creeks to surrender and terminate a war which had proved so disastrous to them. But the British at Pensacola were endeavoring to rally them. Two vessels had anchored at the mouth of the Apalachicola, and had landed five thousand stand of arms and abundant ammunition, and three hundred British troops had commenced a fortification, under the command of a colonel. Runners were sent to all parts of the nation, inviting the Indians to rush to that point for provisions and military supplies, and thither many of the Red Sticks repaired. The condition of the friendly Indians, too, was at this time most wretched, and upwards of five thousand of them were fed at the different American posts.

HISTORY OF CLARKE COUNTY, ALABAMA

ABERCROMBIE,	236	. FORT MIMS 68	. CAMDEN 147,191
JOHN W.	235	ALABAMA TERRITORY, 111	. CAMP HILL 216
ACQUILIUS,	74	. 115,126	. CAMP LOMAX 312
ADAMS,	295	. ST. STEPHENS 115	. CAMPBELL 112,153,248
. A.S.	213	ALABAMA, 37,72	. 250,330
. BENJAMIN F.	185	. ALICEVILLE 61	. CAMPELLE 60
. CORALLY G.	-	. ALLEN 201,250,291-292	. CANE CREEK 248
. RICHARDSON	294	. 330	. CANTON 83
. D.	212	. ALMA 250	. CARLTON 250,330
. DAN	289	. ANDERSON 248	. CARNEY'S FORT 26
. EDWARD G.	182	. ATKINSON 250	. CARSON 267
. FRANK	190	. AUBURN 293	. CATHERINE 294
. GAYLE	294	. AUTAUGA CO. 80	. CHANCE 154,250,330
. JOHN	245	. BAKER'S BLUFF 62	. CHATOM 267
. JOHN CLAUSEL	294	. BALDWIN 36,48	. CHOCTAW BLUFF 201,250
. LUCY	300	. BALDWIN CO. 32,52,77	. CHOCTAW CO. 5,34,190
. NELLIE LOUISE	294	. 115,151,156-157,161	. 198,242,257,261,265
. ORLANDO CHAMBERS	294	. 308,310	. 266
. ROBERT GAYLE	294	. BARBER CO. 160	. CHOCTAW CORNER 60,88
. ROLAND E.	185	. BARLOW BEND 250,271	. 128,130,134-135,141
. S.A.	293	. 330	. 152,187,192,201,300
. WILLIAM EUGENE	294	. BASHI 60-61,129,146	. 301
. WIRT	151,162-163	. 158,248,251,300-301	. CHOCTOW CORNER 131
AGEE,ELMORE E.	181	. BASHI CREEK 61	. CITRONELLE 292
. J.M.	218,246	. BETHEL 150	. CLAIBORNE 113-114,134
. JOHN M.	197	. BIRMILE 188	. 329
. JOHN W.	181	. BIRMINGHAM 188,194,244	. CLARKE CO. 3,19,32,54
. NOAH	119	. 290,293,315	. 56,63,82,84,103,111
. NOAH A.	242	. BLADON SPRINGS 298	. 115,118-121,126,130
ALABAMA MEDICAL COLLEG-		. BLAKELY 152,154	. 135,144,153,157,160
GE, 273	273	. 162-163,315	. 193,198,212,242,244
ALABAMA RIVER,	5,10	. BRAZIER'S LANDING 64	. 246,256,261,284,288
. 34-35,47,49,53,55,61		. BRIDGEPORT 288	. 290-291,308-309
. 63-64,68,73,79-80,82		. BURNT CORN 26,32-33,37	. CLARKESVILLE 110,126
. 83,85-86,118-119,121		. 62-63,72,117,297,343	. 128,195,263-264
. 134,137,142,152,163		. BUTLER CO. 78,158	. CLARKSVILLE 123,131
. 194,296		. CALVERT 303	. 143

HISTORY OF CLARKE COUNTY, ALABAMA

ALABAMA,(cont)	FORT CHARLOTTE 36	GLOVER 251
CLIFTON 152	FORT CLAIBORNE 51	GOOD SPRING'S BEAT 26
COFFEEVILLE 88,112-113	76-77,81-83,194,342	GOOD SPRINGS 248
116,123,131,135,152	FORT DEPOSIT 78,81,312	GOSPORT 119,138,141
153,160,220,244,248	FORT EASLEY 36,62	147,220,248,250,265
250,294,303-304,326	FORT GAINES 151	266,303,330
330	FORT GLASS 26,33-34,57	GRAND BAY 152
COLUMBIANA 251	FORT JACKSON 334,340	GREENE CO. 31-32,82
CORINTH 152	344-345	227-228,279
COTTON GIN 19	FORT LAVIER 33,57	GREENSBORO 262,292
CROCTAW BLUFF 18	FORT MADISON 25-26,34	GREENVILLE 158-159
CUNNINGHAM 248,250	36,57-58,63,69-70,120	GROVE HILL 26,59,84
DALE CO. 153,156	123,297	112,117,126,128-129
159-160	FORT MIMS 26,34,36-38	131,134,138-139,141
DALEVILLE 72	41-42,46,48-52,55,64	142,144,147,149,152
DALLAS CO. 309	65,73,297,340-342	156,159-163,179,195
DEMOPOLIS 121,240,245	FORT MOBILE 36	199-200,202,220,240
279-280,293	FORT MONTGOMERY 56	244,246,248,251-252
DICKERSON 160,250	FORT MORGAN 174	253,259,261,279,282
DICKINSON 156,202,330	FORT PIERCE 36,39,42	283,287,295,297-298
DIXON'S MILLS 160	77	299,308,324,326-327
DUCATUR 146	FORT SINQUEFIELD 26,33	330-331
DUTCH BEND 80	55-58,284,297,323	GUIN 216
EASLEY'F FORT 26	FORT STODDART 44	GULLET'S BLUFF 26
EASLEY'S STATION 33	FORT STONEWALL 174	GULLETT'S BLUFF 33
ECONACHACA 78	FORT WHITE 26,33,129	HATCHECHUBBA 27
ELYTON 194	FORT WILLIAMS 334,339	HEALING SPRINGS 266
ENTERPRISE 293	345	HENRY CO. 163
EUFAULA 160,292	FRENCH'S LANDING 18,64	HICKORY HALL 113
EUREKA 188	FULTON 150-152,179,202	HIXON 262
EUTAW 245	250,261	HOLY GROUND 78,80-81
EVERGREEN 191,292-293	GAINESTOWN 119,131,138	HORSE SHOE BEND 298
FAILSTOWN 251	179,201,244,248,250	HORSE-SHOE BEND 116
FLORENCE 154	GAINESVILLE 161	HORSESHOE 334
FOLSOM CITY 188	GAINSTOWN 18	HUNTSVILLE 115-116,146
FORESTDALE 251	GENEVA 295	222
FORKLAND 292	GLEDEON 330	JACKSON 8,10-11,28,54

HISTORY OF CLARKE COUNTY, ALABAMA

ALABAMA,(cont)	. MAGNOLIA 294	. 273,280,292,298,312
. 58-59,69,88-91,99-100	. MAGOFFIN 123	. 330,338
. 101-102,107-108,112	. MANILA 250	. MONTGOMERY CO. 306,309
. 113,116,123,128,131	. MARENGO CO. 120-121	. MONTGOMERY HILL 310
. 141,151-152,157-158	. 153,158,160,260,275	. MORVIN 248,250
. 160-161,174-176,178	. 276,278-279,283-284	. MOTT'S FORT 26
. 179,194,203-204,206	. 288,290,301,309	. MOUNT VERNON 33,36
. 207,209,211-212,216	. MARIANNA 292	. 46-48,51,76-77,81
. 220,240,244-246,248	. MARION 145,147,162,266	. NANNAHUBBA ISLAND 76
. 250,253,255,259-260	. MARION CO. 216	. NETTLEBORO 160,250
. 261,263,265,269,271	. MAUBILA 18-20,23,25	. NEW PROSPECT 248
. 280,284,288,290-291	. MCGREW FORT 26	. OLD CLARKSVILLE 84
. 292,294,298,302-303	. MCKINLEY 190	. OLD ST. STEPHENS 26
. 305-307,309-310,313	. MCLEODS 248	. 211
. 314-318,322-323,326	. MCVAY 251	. OLD TOWN 82
. 329-330	. MOBILE 8,17,33,36	. OPELIKA 298
. JACKSON SPRING 193-194	. 50-51,54,59,69-70,74	. OPINE 60,251
. JASPER 245	. 75,77,86,89,114,118	. OVEN BLUFF 26,157
. JEFFERSON CO. 276	. 138-140,146-148,152	. 173-174
. JOHNSON'S ISLAND 310	. 153-154,157,161,163	. PARADISE 143
. LANDRUM'S FORT 26	. 174,178,187-188,217	. PEACOCK 251
. LAUDERDALE CO. 72,74	. 221,224-225,230,240	. PENSACOLA 292
. 115,229	. 244,251,256,263,266	. PERDUE HILL 203,265
. LAVIER'S FORT 26	. 271,273,281-282,288	. 329
. LIME HILLS 122,129	. 292-293,297-300,302	. PERRY CO. 131,266
. LIMESTONE CO. 115	. 309,313,315,329-330	. PINE APPLE 212
. LINDEN 279,283,301	. MOBILE CO. 115,211,224	. PINE BELT 130
. LIVINGSTON 227	. 237	. PINE HILL 157,293
. LOFTIN 123,129	. MOBILE POINT 36	. PINE LEVEL 58,88-89,91
. LOWER PEACH TREE 123	. MONROE CO. 5,119,121	. 93,99,103,112,125-126
. 146,156-157,162,281	. 194,203,259,262,265	. PINE LEVELS 62,76
. 300,329	. 266,281,299-300,308	. PINEVILLE 323
. LOWNDES CO. 79,305	. 323,343	. PLEASANT HILL 248
. MACON 126,129,131,138	. MONROEVILLE 262	. POINT CLEAR 151
. 195,252-253	. MONTEVALLO 216	. POINT JACKSON 84
. MACON CO. 80	. MONTGOMERY 146,153,158	. POLLARD 163
. MADISON CO. 115	. 162,223,261,263,271	. POWELL'S FORT 26

HISTORY OF CLARKE COUNTY, ALABAMA

ALABAMA,(cont)   244,248-250,268-269   248,250,265,331
. PRAIRIE BLUFF   83 .   271,280,297,301,304 . WARSAW   315-316
. PRITCHARD   244 .   322 . WASHINGTON   29,135
. REMBERT HILL   292 . SUMMERFIELD   292 . WASHINGTON CO   242
. REPUBLICVILLE   89 . SYMER   251 . WASHINGTON CO.   5,34
. RIVER HILL   248 . TALLADEGA   287 .   110-111,113,115,118
. RIVER RIDGE   262 . TALLADEGA CO.   230 .   221,266-267,284,291
. ROCK CASTLE   271,273 . TALLAHATTA   61 . WEST BEND   112,179,326
.   326 . TALLAHATTA SPRINGS 156 . WHATLEY   154,157,202
. ROCKVILLE   200,244,250 .   204,248,250,295   248,250,284,297,331
. RURAL   250 . TALLAPOOSA CO.   338 . WILCOX CO. 130,152-153
. SALITPA   159,203,244 . TENSAS   310 .   157,159-160,261,278
.   248,250 . TENSAW   38 .   284,288
. SALTIPA   330-331 . THOMASVILLE 10,60,151 . WINN   251,331
. SALTWORKS   248 .   153,159,179,187-188 . WOOD'S BLUFF   60
. SCYRENE   155,250 .   189,191,193-194,201 .   128-129,146
. SELMA   59,117,147,178 .   220,246,248-252,259 . WOODS BLUFF   250
.   187,245,253,271,292 .   260-261,275-276,278 . YELLOW BLUFF   162
.   293,305-307,323 .   295,300-301,331 ALAMABA,
. SHEFFIELD   244 . TOLBERT SPRING   254   UNIVERSITY OF 147
. SHILOH   260 . TOMBIGBEE   -   ALDRIDGE,J.F. 245
. SKIPPERVILLE   156 .   SETTLEMENT   58   ALFORD,JULE   191
. SMITHSVILLE   138 . TROY   305   WALTER   191
. SMITHVILLE 129,131,141 . TURNBULL   281   ALLEN,   201
. SODA SPRINGS   138 . TURNER'S FORT   26 . CHESTER L.   182
. SOLDIER'S RETREAT   48 . TUSCALOOSA 162,191,240 . CY   247
. SPRINGHILL   158 .   280,329 . GEORGE   218,246
. ST. STEPHEN   29,266 . TUSKALOOSA   146 . JAMES   186
. ST. STEPHENS 34,53,62 . TUSKEGEE   316,326 . M.V.B.   149
.   89,110-114,118,211 . UNION   161 . MERRIDA   186
.   221,267,309 . UNION SPRINGS   292 . R.G.   218
. STEVENSON   288 . UNION TOWN   131   ALSTON,L.J.   126
. SUGGSVILLE 25-26,82,84 . UNIVERSITY OF   161,227   LEMUEL J.   128
.   88,112-114,116,119 .   259,262,266,274,276 AMERSON,WALTER J.   182
.   120,123,131-134,136 .   279,295,299-301,306 ANDERSON,   123
.   137,140-142,144,146 . VASHTI   308 . BEN   154
.   147,149,155,178,201 . WALKER SPRINGS 202-203 . BETTIS   182

HISTORY OF CLARKE COUNTY, ALABAMA

ANDERSON,(cont)		. JULIA GAINES	284	. F.W.	148,178,241
. D.C.	151	. MARTHA	284-285	. FRANK	247
. ELIZABETH	280	. MARTHA JANE	285	. JACK	248
. ELIZABETH MCALPIN	279	. OWEN B.	184	. SOL	248
. J.S.	147	. REBECCA KIMBELL	284	BALDWIN,BENJAMIN	80
. JESSE T.	185	. ROBERT	285	BALL,	3,25,58,84,86,89
. JOHN B.	138	. ROBERT STARKEY	285	.	110-111,119,130,144
. JOHN C.	219	. WASHINGTON	285	.	145,200,204,241-242
. JOHN CRAWFORD	279	. WESTWOOD	284-285	.	327
. JULIA	280	. WILLIAM	284-286	. E.H.	144
. MARY BIRD MARTIN	280	. WILLIAM WESTWOOD	285	. ELIZABETH	326
. T.J.	149,160	ASHLEY,JAMES K.	182	. ELIZABETH H.	325
. THOMAS M.	180	ATCHISON,	203	. HERVEY	328
. WILLIAM	128	. SAM	247	. JANE AYRAULT	328
. WYATT F.	185	. WILLIAM F.	331	. T.H.	144,326,328
ANDREWS,JAMERSON	126	AUBURN UNIVERSITY,	261	BALLARD,	31
. S.H.	217,246		262,294	BAREFIELD,HARRIS	245
. WALTER W.	185	AUSTILL,	65-69,73	BARGE,H.P.	218
APALACHE RIVER,	71	. EVAN	70,82	BARLOW,BRONSON	119
APALACHICOLA RIVER,	345	. JERE	65,70	BARNARD,	
ARKANSAS,ELKHORN	152	. JEREMIAH	64,69-70	FREDERICK A.P.	227
ARMISTEAD,ANN CARNEY	285	AUSTRALIA,	319-320,322	BARNBY,T.	98
. ANN HEARIN	285	SIDNEY	318-319	BARNES,	119
. BRYAN	285	AUTREY,JAMES A.	185	. ALFRED	247
. CHARLES	285	AUTRY,	71	. ANNIE MAE	271
. ELIZABETH	284	JOHN E.	331	. B.S.	117,244,271
. ELIZABETH BOROUGHS	284	AUTTOSE,	37	. BENJAMIN S.	269,280
	285	BAGBY,	131	. BENJAMIN SHIELDS	268
. ELIZABETH LEE	285	BAGLEY,WILEY D.	183	. C.E.	271
. ELLIS N.	184	. WILLIAM A.	181	. FREDONIA A.	-
. EMMA	285	. WILLIAM W.	181	. LANKFORD	304
. J.R.	211,244	BAILEY,	30,32,36,43,56	. J.E.	271
. J.W.	241,244	. DANIEL	42	. JOHN B.	181
. JAMES	246	. DIXON	28,41,44,64	. MILTON	247
. JAMES W.	285	. JAMES	42	. R.E.	271
. JANE WESTMORELAND	285	. TOM	44	. S.B.	247
. JOHN KIMBELL	284-285	BAKER,		176 . S.T.	271

HISTORY OF CLARKE COUNTY, ALABAMA

BARNES,(cont)
. SAMUEL T.   268
. W.M.   271
. WILLIAM K.   304
BARRINGTON,JOHN   266
BARTON ACADEMY,   224
BASHI CREEK, 113,122,124
            138,297
BASHI SKIRMISH, 26,60-61
            63
BASS,OCIE   186
  WILLIAM   106
BASSETT CREEK, 8,10,58
BASSETT'S CREEK,   84
    112-113,137,151
BATCHELOR,   36
BATES,   76
  JOSEPH   119
BATTLE OF ANTIETAM, 287
BATTLE OF APPOMATTOX,
            164
BATTLE OF ATHENS,   158
BATTLE OF ATLANTA,   150
            154,158
BATTLE OF BEAR CREEK,
            151
BATTLE OF BLAKELY,   151
BATTLE OF BROWNSVILLE,-
    ,   151   151
BATTLE OF BULL RUN,   164
            287
BATTLE OF BURNT CORN, 26
            27,31
BATTLE OF CALEBEE,   340
BATTLE OF CEDAR MOUNTA-
    AIN,   287   287

BATTLE OF CHANCELLORSV-
    VILLE,   287   287
BATTLE OF CHATTANOOGA,-
    ,   153 153,158
BATTLE OF CHICAMAUGA,
    . 150-156,158,160,163
    .   289,302
BATTLE OF DALTON,   150
        155,158
BATTLE OF DECATUR,   151
BATTLE OF FORT MIMS,   26
BATTLE OF FORT MORGAN,-
    ,   161   161
BATTLE OF FORT SINQUEFI-
    IELD,   26   26
BATTLE OF FRANKLIN,   150
    151,155,158,160,306
BATTLE OF FREDERICKSBU-
    URG,   287   287
BATTLE OF GETTYSBURG,
            159,287
BATTLE OF HOLLY SPRING-
    GS,   153   153
BATTLE OF HOLY GROUND,-
    ,   340   340
BATTLE OF HORSE-SHOE BE-
    END,   88   88
BATTLE OF HORSESHOE BE-
    . END,   334   334
            337-340
BATTLE OF HUNTSVILLE,
            158
BATTLE OF JONESBORO, 150
    155,158,160
BATTLE OF LITTLE SYPSY-
    Y RIVER,   151   151
BATTLE OF LOOKOUT MOUN-

. NTAIN,   150 150,153
            155,158
BATTLE OF LUVERNE,   158
BATTLE OF MISSIONARY R-
. RIDGE,   150   150
. 153-155,158,160,163
.   289,310-311,313
BATTLE OF MURFREESBORO-
    O,   158   158
BATTLE OF NASHVILLE, 150
            155,158
BATTLE OF NEW HOPE CHU-
. URCH,   150 150,155
.   158-160,163
BATTLE OF NEW ORLEANS,-
    ,   194   194
BATTLE OF OKOLONA,   158
BATTLE OF PEACH TREE C-
    CREEK,   150   150
BATTLE OF PORT GIBSON,-
    ,   151 151,153
BATTLE OF RESACA,   150
    155,158,160,163
BATTLE OF ROCK FACE MO-
    OUNTAIN,   153 153-154
BATTLE OF ROCKY FACE M-
    MOUNTAIN, 160   160
BATTLE OF SAN JACINTO,-
    ,   135   135
BATTLE OF SHILOH,   152
            161,302
BATTLE OF SPANISH FORT-
. T,   151   151
.   158-161
BATTLE OF SPOTTSYLVANI-
    IA,   287   287
BATTLE OF STONE MOUNTA-

HISTORY OF CLARKE COUNTY, ALABAMA

BATTLE OF STO(cont) AIN, 158	CARMICHAEL 296 . SUSIE BLACKWELL 295	BIDDELL,BENJAMIN I. 98 BIDDILL,BENJAMIN J. 110	
BATTLE OF TENSAW RIVER- R LANDING, 159	. T.J. 242,245,261 159 . TRAVIS JESSE 295	BIDDLIX, 126 BIDGOOD, 104-106	
BATTLE OF TUSCUMBIA, 158	. TRAVIS LINYER 295	BIENVILLE, 339	
BATTLE OF WILDERNESS, 287	BEDWELL,J.D. 150 . J.W. 212	BIGBEE RIVER, 60 BIGGERS,W.R. 217	
BATTLE OF YAZOO CITY, 151	. JAMES W. 314 . JOHN D. 153	BISHOP,ARTHUR 182 EDDIE 182	
BAUGH,JOHN T. 183	. LULA WING 314	BLACK WARRIOR RIVER, 86	
BAUGHN,HUBERT 293	BELGIUM, 293	BLACK,ARTHUR 185	
BAYARD, 111	BELL,ADLIE 180	BLACKFORD, 157	
. P.F. 99-100	. CARRIE SAVAGE 330	BLACKMAN,HENRY 182	
. PERCY T. 98	. FISHER 330	BLACKWELL, 201	
. PEREGRINE F. 104	. HENRY 148	SUSIE 295	
. PERIGRINE F. 103	. JOSEPH E. 183	BLOUNT, 77	
. PERREGRIN F. 91	. T. 148	FREDERICK S. 147	
BEALE,WALTER 98	BELMAN,H.C. 328	BLUE, 51	
BEALL,WALTER 106	BENNETT, 191	BODGOOD,W. 98	
BEAR CREEK, 158	BENSON,BILLY 247	BOLEN, 178,310	
BEASLEY, 37-40,52	. COLUMBUS E. 185	. ARCHIE 290	
DANIEL 36	. FRED W. 181	. E.J. 290	
BEAVER CREEK, 138	BERRY, 203	. H.H. 290	
BECK, 160	BESTOR,DANIEL P. 228	. HORACE 290	
. CLARENCE 181,185	BETTIS,W.W. 192	. J.A. 290	
. FRANK 160	Z.L. 127,243	. JOHN A. 150,288	
. THOMAS G. 330	BETTS,LONNIE 330	. JOHN C. 182	
BECKHAM,SENAH 186	W.F. 293	. JOHN R. 182	
BEDELL,B.J. 100	BEVERLY,	. MARY J. THOMPSON 289	
. BENJAMIN I. 91,99	CHRISTOPHER C. 185	. 290	
. BENJAMIN J. 103-104	BEVILL,W.G. 217	. SID 290	
.	106 BEVILLE MERCANTILE COM-	. TOM 247,288,290	
BEDSOLE,EDWARD 295	MPANY, 176	. WILLIE G. 183	
. J.G. 211	BIBB, 115	BOROUGHS,	
. JAMES G. 185	BICKELL,E.J. 251	. ANN ELIZABETH 286	
. MARTHA GOODMAN 295	. FLOSSIE 251	. BESSIE 309	
. MARY ELLIS -	. W.E. 251	. BRYAN 211,244,307,309	

BOROUGHS,(cont)		. EVIE KIMBELL	260,323 . J.W.	149,152
. BRYAN MORRIS	309	. JANIE MAY CLARKE	300 . JOHN B.	181
. CALEB	186	. JESSE	300 BREWSTER,	130
. EDWIN ARMISTEAD	309	. JESSE V.	300 BRICE,	188
. ELIZABETH	284-285	. KIMBELL	260 BRIGHT,HENRY	111
. FRED	184	. LUCY ADAMS	300 BRITTINGHAM,S.S.	141
. FREDERICK	309	. N.B.	192,300 BRODNAX,ROBERT	242
. IMOGENE	308-309	. THOMAS	260 BROOKS,AMOS	181
. JAMES DICKINSON	308	. THOMAS K.	182 . HOWELL	181
	309	BRADBERRY,	31,343 . JAMES J.	181
. LILLIAN	309	. JAMES	125 . JOHN	148
. MARTHA	323	. WILLIAM	29,62 BROUGHTON,ANNIE C.	213
. MARTHA J.	284	BRADFORD'S POND,	83 .	215
. MARY ELIZ.	-	BRADFORD,BRASELL	182 . ANNIE CELESTE	216
. DICKINSON	308	. M.D.	149 . J.C.	216
. MAZIE SMITH	286	. THOMAS F.	185 BROWER,FRANK B.	331
. REBECCA K. MORRISS	285	BRADLEY,CHARLES	247 BROWN,ALONZO	186
. REBECCA KIMBELL	-	. FRANK	247 . T.	138,141
. MORRISS	286	. HENRY F.	184 . TOM	131
. REBECCA M. MORRIS	309	. JOHN	247 BRUMBY,THOMAS	105
. THOMAS	284-286,309	. ROBERT	148,247 BRUMLEY,THOMAS	106-107
BORROUGHS,ALFONSO	186	. ROBERT S.	185 BRUNSON,FATE J.	183
CARRIE L.	186	BRADY,	65 JAMES H.	182
BOSWELL,WILLIAM C.	182	WILLIAM C.	185 BRYANT,A.S.	247
BOTTOMS,JAMES	145	BRAGG,	161 . DURR	247
BOWLING,SALLIE	267	BRAXTON	155 . JACOB	147
BOWYER,	77	BRAND,J.W.	192 . JIM	248
BOX-MAKER CREEK,	118	BRANDENBURG,	156 BUCHANAN,GEORGE	107
BOYKIN,B.O.	265	. HENRY L.	183 BUCHANAND,GEORGE	98
. J.F.	174,242	. M.E.	149 BUCK,ROBERT J.	187
. SOLOMON	128	. MARTIN E.	155 BUCKNER,	156
BOYLES,ALICE	260	BRANSON,N.	104 BUFORD'S ISLAND,	46
. ALICE GRACE	317	BRASSELL,FLETCHER F.	184 BUFORD,	47
. BRUCE	260	BRATTON,TOM	246 JOHN	46
. C.W.	59,212,217,248	BRECKENRIDGE,	289 BULLOCK,STEVE E.	181
	259,317	BREWER,	128,153,241 BUMPERS,BEN	156
. DOUGLAS	260	. J.R.	220 . EMMA LEE	292

BUMPERS,(cont)		. CHRISTIAN	306	. M.	122
. HOWARD L.	184	. CHRISTINE	291	. W.G.	159
. JOHN	247	. CORY L.	185	CANADA,QUEBEC	337,339
. LANE	156	. DUNCAN	306	CANNADY,W.B.	217
. MIMA	292	. E.O.	241	W.P.	212
. R.S.	292	. ELLIS B.	185	CANNON,JOEL E.	98-99,106
. RALEIGH J.	183	. HERBERT A.	180	CANOE FIGHT,	26
BUNN,OTIS	187	. HUGH	213	CARL,MAYNARD	185
BURGE,C.W.	149	. JAMES D.	182	CARLETON,GEORGE A.	279
. CHARLES W.	151	. JOHN	246,264	MORGAN	241
. H.W.	218	. L.C.	212	CARLTON,GEORGE A.	252
. N.P.	197	. LAFE C.	185	CARMICHAEL,	
. WILLIAM B.	183	. MALCOLM	213	. JOHN DUNCAN	296
BURNT CORN CREEK,	29	. NEAL	246	. LEONA ELLIS	296
BURNT CORN SPRING,	48	. O.V.	213	. MARY ELLIS	296
BUROUGHS,W.M.	280	. RAYMOND	186	CARNEY,ANN	285
BURR,AARON	32	. W.A.	212,254	. JOHN	59
BURROUGHS,	162	. W.O.	213	. JOSIAH	58,106-108
. BRYAN	161	. WALLACE E.	184	. JOSUAH	98
. BRYANT	150	CALIFORNIA,	6	. MARTHA T.	58-59
BURSEY,CHARLES	160	CALLAR,	297	. R.P.	241
BUSBEE,LIZZIE W.	260	CALLEAR,L.A.	312	. SARAH	59
BUSH,	246	CALLER,	30,32	CARSON,	26,34,36,56,58
. CHARLES	215	. ALICE	326	.	63,70,78,81
. PRESTON R.	220	. JAMES	28,110,326	. JOSEPH	110
. T.G.	188	. JOHN	125,326	CARTER,	266
BUTLER,EDMUND	128	. MARIAH	326	. C.H.	212
BYRNE,	77	. MARY ALICE	326	. DAVE	218
CAESAR,	65,67-69	. ROBERT	29,98,110,113	. ROBERT	193
CAHALL,BARNEY	106	CALLIER,ROBERT	103	. THOMAS H.	287
CAHAWBA RIVER,	82-83,115	ROBERT L.	186	CARTWRIGHT,DAVID	29
	345	CALVERT,W.H.	141	CASSELS,	78-79,81
CALHOUN,	143,200	CALVIN,	170	CASSITY,SATIRA	292
. ANDREW	264	CAMP,GARFIELD	311	CEDAR CREEK,	112,119,140
. BILLY	156	CAMPBELL,ARCHIBALD	122		142
. C.E.	212	. DANIEL	98,104,106	CHAMBERS,	129
. CHARLES W.	184	. E.K.	252	. J.B.	112

HISTORY OF CLARKE COUNTY, ALABAMA

CHAMBERS,(cont)		. JESSE	218,244	CHRISTMAS,FELIX G.	147
. JOSEPH	119	. JESSE P.	324	NATHAN	126
. JOSEPH B.	126,242	. JESSE PUGH	325	CHUNN,A.E.	212
. MARY LOUISE	294	. JOHN	331	ZELL	217
. NELLIE L. ADAMS	294	. JOHN C.	59,176,241,247	CLAIBORNE,	27,32-37-38
. WILLIAM	294	. KOSSIE WILSON	282	.	44,48-49,51-52,61-62
CHAMBLISS,	47	. LEILAND	244	.	69,76-82,108,297
W.R.	46	. LEILAND WOODARD	325	. F.L.	34
CHAMPION,H.J.	317	. LEONARD	248	. FERDINAND LEIGH	32
. ROBERT L.	181	. MAMIE	329	. JOHN H.F.	72
. RUBY	317	. MARY FRANCES	-	CLANTON,JAMES H.	159
CHANCEY,CONDIE	180	. FLUKER	324	CLARK,AMANDA WALES	316
CHAPMAN,	129,143,176,200	. MARY SUMMER	324	T.C.	316
. ACHSAH PUGH	324	. MITFORD	187	CLARKE,JANIE MAY	300
. AMELIA	299	. RAYMOND	185	. PAUL	191
. ARTHUR L.	186	. S.P.	246	. W.E.	219
. CALEB	185	. SARAH JACKSON	324	CLAXTON.	162
. CECIL S.	181	. SOL	186	CLAY,	232
. CLAUDE	330	. STEPHEN P.	156	W.W.	185
. COSSIE	186	. STEVE	246	CLAYTON,	289
. E.M.	150,163,240	. SULLIVAN	186	CLEILAND.	203
. ELIJAH	186,264,324	. VAUGHAN	245	CLEMENTS,A.W.	189
. ELIZABETH MARTIN	324	CHARAMILLA,	20	BENJAMIN	105
. EUGENIE AYRAULT	325	CHARLESTON COLLEGE OF	-	CLEMINTS,BENJAMIN	98
. EUGENIE H. WOODARD	325	MEDICINE.	280	280 CLEVELAND,	273
. FRANCES ELIZABETH	325	CHATTAHOOCHEE RIVER,	154	. BESSIE	117
. G.S.	211,244	CHATTAHOOCHIE RIVER,	71	. GROVER	188
. GILES	324		345	. JERE	117
. GROSS SCRUGGS	323-325	CHEROKEE NATION,	70	. JOSEPH S.	184
. HELEN ADELAIDE	325	CHERRY,W.H.	247	. S.B.	149,247
. J.C.	178	CHILES,WALTER	105-106	. STEPHEN B.	241-242
. J.M.	59,134,269,271	CHINN,A.E.	217	. STEVE B.	256
. JAMES	186	CHIPPENDALE.	268	. WILLIE	186
. JAMES HORTON	325	CHOCTAW INN,	17	CLINCH RIVER,	71
. JAMES MONROE	178	CHOLOCCO LITEBIXEE,	51	CLOTHIER,GEORGE	117
. JAMIE	213	CHOTARD,H.	81	COALE,SKIP	176
. JEANETTE BALL	325	CHREITON,HIRAM	213	SKIPWORTH	217

COATE,	142	. W.W.	150	CREAGH, 65-66,119
. ANN ELIZ. BOROUGHS	286	. WILLIAM	128	. G.W. 34,82,117,133-134
. C.A.	218	COLLEY,E.L.	253	. 141,242
. CHARLIE	185	COLLIER,FRANCIS	106	. GERARD W. 150
. H.M.	243	COLLINS,	190	. GERARD WALTHALL 117
. H.W.	127	JOHN	247	. GIRARD W. 29,31-32,63
. HENLEY WASHINGTON	286	COLUMBIA COLLEGE,	227	. 69,78,83,241
. JAMES BUCHANAN	286	COLVEN,C.H.	159	. JOHN G. 98,105,127,135
. MARTHA ELIZ.	286	COMER,B.B. 248,293		. 241,243
. MAZIE REBECCA	286	CONNOR,EPHRAIM	294	. THOMAS B. 110
. RICHARD SMITH	286	COOLOOME,	37	CRENSHAW, 123
. WILLIAM 110,112,128		COOPER,EVA P. GRAHAM	317	CROCKESS,J. 104
COATES,C.A.	218	. EVA PEARL GRAHAM	316	CROWN POINT INSTITUTE,-
. GUS	331	. GRAHAM	317	, 327 327
. LESTER L.	181	. JOHNNY W.	215	CRUELL'S FERRY, 69
. ROBERT	330	. LAURA TERESA	317	CRUMPTON,W.B. 190
COATS,BUSTER	182	. SAMUEL A.	316-317	CUBA, 19,293
NETTLES D.	181	COOSA RIVER, 38,50,162		HAVANA 37
COBB,EARL F.	183		334,339	CULLUM, 74
. ENOCH	218,246	CORQUODALE,CHALRES	248	CUNINGHAME,J.W. 218
. J.M.	244	ERNEST	248	JAMES G. 191
. MAL	218,246	COWAN,DAVE	246	CUNNINGHAM,GEORGE W. 183
. S.R.	218	. GRADY	212	. J.D. 248
COCAS ISLAND,	320	. J.R. 241-242,246		. J.G. 244
COCHRAN,WILLIAM 106,126		. MINNIE COLE	302	. J.W. 219
COCKE,MARY BINTON	266	. SAMUEL A.	213	. JOHN D. 314
COCKS,JACK FREMING	266	. T.J.	246,302	. LULA WING 314
COFFEE, 113,116,334-336		COWETA,	37	CUNNINGHAME,
COGBURN, 117,141		COX,	143	EMMA ARMISTEAD 285
COLE,M.E.	303	. C.E.	218	CURNELLS. 27
MINNIE	302	. JOE	246	VICEY 48
COLEMAN,	203	. MATTHEW	213,246	CURRIE,MARTHA 296
. ARCHIE	212	COXE,JOHN	48	CURRY, 231
. DAN L.	180	COXWELL,FRANKLIN H.	184	. DAN 218
. EUGENE	212	JOHN T.	184	. JABEZ LAMAR MONROE 230
. GARY M.	180	CRAIG,JOHN	185	CURTIS,JIM 211
. JOSEPH W.	330	CRAWFORD,	36-37	DADE,

HISTORY OF CLARKE COUNTY, ALABAMA

DADE,(cont)		. HARWELL	245	MANCY	186
BENJAMIN FRANKLIN	161	. HARWELL GOODWIN	276	DENT,	34
DAFFIN,D.	144	. HENRY G.	202,244,247	DESHA,	193
. DERUSHA	151,252-253			DESOTO,	18,20-25,118
. JACK	247	. J.W.	197	FERNANDO	19
. JEFF	249	. KATE SMITH	285	DEWES,	
. ROGER	186	. LOUISA	301	LAURA S. WALKER	145
. W.W.	195,218,253	. MOLLIE GOODWIN	276	DEWITT,	123
DAHLBERG,	250	. ORMAND L.	184	. HARRIET	151
F.W.	178,249	. THOMAS W.	245,276	. R.J.W.	150,157
DAHLBERT,	176	. W.M.	150,160	DICKERSON,	149
F.W.	176	. WILLIAM C.	181	. CHARLIE J.	186
DALE FERRY,	113	DAWSON,	116,203	. COLONEL	186
DALE,	30,64-66,68-69	HENRY	247	. PRESIDENT	186
	73-76,78	DAY,BRYANT	185	. R.L.	218
. SAM	34	. CHARLES	247	DICKINSON,	129,287
. SAMUEL	29,63,67,70-72	. SOLON	184	. ANTHONY	212
	75,82,84	. WILLIAM T.	183	. J.S.	245,247
DALTON,DAVE	218	DEAL,A.J.	216	. JAMES S.	242,308
DANCING RABBIT,	74	. HELEN	213	. MARY ELIZ.	308
DANIELS,	143	. HELEN MARGARET	216	. RICHARD	241
DANZEY,FREDERICK L.	182	DEAN,JOHN	110,125-126	. RICHARD Q.	135
DARIEN,	19	DEAS,ALBERT S.	180	DINSMORE,SILAS	111
DARRINGTON,	140	. IVY C.	184	DISMUKES,D.B.	212
JOHN	142	. J.S.	248	DIXON'S MILLS,	60
DAUGHTRY,JESSE H.	183	. MATTIE	117	DOLBEAR,	176
DAVIDSON,J.S.	251-252	DEASE,JAMES W.	330	. DRAKE	176
DAVILLA,PEDRAIAS	19	DEGALLEGOS,BALTASAR	21	. ROBERT	247
DAVIS,	161,248,282	.	22	DORMAN,DURRY LEE	180
. ALLEN	186	. FRAY JUAN	22	DORTCH,JAMES C.	184
. ARTHUR S.	184	DELLET,JOHN	265	JOHN C.	181
. CLAY A.	183	DELOACH,BERNARD C.	181	DOSSEY,A.B.C.	141
. CLUB-AX	305	DENKINS,	82-83	DOTY,	176
. EDWARD J.	184	J.E.	81	E.J.	176,247
. EDWIN B.	183,185	DENNY,	176,178	DOUBLE SWAMP,	78
. H.C.	150,162	A.	141,325	DOUGHERTY,	345
. H.G.	273	DENSON,EUGENE	186	DOWE,LORENZO	209,211,258

HISTORY OF CLARKE COUNTY, ALABAMA

DOWEY,RAYBOURN	331	DUMAS,FRED	181	. MARTHA CURRIE	296
DOWLING,		RAYMOND	184	ELMORE,BENJAMIN F.	219
KATHLEEN PUGH	299	DUNCAN,BENJAMIN	119		245
DOWNEY,OCIE L.	181	THOMAS D.	172-173	EMMONS,	119
. OZIE B.	330	DUNGAN,ERBY A.	184	JONATHAN	112
. ROBERT L.	180	. GRADY B.	184	EMORY UNIVERSITY,	292
DOWNING,	265	. TRAVIS R.	184	ENGLAND,	265,293,319,322
DOYLE,	193,203	DUNN,	36	. LONDON	318,321
. J.B.	218	. HENRY J.	184	. MANCHESTER	318
. J.D.	241	. W.D.	197,218,242,245	ENGLISH,MARY	217
. JESSE B.	182	.	248	ESKRIDGE,	112
. WILLIAM B.	182	DUNNING,	60	ESPIRITU SANTO,	19
DOZIER,MANAH	181	. JAMES B.	182	ESTIS,W.	181
DREW,	203	. OTHA H.	183	ESTREMADURA,	19
N.E.	195,247	DURANT,SOPHIA	79	ETHERIDGE,AGNEW	181
DRINKARD,	60	DUVAL,	233	. CLARENCE C.	184
. G.W.	150,153	G.B.	231	. MIT C.	181
. J.L.	150	DYKES,ELIAS	247	ETHRIDGE,E.	105
. JEREMIAH	148	GARRETT	248	EUROPE,	169-170
. JOHN M.	180	EARLE,	122	EVANS,	63
. LEMUEL	148	JOSEPH B.	128,242	. HARRIET E. GRAYSON	301
DUBOIS,SEWALL	176	EASLEY,WARHAM	110	. J.F.	212
DUBOSE,	176	WILLIAM	110	. JEHU	150
. ABEL	241	EASTMAN BUSINESS COLLE-		. LOUIS G.	301
. C.C.	251	EGE,	329	329 . SUSAN EMMA	300
. CORA	313	ECUNHUTKE,	37	EVINGHAM,	105
. ELIAS H.	241	EDDIN,	106	EWING,	197
. J.E.	178	EDGE,WILLIE	184	JOHN	148
. JACK	247	EDISON,JAMES E.	185	EZELL,R.L.	195
. LEO	182	EGGLESTON,	189	. W.	119
. M.B.	294	EGYPT,ALEXANDRIA	320	. WILLIAM F.	128
. MATTIE	178	CAIRO	318	EZELLE,FRANK	186
. O.H.	247	ELAM CHURCH,	85	FAILE,GEORGE	182
. PETER	176,241,310	ELLIOTT,	85,219	SIDNEY B.	184
. SEWELL	178	JOHN	65	FARRAGUT,	162
. STELLA	178	ELLIS,GEORGE	⁻296	FARRAR,A.	101
DUKES,WILLIE	180	. LEONA	296	ABLE	102,105

HISTORY OF CLARKE COUNTY, ALABAMA

FARRER, ABLE	98	. JACKSONVILLE 244	. SAMUEL 241,285-286
FAVOR, JERRY W.	185	. PENSACOLA 27-29,31,37	FOSCUE, CLAYTON 116,195
FEAGAN, J.F.	213	. 43,45,48,73,77,84,114	. 197,219,243,248
FENDLEY, ALBERT	183	. 174,194,293,297-298	. J. 246
. DANIEL E.	184	. 345	. JOHN 181
. HARRIET DEWITT	151	. TAMBA BAY 19	. JOHN C. 151
. JOHN H.	150	. TAMPA 317	FOSH, 71
. NAPOLEON	181	FLOURNOY, 27,33,61-62,76	FOSTER, 62,82,146
. ROBERT J.	182	82	. ARTHUR 103
. WILLIAM B.	183	FLUCTABUNA CREEK, 85	. B.C. 133-134,146
FEW, GEORGE P.	180	FLUKER, ARTHUR 186	. BEN 156
FIGURES, J.T.	144	. EDWARD 186	. BENJAMIN 63
JAMES T.	252-253	. MARY FRANCES 324	. JAMES 246
FILES,	247	FONTAINE, GEORGE 212	. JOHN W. 242
DAVID	70,111	GEORGE F. 151	FOUNTAIN, TERREL 246
FINCH,	141	FOOSHATCHE, 37	FRANCE, 293,321
. CHARLES	218	FORBES, 140	PARIS 169
. H.	119	FORD, T.J. 218	FRANCIS, 37,55,57
. LEM W.	185	FOREMAN, GUY W. 184	JOSIAH 27
FINDLEY, THOMAS M.	185	FORGUSON, JACOB 104	FRANKLIN ACADEMY, 132
FISHER,	119,189	FORREST, 164	144
PAUL	213,215	FORSTER, BETTIE 187	FRANKLIN COLLEGE, 326
FITTS, JAMES	207,241	FORT DECATUR, 339	FRAZER, G. STANLEY 293
JIM	209,211	FORT DELAWARE, 287	. J.W. 293
FLEMING,	141	FORT DETROIT, 32	. JOHN STANLEY 292
. CALEB	246	FORT GREENVILLE, 32	. KEENER CHAPMAN 293
. E.S.	91	FORT MATHEWS, 71	. SATIRA CASSITY 292
. G.W.	91	FORT MORGAN, 162	. WILLIAM EMSLEY 292
. J.W.	244	FORT STONNART, 33	FRAZIER, J.S. 212
. L.W.	247	FORT SUMTER, 149	FRENCH, JOHN 119
. SOL	181	FORT TOULOUSE, 339	FRIDDLE, ALVER 331
FLETCHER,	39	FORT WASHINGTON, 32	. D.L. 150
JOSIAH	45	FORWARD, SAMUEL 247	. DANIEL LOUIS 158
FLINN, R.H.	218,247	FORWOOD, 141	FRISBIE, HORACE 176,311
FLORIDA,	19,72,133,303	. MARTHA ELIZ. COATE 286	322
	340	. MARTHA JANE -	FROWNER, GEORGE H. 186
. HOLLYWOOD	152	. ARMISTEAD 285	FULLER, JOHN B. 312

FURR, JACK	185	. MARIETTA 157	NATHANIEL T. 98
PEARL	182	. MILIDGEVILLE 100-101	GOODWIN, EMMITT 187
GAILLARD,	282	. NEW HOPE 159	MOLLIE 276
GAINES,	55	. RESACA 156,163	GORDON, J.A. 150
. GEORGE S.	110,242	. ROME 154	GRACE, 156
. JULIA	284	. SAVANNAH 84	GRAHAM, 320
GALPHIN, GEORGE	35	GERMANY, 170,172,319,321	. ALICE BOYLES 260
GARFIELD CAMP,	313	. BERLIN 168,299	. ALICE GRACE BOYLES 317
GARRETT,	228	. SEICHEPREY 168	. AMANDA WALES CLARK 316
. COMA	218,243,259	GIBBY, JAMES 330	. BOBBIE 319
. GEORGE G.	182	GILBERT, JAMES 148	. CHARLES EDWARD 317
GARRICK, EMMETT W.	182	GILL, 203	. DAVID 319
. ENOCH M.	181	. JACK 247	. EDWARD C. 260,317
. FLOYD A.	182	. WASH 247	. EDWARD CARR 315
. WILLIAM L.	185	GILLIS, J.F. 197,218,220	. EVA P. 317
GATES, ENOCH C.	183	. 305	. EVA PEARL 316
. GUS T.	182	. MARGARET J. MILES 305	. JOHN CHAMPION 317
. MONROE	181	. NEIL 305	. JOHN P. 317
GAVIN, C.W.	213	GILMORE, G.W. 138	. JOHN PITTMAN 315
GAYLE, JOHN	265	STEPHEN 213	. JOHN S. 150,217,242
S.	141	GIRARD, 153	. 245,253,316-319
GEARING, SAMUEL	338	GLASS, 33	. JOHN SIMPSON 314
GEORGIA,	37,70,72-73,76	GLEN, B.C. 212-213	. OPHELIA J. HOUSTON 315
.	84,86,88,115,122,139	GLENN, BENNIE M. 183	. RUBY CHAMPION 317
.	154,223,230,289,297	THOMAS E. 182	. RUFUS L. 315,318-319
.		301 GODBOLD, CADE M. 242	. SARA BELLE PITTMAN 315
. APPLINGTON		140 W.T. 183	. SARAH MARGARET 317
. ATLANTA	153-157,160	GODWIN, MARY 171-172	. TERESA 319
.	163,174,293	GOODE, 240	. TERESA H. TAYLOR 315
. AUGUSTA	58,302	. JAMES J. 241	. WILLIS WILLIFORD 316
. CARMICHAEL'S	-	. WILLIAM 128	GRANT,
.	STATION 71	GOODMAN, EVEY R. 183	. ELIZABETH HELEN -
. COLUMBUS	159	. MARTHA 295	. NEWBOLD 283
. FORT REPUBLIC	71	. MARY ANN SHEFFIELD 295	. ISAAC 127,151,197
. GREENSBOROUGH	71	. MATTHEW 295	. 240-243,246,253,282
. JONES CO.	71	. O.J. 212	. 283
. MACON	153,293	GOODRICH, DELD. W. 98	GRAY, O.L. 219

GRAYSON,A.H. 150,158	. ROBERT E. 181	HAWK,CLAUDE 180
. H.C. 241	. THOMAS B. 182	HAWKINS CREEK, 138
. HARRIET E. 301	HAILS,GEORGE W. 306	HAWKINS, 72,341,345
. L.A. 252	HALL'S LAKE, 86	. CARVIN 186
GREEN ACADEMY, 221	HALL, 191	. T.B. 138
GREEN,NICK 186	. ALEX 190	HAYDEN'S CREEK, 194
GREENE SPRINGS ACADEMY-	. BILLY 156	HAYDEN, 113,119
Y, 227	227 . CALLIE 190	. ABERDEEN 186
GREENE,J.A. 213	. HENRY 302	. ROBERT G. 112
GREENLEE, 112,119	. J.M. 149	HEAD,T.L. 219
GREENLEES,W.G. 204	. LULA 261	HEARD, 78
GREGORY,JAMES R. 181	HAMILTON,C.D. 148	. BAILEY 29
GRIFFIN,A.B. 61	. W.R. 134,147	. R.C. 197,219
. ELLIS G. 182	. WILLIAM R. 127,243	. ROLAND C. 185
. F.F. 61	HAMLET, 283	HEARIN,ANN 285
. IVY 182	HAMMON,M.W. 158	. THOMAS 134
. IVY THOMAS 60	HAMNER,J.W. 213	. W.J. 241
. J.G. 61	HANLEY,J.S. 191	HEARN,JOSEPH 122,128
. JOHN 60	HARDY, 191	HEARNE,J. 104-105
. MANLEY B. 183	HARE,JOE 183	HEATON, 55
. T.W. 60	HARPER,JAMES M. 184	ISAAC 57
. W.H. 60	HARRELL,ARTHUR 180	HEMPHILL LUMBER MILL,
. WILLIAM 60	HARRINGTON,SALLIE 299	175
GROVE HILL ACADEMY, 324	HARRISON, 219	HENDERSON, 251,344
GRUNDY,FELIX 337	. MARGARET SMITH 286	. DUNCAN 343
GULF OF MEXICO, 8	. N. 138	. OLLIE S. 184
GUNN,JOHN H. 184	HARVARD UNIVERSITY, 230	. W.L. 188
NORMAN 190,242,245	HARWELL,ISHAMAEL P. 104	HENDLEY,L.B. 150
GUY,J.D. 212,246	. J.H. 104	HENDRICKS,JOHN H. 182
. ROBERT CURTIS 180	. ROBERT R. 58	HENLEY, 190
. WILLIE RAY 181	HASKEW,D.W. 212	. JOHN D. 182
GWIN, 203	HIRAM GENERAL 180	. L.B. 151
. C.E. 150	HASSEL,	HENSHAW,A.L. 241
. CHARLES W. 182	. BARBARA SAVAGE 330	HENSON,J.S. 197
. JOSH 247	. PEARSON 330	JOHN S. 261
. MASSEY A. 184	HAUK,JOHN 90	HERRIN,W.J. 154
. PETER 247	SEBESTIAN 90	WILLIAM 155

HISTORY OF CLARKE COUNTY, ALABAMA

HERRING,ELIZABETH	215			45,48	. HARRY	186
HIBERT,H.	105	HOLTAM,PLEZ A.	183		. HENRY	186
HICKORY GROUND,	38	HOLTZCLAW,	152,160		HUDSON RIVER,	9
HICKS,	176	HONEYMON,	207,209,211		HUDSON,C.W.	193
. DEWEY	329			258	WILLARD E.	181
. GEORGE D.	184	HOOD,	155,157		HULL,	197
. J. CARNEY	245	HORN,EDDIE		185	HUNT,	191
. J.C.	329	. JOHN		186	HUSTON,	120
. KIMBELL	211,244,329	. PETE		191	ILLINOIS,	189
. L.O.	178,211,244,247	HORSE CREEK,		122	. ALTON	153
.	329	HORSESHOE,		50	. CHICAGO	251,327
. MAMIE CHAPMAN	329	HOUPT,HENRY		99	. ROCK ISLAND	289
. WELTON G.	182	HOUSTON,OPHELIA J.		315	INDIANA,CEDAR LAKE	328
HIGH-HEAD JIM,	27	HOVEN,ATWOOD		182	. CROWN POINT	326-327
HIGHTOWER,	101-102	. BENJAMIN		52	. HAMMOND	328
HIGLEY,JOHN H.	151	. ELMER E.		181	. LAKE	327
HILL,ACIE E.	181	. GROSS		184	. LAKE CO.	327-328
. ALFONSO B.	185	. JAMES E.		181	INGOLSTADT,	
. BOB	185	. JOHN	46,52-54		UNIVERSITY OF	171
. CLEMENT C.	183	. JOHN E.		248	IRELAND,	213,265
. FELIX	184	. KING		54	IVY,CHARLES	106
. O.H.	252	. LEO H.		182	JACK,	36,41-42
. SAMUEL	110	. SOLLIE		184	JACKSON ACADEMY,	240
HIND.	62	. W. HENLY		52	JACKSON FERRY,	108-109
HINDS,	34,76	. WILLIAM	52,54		JACKSON,	50,73,76,108
HINSON,J.S.	241	HOWARD COLLEGE,	287		.	113,116,136,298,334
W.H.	190	HOWARD,CHARLES	176,178		.	335,338-342
HIXON,CORNELIA	262	.		310	. ANDREW	89,193-194
HOITHLEWALE,	37	. J.M.		247	. BERNARD	184
HOLDER,	119-120	HOWEL,HENRY		99	. BERNICE P.	215
. WILLIE	150	HOWELL,		201	. JAMES M.	286
. WILLIS	157	. A.H.		247	. NATHANIEL B.	184
HOLLAND,	60	. DAN H.		247	. OCIE A.	184
HOLLIS,T.J.	261	. HENRY		98	. OLD HICKORY	89,297
HOLMES,	44,46-47	HOWILL,H.		107	. SARAH	324
. MIKE	159	HOWZE,ALEC		186	. STONEWALL	174
. THOMAS G.	32,36-37,43	. ALF		186	. TOMMIE	186

JACKSON,(cont)		. WILLIAM ENGLAND	301	JOURDAN,	29
. W.R.	150	. WILLIAM JAMES	300	JOWERS,THOMAS B.	183
JACKSONS CREEK,	112	JOHNSTON,	160	JUDSON COLLEGE,	294
JAMES,ABNER	55	JOSEPH E.	155	JULY RUSSEL	187
. ED	186	JOINER,HILTON K.	183	KEEL,JOHN B.	182
. J.H.	213	LEANDER	181	KEIL,WAYMAN D.	182
. LORENZO	241-242	JONES, 46,63,65,101-102		KELLEY,GEORGE	184
. MARY	55	.	203	KELLY,T.P.	288
. ROBERT	51	. A.M.	212	KEMBALL,ISHAM	55-56
. SARAH	56	. ANN TAYLOR	301	RANSOM	55
. THOMAS	55	. ARTHUR PAUL	286	KENNEDY,	52,76-77
JAPAN,	330	. C.B.	274	. EDWARD	127,241,243
JARIS,WILLIAM G.	180	. DANIEL E.	180	. JOSEPH P.	51
JAY,	324	. G.E.	241,274	. JOSHUA	36
JEFFERSON,THOMAS	221	. HENLEY B.	184	. WESLEY BECK	180
JENKINS,JAMES S.	242	. J.P.	212	KENNIS,JOHN	186
JERSEY CITY,	330	. JAMES TAYLOR	219	KENTUCKY, 86,114-115,145	
JETT,	217	. JOHN	121	.	213,298
JEWETT,O.S.	242	. JOSIAH	247	. AUGUSTA	303
ORA	248	. KATE	273-274	. LOUISVILLE	278
JOHNS HOPKINS UNIVERSI-		. LON MAY	274	KERRIDGE,	
ITY,	293	293	. MAZIE REBECCA	- FLOSSIE BICKELL	251
JOHNSON ISLAND,	302	.	COATE 286	KERSH,	191
JOHNSON'S ISLAND,	313	. PAUL S.	184	KETCHEN,	155
JOHNSON,	345	. R.	69	KETCHMAN,	163
. A.S.	241,245,249,301	. SAM R.	184	KIDD,ELMER	330
. ALBERT	189	. STARKEY	286	KILBY,THOMAS E.	276
. ALBERT SIDNEY	300-301	. W.F.	133,241	KILPATRICK,ALEXANDER	128
. LOUISA DAVIS	301	. WALTER	301	. BANDY	158
. MIKE	124	. WILLIAM	301	. JOHN Y.	241-242
. PERRY	186	. WILLIAM T.	127,243	. RUFUS H.	147
. S.J.	246	JORDAN,CHARLES A.	181	KIMBALL,	
. STELLA DUBOSE	178	. CONNIE E.	184	. MARTHA T. CARNEY	58
. SUSAN EMMA EVANS	300	. MARY A.	306	. T.I.	325
. W.E.	246,313	. ROBERT	182	KIMBELL,	176
. W.J.	245	. WATT T.	183	. ALICE	178
. WILLIAM	301	. WILLIAM	110	. BENJAMIN	284

HISTORY OF CLARKE COUNTY, ALABAMA

KIMBELL,(cont)		. THOMAS	212	. JAMES A.	304
. CARRIE	59	. THOMAS J.	183	. JEAN RUTHERFORD	304
. EVIE	260,323	. TINNIE EUGENE	309	. JOSEPHINE A.	304
. ISHAM	58-59-60,139,176	. TINNIE MCDONALD	309	. R.A.	155
	211,244,247,284-285	KLYCE,T.C.	213	. RUFUS	149,160
	323	KNIGHT,	123	. THOMAS	304
. JOHN	59,285	. CLAYTON W.	185	. VICTORIA LAULETTE	304
. MARTHA BOROUGHS	323	. HENRY E.	183	LARRELE,MOSES	110
. MARTHA J. BOROUGHS	284	KROUSE,	247	LARRIMORE,DAVID D.	180
. MARTHA T. CARNEY	59	. EMMA RIVERS	117	. THOMAS J.	183
. MARY	59	. MAY RIVERS	322	. THOMAS W.	180
. MARY RANSOM	284	. THEO	247	LAUNDRUM,JOHN	110
. MORRIS	59,323	LACKLAND,J.T.	219,245	LAVAL,	342-343
. RANSOM	58,284		248	LAVENDER,JOHN R.	330
. REBECCA	284	LAFLORE,WILLIAM B.	180	LAVIER,	33
. T.I.	247	LAKE GENEVA,	170	LAW,CARSON	187
. THOMAS I.	59,156,322	LAKE TENSAS,	221	GEORGE	187
. THOMAS ISHAM	284	LAKE TENSAW,	34-35,49,77	LAWLIS,JAMES	185
. WILLIE	59	LAMBARD,J.S.	202,247	LAWRENCE,J.O.	212
KIMBROUGH,		LAMBERTH,ERVIN	181	LEA,	247
. JOHN AUSTIN	278	. JESSE R.	185	LEAKE,	287
. RELEVIA	278	. ROBERT A.	185	. SHELTON F.	286
. ROY W.	181	. ROBERT L.	183	. WILLIAM D.	286
. STELLA OAKLEY	278	LANDRUM,JOHN	125-126	LECHLAN,WILLIAM	99
. V.J.	190	LANGHAM,THOMAS	98	LEE,	162,287
. W.A.	211		105-106	. JOHN B.	183
. WILLIAM T.	278	LANKFORD,	116	. L.H.	197
KING INSTITUTE,	240	. A.R.	148,302	. NED D.	183
KING,J.	119	. AMANDA C.	303	. ROBERT	127,243
KINMAN,OCIE W.	183	. AMANDA CAROLINE	302	. SHELLIE	180
KIRK,CECIL B.	182	.	304	LENSIR,	141
RICHARD C.	329	. AMELIA EUGENIA	-	LEONARD,	331
KIRKPATRICK,JAMES	125	. TAYLOR	304	. ERBY A.	181
	126	. AUGUSTUS RUFUS	302,304	. EVIE C.	181
KIRVEN,B.E.	309	. FREDONIA ADELINE	304	LESTER,	79
. IMOGENE BOROUGHS	309	. HENRY	302	LETT,FRED	309
. T.C.	211,244,309	. HENRY HUGH	304	LILLIAN BOROUGHS	309

LEWIS,ELIZABETH	284	LYNCH,EDWARD O.	184	. GIDEON B.	252
MARGARET SMITH		286 LYNUM,ROBERT	186	. JOHN	317
LINDSAY,C.	141	MACON MALE & FEMALE AC-		MATHERS,CHARLES S.	180
JOE D.	182	CADEMY, 147	147	CREAGH B.	183
LIPSCOMBE,NATHAN	122	MACON,	195	MATHEWS,	45
LISENBE,HUGH H.	183	J.E.J.	138	. CONDIE W.	183
LITTLE RIVER,	28,34,76	MADISON.	338	. DAVE C.	220
	342	MAGILVERY,A.	104	. DAVID	242,291
LITTLE,O.M.	150	M.	104	. DAVID CHAPMAN	291
LIVINGSTON,	191	MAGOFFIN'S STORE,	112	. ELIJAH	150,162
LOCKHART,JOE T.	182		129	. EMMA LEE BUMPERS	292
LOCKLIN,MINNIE	329	MAGOFFIN,JAMES	112,241	. FRANCES I. MCLEOD	291
LOFTIN,JOHN	122,128	MALLET,J.W.	227	. J.W.	197,241
LONG,CONNIE	181	MALONE,ALBERT	186	. JAMES WALDRUM	291
. JOHN	105	THOMAS	110	. REBECCA WALDRUM	291
. T.A.	197,241	MANLY,BASIL	227	MATLOCK,THOMAS	126
LONGSTREET,	156-157	MANOWA,	336	MAUBILA,	201
LORD BYRON,	171	MARION MILITARY INSTIT-		MAURREY,HARRY	158
LOUISIANA,	143,285,289	TUTE, 266	266	MAY,CHARLIE COBLE	180
.	298,315	MARSH,H.B.	59	. LON	274
. BATON ROUGE	33	MARSHALL,GEORGE	186	. PATRICK 29,31-32,78,82	
. CROWLEY	317	. JOHN E.	183	. WILLIE J.	330
. NATCHITOCHES	152	. SALLIE	281	MAYER,FANNIE	281
. NEW ORLEANS	48,114,151	MARTIN,	190	MAYTON,JAMES	183
. 278,287,304,308,329		. ELIZABETH	324	THOMAS K.	184
LOUISVILLE MEDICAL COL-		. HENRY	186	MCALPIN,ELIZABETH	279
LLEGE, 308		308 . MARY BIRD	280	MCCALL,CHARLEY	190
LOVE,ROBERTUS	128	. P.L.	213	MCCANN,J.W.	213
TILLIS	186	. ROBERT G.	185	MCCARY,	132
LOVEJOY,	158	MARYLAND,	283	MCCASKEY,T.H.	152
LOVELADY,JOHN	338	. BALTIMORE	293	MCCASKY,T.H.	150
LOWDER SPRINGS,	145	. PINE LOOKOUT	157	MCCLELLAN,MARION	200
LOWDER,	146	. SNOW HILL	337	MCCLINTON,ARTHUR J.	181
GEORGE	145	MASON,	178	MCCLURE,HOWARD K.	181
LUCKET,	80	MASON-DIXON LINE,	149	WILLIAM	138
LYLES,EMMETT M.	183	MASSACHUSETTS,BOSTON	326	MCCONNEL,THOMAS	119
LYNAM,JOHN W.	186	MASSEY,	326	MCCORQUDALE,CHESTER	218

MCCORQUDALE,(cont)	MCKINSTRY,	288 MCVAY,	203
W.W.	212 ALEXANDER	158 . CURTIS	181
MCCORQUODALE,	203 MCLAIN,CHARLES P.	182 . DACY B.	182
MCCORVEY,	240 MCLENDON,J.T.	150 . FAYETTE	247
MCCRARY,CLAUDE	217 MCLEOD,	200 . G.W.	264
G.C.	211 . A.L.	241,245,248 . HUGH L.	290
MCCRAY,	159 . ALLEN	248 . JOE	247
MCCURDY,A.J.	150 . ARCHIBALD LONZO	305 . LEON	244
MCDONALD,D.S.	212 . ARCHIE L.	253 . MITCHELL C.	184
. JOSH	247 . CHRISTIAN CALHOUN	306 . NANCY	264
. SIDNEY A.	183 . CHRISTINE CALHOUN	291 . ROBERT M.	184
. TINNIE	309 . DANIEL	149 MCWHORTER,	
. V.M.	190 . E.M.	264 GEORGE A.P.	185
MCDUFFEE,JOHN	219 . ELIZABETH FURNISS	306 MEEK,	148,231
MCDUFFIE,	. ERBY L.	180 ALEXANDER B.	230
. CORNELIA HIXON	262 . FLETCHER	212 MEGGINSON,G.W.	252
. JOHN	262 . FRANCES I.	291 . PERCY C.	184
MCFADYEN,AUGUST F.	183 . H.M.	217,220 . THEO W.	184
MCFARLAND,C.B.	150 . JESSE A.	181 . W.T.	252
MCFARLIN,	29 . JOHN	291,306 MERRILL,SARAH JAMES	56
MCGILL,FRANK	213 . L.E.	212 MERRIWEATHER,	123
MCGILLIVRAY,SEHOY	38 . L.L.	219 MEXICAN CENTRAL RAILWA-	
MCGIRTH,	49,51 . L.Y.	200 AY, 273	273
. DANIEL	48 . MARY A. JORDAN	306 MEXICO,	19,148,293
. JAMES	48 . NORMAN	212 TAMPICO	273
. VICEY	50 . W.A.	240 MEYERS,J.F.	193
. VICEY CURNELLS	48 MCMULLEN,FRANK	185 MIDDLETON,	36,39,41
. ZACHARIAH	38,48 MARION C.	185 MILES,AMBROSE	31
MCGOFFIN,J.	105 MCNAC,	32 . AQUILLA	305
MCGOWAN,WILLIAM	280 . HANNAH WEATHERFORD	38 . EDMUND	61
MCGREW,	58,62,114 . SAM	81 . MARGARET J.	305
WILLIAM	29,61,125 MCNEAL,D.H.	293 . W.M.	150
MCINTYRE,AGNEW A.	185 MCNIDER,ELLIS	182 MILLER,HARRY H.	181
. EWELL D.	182 JOSEPH	183 MILSTEAD,ALBERT R.	184
. TOLLIE E.	184 MCPHETERS,T.B.	204 SAMUEL B.	181
MCIVER,	190 MCQUEEN,	28-30,37 MILTON,	339
MCKINLEY,REUBEN F.	184 PETER	27 MIMS' FERRY,	76

HISTORY OF CLARKE COUNTY, ALABAMA

MIMS,	35	. B.R.	133	. ELIZABETH LEE	-
DAVID	43	. JAMES	247	. ARMISTEAD	285
MISSISSIPPI RIVER,	9,11	. ORMOND O.	184	. JOHN	284
	19,84,304	. ROBERT	248	. REBECCA K.	285
MISSISSIPPI TERRITORY,	5	. W.M.	197,248	. REBECCA KIMBELL	286
. 32,71,77,84,88,103		. WILLIAM	241	MORRY,HARRY	288
. 111,125-126,221		MOLTON,	203	MOSELEY,	190
MISSISSIPPI,	5,45-46	MONCRIEF,CALEB	84	MOSLEY,ROBERT B.	182
. 62-63,69-70,72,78,81		MONGTOMERY,	65	MOSS,JOHN	330
. 85,111,153,161,178		MONK,ANGUS	150,163	MOTES,THOMAS	181
.	179,189,285	ELVIN C.	181	MOTT,	190,192
. CORINTH	154,173,314	MONTGOMERY, 63,338-339		. DAVID T.	183
.	316	. HUGH	337	. FLOYD C.	183
. IUKA	152	. L.P.	337	. MARION M.	182
. JACKSON	289	. LEMUEL PURNELL	337	MOULTON,	337
. LAUDERDALE SPRINGS	158	. RICHARD	148	MOURRICE,	45,47
. MERIDIAN	151-152,315	MOOKLAUSA,	37	MOYLER,F.M.	218
. MORTON'S STATION	289	MOORE,CHAUNCEY	182	MT. NEBO SCHOOL,	324
. NATCHEZ	32-33	. G.H.	211	MUD TAVERN,	113
. PASCAGOULA	59,244,323	. GEORGE H.	217	MURPHY,J.F.	247
. PERLINGTON	77	. JOHN S.	247	. JOHN	265-266
. TISHOMINGO CO.	314	. T.L.	150	. JOHN F.	203,265
. TUPELO	157	. TOM	247	. MURDOCK	265
. VICKSBURG	152,157,159	MORGAN,	335	. NEIL	265
.	289	. CHARLES L.	185	. ROBERT	265
. WEST POINT	316	. CLINTON J.	185	MURRAY,	223,304
MISSOURI,SPRINGFIELD	152	. GARFIELD	180	WILLIAM	54
ST. LOUIS	245,262	MORRIS,ALBERT	186	MURREL,WILLIAM	126
MITCHEL,	203	. GILBERT	186	MURRELL,	284
MOBILE & WEST ALABAMA	-	. JOHN	285	WILLIAM	241
RAILROAD, 188	188	. REBECCA M.	309	MUSHULLATUBBA,	76
MOBILE BAY,	151-152	. ROBERT	309	MYRICK,	203
MOBILE CREEK,	250	. SIMON	185	. A.M.	247
MOBILE MEDICAL COLLEGE-		. W.H.	213	. WILLIAM A.	247
E.	324	324 MORRISS,		NABOURS,NATHAN	98
MOBILE RIVER,	33,85	. ELIZABETH	-	NAPOLEON,	170,297
MOBLEY,	134	. ARMISTEAD	284	NELSON,F.N.	215

NELSON,(cont)		S.P.	190	RICHARD	153
FRED N.	215	NOBLES,MANUEL	185	OVERSTREET,AMOS L.	183
NETTLES,	293	. RIAL	246	. CARLOS	183
GEORGE	246	. S.B.	246	. HENRY F.	184
NEVILLE,		NORRIS,REESE	202,247	. JAMES S.	330
CARRIE H. TAYLOR	178	NORTH CAROLINA,	31,58-59	. SAM	184
NEW MEXICO,	294	. 84,86,88,114-115,223		. WILLIE C.	331
NEW YORK,	188,227,326	. 265,296,306,337,345		OWEN,THOMAS M.	330
WEST POINT	281	. BENTONVILLE	153,160	PACE,A.J.	195
NEWBOLD,		. HALIFAX CO.	284	T.B.	17
ELIZABETH HELEN	283	. MOORE CO.	285	PAINE,	123
NEWMAN,		. ONSLOW	283	PANAMA CANAL,	8
. ANN ELIZ. BOROUGHS	286	. RANDOLPH CO.	284	PARIS,WILLIAM L.	126
. ANN ELIZABETH	-	. SALISBURY	160	PARKER,	176,213
. BOROUGHS	286	. UNIVERSITY OF	161	. CARLOS T.	184
. GEORGE	159	. WARREN CO.	157,284	. JUDITH CARR	302
. JAMES ADDISON	284,286	NUNNALLY,BILL	324	. S.J.	218,247
. JAMES BRYAN	286	NUNO TOBAR,	24	. S.W.	247
. THOMAS REUBEN	286	OAKCHOIEOOCHE,	37	. SARAH J.	303
. WILLIAM B.	284	OAKLEY,STELLA	278	. SEARCY M.	183
. WILLIAM BOROUGHS	286	OAKTUPA,	34	. W.A.	190
	287	OATES,	279	. W.S.	176
NICHOLS,	206,271-272	OCFUSKE,	37	. WILLIAM E.H.	186
. COBB	244,273,282	OCHEBOFA,	37	PATE,	253
. EARL C.	185	ODOM,HENRY BOWEN	185	PATRICK,	42-43
. EARLE	274	. J.B.	150,162	PATTON,	230-231
. JOHN COMA	274	. WILLIAM F.	181	ROBERT M.	229
. JOHN W.	273	OGYWN,JAMES	310	PAYNE,AB	246
. KATE JONES	273-274	OHIO,CAMP CHASE	156,160	. DAN	246-247
. PEARL LEE WILSON	273	EAST LIVERPOOL	311-313	. FRANK	247
. PEARLEE WILSON	282	OLIVER,HARRY L.	185	. J.D.	247
. PORTLAND	186	JOHN W.	330	. SIDNEY A.	181
. WILLIAM	273	ONEAL,EMMET	261	PAYNNE,A.L.	218
NICHOLSON,	106	ONEIL,	42	PEACOCK,WILLIAM	77
NIXON,GEORGE HENRY	77	ORTIZ,JEAN	20	PEARSON,	106
HENRY	193,197	OSBORNE,	36,42,76	PEAVY,NICK	185
NOBLE,	123	OTT,COLONEL M.	184	PENDELTON,CLARENCE	185

HISTORY OF CLARKE COUNTY, ALABAMA

PENDLETON ACADEMY,	131	SARA BELLE	315	. SALLIE BOWLING	267
PENNSYLVANIA,	90,312	PLUMMER,	36	POWERS,	153
. PHILADELPHIA	28,91,268	POCKUSCHATCHE,	37	. TERREL	139,147
	270	POE,	160	. TERRELL	127,243
. PITTSBURG	32	POGUE,PINK H.	156	PRATT,FRANCIS B.	213
. UNIVERSITY OF	270	POLK,	230	PRICE,J.P.	105-106
PERDIDO CREEK,	77	POOLE,	192-193	JAMES P.	98
PERDIDO RIVER,	84	. CHARLES	246	PRIM,ALBERT	59,323
PERRY,JOSEPH	45,47	. F.E.	241	T.J.	247
WILLIAM F.	229,231	. FRANK E.	245	PRITCHETT,	117
PERSHING,JOHN J.	276	. HENRY C.	181	. C.C.	246
PERU,	19	POPE,ARCHIBALD H.	147	. CHARLES G.	150
PETRIE,GEORGE	223	BARNEY	122	. G.	159
PETTUS,	160	PORT GIBSON,	153	. HADDEN S.	182
PHILEN,MADISON	150	PORTER,	203	. JAMES	217
PHILIPPINES,	315,318	L.A.	248	PROSSER,	
PHILIPS,	57	PORTIS,	119,141	JOSIE D. TAYLOR	178
ZACHARIAH	29	. E.M.	59	PUCKETT,W.F.	200
PHILLIPS.ELISHA	212	. EDMOND	247	PUCKUNTALLAHASSEE,	37
. J.	84	. H.W.	245	PUGH,	129,143,190,200
. JOSEPH	110,126,140	. IDA	126	.	203
. LEWIS H.	183	. IRA	245	. ACHSAH	324
. T.M.	246	. J.P.	133	. ALBERT	244
. WILLIAM E.	181	. JOHN W.	117,241,247	. ALBERT S.	298
PIAZARRO,	19	. JOSEPH P.	127,243	. ALBERT V.	182
PICKENS,JAMES	111	. RIVERS	245	. ALFRED B.	298
JOE R.	182	. THOMAS	126	. ALFRED BETTIS	183
PICKETT,	3,19,26,34,55	POST,LYON	311	. AMELIA CHAPMAN	299
	61,63,69,115,147,221	POTTER,	105	. ARCHIE A.	186
PIGEON CREEK,	266	POTTS,HENRY	98,103-104	. BELAH	185
PILATE.	132	POWE,GEORGE W.	217,264	. C.C.	244,298
PINCKNEY,	344-345	POWELL'S FERRY,	79	. CLEM	244
PINE CREST CEMETERY,	323	POWELL.	223	. E. STUART	299
PINE LOG CREEK,	46	. DANIEL T.	267	. E.S.	298
PIPPEN,E.	150	. FLORIDA GARNER	267	. EARL	181
PIPPIN,E.	156	. JOE	248	. EARL E.	183
PITTMAN,E.D.	315	. R.D.	215	. EDDIE G.	181

HISTORY OF CLARKE COUNTY, ALABAMA

PUGH,(cont)		QUISENBERRY,	286	. THOMAS	247,322
. ELIJAH	126,186	RABBIT CREEK,	8	. THOMAS B.	241
. ERBY V.	180	RAINEY,GROSS	186	. VIRGINIA	322
. GEORGE C.	183	RANALDSON,J.	105	. WILL	248
. ISAAC	241-242,296-299	RANDON'S CREEK,	64	RIXEY,	286
. J. PICKENS	240,298	RANDON,	41,65	ROBERTS,A.J.	150
. J.E.	150	. JOHN	39	. JOHN F.	183
. J.L.	298	. PETER	37,45,48	. JOHNNIE	182
. J.P.	150	RANSOM,MARY	284	. M.I.	150
. JAMES P.	220	RAYBOURN,ALBERT G.	181	. STONEWALL J.	183
. JESSE	298	RLMORE	182	ROBERTSON,WILLIAM A.	128
. JESSIE STUART	299	REED,HENRY	330	ROBINS,JOE	152
. JOHN ELIJAH	159	REEVES,ELBERT	181-182	ROBINSON,	192,203
. JOHNNIE	184	. GEORGE B.	180	. A.N.	244
. KATHLEEN	299	. WILLIAM LESTER	180	. CHARLIE	185
. LILIAN	217	REID,DAVID T.	183	. D.W.	197
. MARGARET	299	. J.T.	60	. FRED	186
. MAYBEN B.	183	. J.W.	60	. G.E.	197
. MORGAN B.	181	REINHARDT,JOHN	217	. JAMES	148
. OCIE B.	183	RICE,ROBERT E.	182	. JESSE	148
. RANSOM	298	RICHARDSON,		. JOHN E.	183
. REUBEN	186	CORALLY G.	294	. LIGE	186
. ROBBIE B.	183	RICKER,W.E.	150	. MILES	186
. SALLIE HARRINGTON	299	RIGDON,MARTIN	45,47	. WILLIAM	105
. SIDNEY	298	RIPLEY,D.P.	111	. WILLIAM A.	98
. SIDNEY S.	299	RIVERS,	119	. WILLIAM G.	180
. STEPHEN	240	. BLOUNT	322	. WILLIE M.	181
. STEVE L.	186	. ELLEN	322	ROCKER,W.E.	154
. T.J.	244	. EMMA	117	ROCKY FALL MOUNTAIN,	152
. THOMAS	296,298	. EMMA LENA	322	RODGERS,A.H.	212
. W.S.	150	. J.C.	59,176,204,322	. HAIS	82
. WALTER S.	161	. JOSEPH	322	. THELMA	217
. WOODIE S.	298	. MAY	322	ROE,WALTER E.	183
PURNELL,	337	. ORIE S.	184	ROGERS,	240
PURVIS,GRADY	180	. PAULINE	322	ROPER,	212
PUSHMATAHAW,	76	. SARAH C.	322	ROTCH,ALVIN	184
PUSHMATTAH,	296-297	. T.B.	117,141	ROUSSEAU,	170

ROZIER,	190	. MARY	330	SHELLY, THOMAS	187
RUSH, ELLEN RIVERS	322	. MINNIE LOCKLIN	329	SHELTON,	287
MONROE	183	. POMEROY	330	SHEPARD, O.A.	252
RUSSELL, 77,79,81-83,335		. T.B.	325	SHEPHARD, J.W.	160
GILBERT C.	76	. THOMAS B.	241	SHEPHERD, J.W.	150
RUSSIA, ARCHANGEL	318,321	SC., CHARLESTON	140	SHERTZER, L.L.	293
MOSCOW	321	. EDGEFIELD DISTRICT	291	SHETLAND ISLANDS,	321
RUTHERFORD, JEAN	304	.		SHIELDS,	148
RUTLEDGE, L.	150	. OCONEE STATION	70	SAMUEL B.	126,128
SACOLD, REUBIN	105	. PENDELTON DISTRICT	70	SHIP ISLAND,	152,159
SAFFOLD, R.	99-100	. POVOTAGLIO INLET	287	SIMPKINS, WOODIE T.	182
. REUBEN	110	SCARBOROUGH, JOHN	85	SIMS, SAMUEL	34
. REUBIN 103-104,106,108		SCHULTZ, EMMETT	184	SINGLETON SPRING,	254
. RUBEN	91	SCOTLAND, 265,293,304		SINGLETON, JOE T.	247,254
. RUBIN	98	SCOTT, 34,191		REUBEN R.	184
SALUDA HILLS,	162	EDWARD A.	144	SINQUEFIELD,	33,58
SAMPY, W.A.	212	SCRUGGS,	116	SISEMORE'S FERRY,	28,63
SAN LUCAR,	19	. JOHN L.	220	SISEMORE,	44
SANDERS, JOHN R.	181	. WILLIAM	246	SKINNER, HENCHEY M.	183
WILLIAM	181,247	. WILLIAM L.	180	HENRY	330
SANDERSON,	158	SEABROOKE,	287	SKIPPER, J.C.	212
SANOTA,	50	SEARIGHT, ARCHIE	312-313	SLATER,	119
SAUNDERS,	192	SELLERS, JIM M.	182	JOHN	112
THOMAS	241	SEWALL, ELLA	179	SMITH'S CREEK,	112
SAVAGE HOTEL,	17	LEWIS	110	SMITH, 66-67,69,73,155	
SAVAGE,	259,286	SEWELL, F.I.	247	.	190
. ANDREW	329	. F.L.	211	. C.L.	150,154,213
. ANNA	329	. L.E.	247	. CONNIE	183
. BARBARA	330	. LEWIS H.	180	. EDWARD	104
. CARRIE	330	. ROBERT L.	184	. H.H.	150,159
. CHARLES	329	SHEFFIELD, MARION	185	. HENDRICK C.	180
. H.J.	203,329	MARY ANN	295	. J.Q.	276
. J.A.	212	SHEHAN, KOSS U.	184	. JAMES	65,70
. J.C.	218	. SIDNEY	185	. JANE W. ARMISTEAD	285
. JAMES C.	218	. SULLIVAN	184	. KATE	285
. JOHN A.	329	SHELLEY,	171	. MARGARET	286
. LAWRENCE	330	MARY GODWIN	171-172	. MAZIE	286

HISTORY OF CLARKE COUNTY, ALABAMA

SMITH,(cont)	SOUTHERN UNIVERSITY, 262	. NANCY MCVAY	264
. N. 98	292-293	. S.A.	217,264
. NEAL 98-99,103,108	SOUVANOGA, 37	. TOOMA	217,264
241-242,285-286	SPAIN, 19	. VELMA	264
. ROBERT 286	SPANISH FORT, 152,154	. W.C.	264
. SAMUEL 45,47	157,162	. W.V.	264
. WILLIAM ELBERT 185	SPINKS,ASHLAND C. 182	STIFFLEMIRE,G.W.	150
SMOOT, 30,79,176,250	. DAVID M. 185	STOKES,CHARLES	119
. A.S. 59,247	. GEORGE T. 184	HANCE F.	330
. ARCHIBALD 302	. JOHN C. 182	STRINGER,	176
. ARCHIBALD S. 249	. LEWIS 122	. A.R.	150,160
. AURULIA TAYLOR 302	. SAMUEL L. 185	. ALEX	213,247
. B.S. 111	SPURLIN,ELLA 215	. J.V.	247
. BENJAMIN 29,78	ST. STEPHENS ACADEMY,	. JIM	213
. BENJAMIN S. 110	115,221	. JOHN R.L.	247
. S. 176	STABLER,MARION 182	. S.P.	176
SNELL,CLIFFORD J. 181	STALLWORTH,LON 186	. SETH P.	247
. NATHANIEL 186	STANLEY,COBLE H. 184	STRINGERS FERRY,	94
. WILLIAM C. 181	HARVEY B. 184	STRONG,THOMAS I.	98
SNYDER,EVA P. GRAHAM 317	STATE NORMAL SCHOOL, 227	STUART,	160
HOMER 317	STEADHAM,BENJAMIN 44	STURGES,B.H.	132
SOLOMON,T.H. 150	. EDWARD 45,47	STUTTS,BALDWIN	201
SOUTH ALABAMA INSTITUT-	. HESTER 44	EUGENE P.	193-194
. TE, 259 259,276	. JESSE 45,48	SUEZ CANAL,	320
301	STEELE,J.C. 15	SUMMER,MARY	324
SOUTH CAROLINA COLLEGE-	THOMAS H. 182	SUMMERFIELD INSTITUTE,-	
E, 265	265 STEPHENS, 240	, 292	292
SOUTH CAROLINA, 31,52,58	HENCHIE W. 183	SUTTON,R.E.	254
. 77,84,86,88,114-115	STEPHENSON, 160	SWITZERLAND,GENEVA	169
. 223,264-266,280,288	STEWART, 120		170,172
. 316,345	. BOB H. 264	SYKES,JAMES	248
. COLUMBIA 230	. CARLEY 264	TAIT,DAVID	28,38
. NEWBERRY 324	. DOOG 264	TALBERT,	138
. SPARTANBURG 279	. DUGE 156	TALLAHATTA CREEK,	113
SOUTHERN RAILROAD, 10,13	. J.C. 176,212,263-264	TALLAHATTA SPRINGS,	142
17,108	. JOHN C. 182		145-146
SOUTHERN RAILWAY, 188	. NANCY 264	TALLAPOOSA RIVER,	37,334

HISTORY OF CLARKE COUNTY, ALABAMA

TALLAPOOSA RI(cont)	. MARY ESTELLE 303	. KNOXVILLE 157,216,337
338-339	. MINNIE COLE 302	. LIVINGSTON 163
TALLASE, 37	. ROBERT 148,302	. LUVERNE 288
TANSEY,J.K. 212	. ROBERT H. 186,302-303	. MARYVILLE 216
TARLETON,SOLOMON 181	. S. PARKER 178,302	. MARYVILLE COLLEGE 216
TATE, 32	. S.J. 248	. MISSIONARY RIDGE 289
STEVE 250	. S.P. 176	. MURFREESBORO 156
TAYLOR, 176	. SARAH 178	. MURFRESBORO 289
. AMANDA 315	. SARAH J. PARKER 303	. NASHVILLE 153-154,160
. AMANDA C. LANKFORD 302	. SARAH SMOOT 303	. 163,312
303	. SKIPWORTH C. 303	. RANDALSBURG 304
. AMELIA EUGENIA 303-304	. TERESA H. 315	. TULLAHOMA 288-289
. AMELIA EUGENIE 302	. TERESA HALO- -- 303	TENNESSEE-MOBILE RAILR-
. ANN 301	. W. JESSE 302	ROAD, 139 139-140
. AURULIA 302	. W.J. 195,218	TENSAW LAKE, 28,46
. AURULIA A. 303	. WALTER 91,176,204,247	TENSAW RIVER, 159
. CAROLINE HOLT 303	. 263,302-304,315	TEXAS, 11,59,131,133
. CARRIE H. 178	. WILLIAM JESSE 302-303	. 135-136,143,286,298
. COLUMBUS 301	TECHUMSEH, 75	. 315
. D. 99	TECUMSEH, 72	. DALLAS 303
. DAVID 91-92,98,103	TENNESSEE RIVER, 137,154	. FORT ALAMO 131
106-108,301-303	222,345	. FRANKLIN 287
. DICK 161	TENNESSEE, 76,86,88,115	. HOUSTON 316
. EVA CARR 303	. 145,154-155,157,160	. SAN MARCOS 280
. FLORENCA A. 303	. 194,223,297,316,338	. TAYLOR 304
. FREDONIA A. 303	. 344	. WASHINGTON CO. 285
. GEORGE W. 219	. BRISTOL 157	THOMAS,HENRY 186
. JOE 187	. CAMP BLOUNT 345	. JOHN 105
. JOHN 302-303	. CHATTANOOGA 153	. S.E. 247
. JOHN B. 302	. 288-289	. SAMUEL 188
. JOSEPHINE LANKFORD 303	. COLUMBUS 163	THOMASVILLE INSTITUTE,-
. JOSIE D. 178	. CONCORD 216	, 188 188
. JUDITH 302	. FARRAGUT HIGH -	THOMASVILLE OPERA HOUS-
. JUDITH C. 303	. SCHOOL 216	SE, 189 189
. JUDITH CARR PARKER 302	. FAYETTEVILLE 345	THOMPSON,JOSEPH 105
. LELAND 303	. FRANKLIN 153-155,291	. MARY J. 289-290
. M.E. COLE 303	. HERMITAGE 345	. WILLIAM N. 98

THORNTON, E.S.	241	TRUITT,	213	TUSCALOOSA,	20
. ELI S.	242,246	TUCKER, A.B.	252	TUTWILER, HENRY	227
. JOHN	180	. ALEXANDER	120	JULIA S.	227
. JOSEPH	186	. ANNIE MARSHALL	-	TYRE, GEORGE H.	330
. L. EARLE	147	. WILSON	282	TYSON,	246
. W. JAMES	147	. AUSTICO BUSBEE	260	HADLEY	242
TIPSON, CHARLES	215	. HENRY G.	184	ULCARNUSH BAPTIST CHUR-	
TODD, JAMES	186	. J. LEE	260	RCH, 294	294
ODELL	186	. J.W.	191,220,275	UPCHURCH,	129
TOLBERT, F.M.	150	. JAMES WILSON	275	URQUHART, HENRY	212
TOMBECKBEE RIVER,	85-86	. JOHN F.	183	VANHEUVEL, M.	198
	111,118,121	. LIZZIE W. BUSBEE	260	VANLOON, HENDRICK	168
TOMBIGBEE RIVER,	5,8-9	. LULA HALL	261	VAUGHN,	159
. 10-11,13,19,26,28,55		. Q.W.	245	VICKERS, DONNIE A.	181
. 58,61-62,73,84,89,108		. QUINCY W.	282	GORDON B.	182
. 110-111,116,119,121		. WILLIAM S.	150,157	VIRGINIA, 77,115,157,161	
. 122,174,177,206,249		TULANE UNIVERSITY,	299	.	223
.	261,296		308	. CITY POINT	153
TOMBIGBEE TIVER,	53	TUOMEY, MICHAEL	227	. DREWRY'S BLUFF	157
TOMBIGBY RIVER,	33	TURKEY CREEK,	138	. ELIZABETH CITY CO.	284
TOMMY, HIRAM	129	TURKEY, GALLIPOLI	320	. FRIES	216
TOMPKINS, FRANK Q.	181	TURNER,	110	. GLADE HOLLOW	71
. J.J.	246	. ABNER	26	. GUM SPRING	286
. JOHN R.	219	. ARGYLE	287	. HATCHER'S RUN	157
. THOMAS P.	185	. BEN D.	219	. LEXINGTON	161
. W.J.	197	. BENJAMIN D.	266	. NORFOLK	32
. WALLACE A.	183	. BENJAMIN DICKERSON	266	. ORANGE	286
TOOKABATCHA,	72	. CHARLES	287	. PETERSBURG	157
TOULMIN,	33	. FLORIDA GARNER	-	. RICHMOND	32,153,157
HARRY	219	. POWELL	267	.	287
TRANSYLVANIA UNIVERSIT-		. GROSS S.	185	. ROCKBRIDGE CO.	71
TY,	303	303 . JIM H.	182	. RUSSELL CO.	229
TRAVIS, WILLIAM B.	131	. JOE	186	. SHENANDOAH VALLEY	302
TRAYMAN. RUBIN	99	. MARY BINTON COCKE	266	. SPOTTSYLVANIA	287
TREASTER, FOSTER R.	182	. T.J.	150	. SUSSEX CO.	32
TRIMBLE.	337	. WILLIAM	287	. UNIVERSITY OF	227
TRIPLET,	106	TURNIPSEED, S.U.	204	. WASHINGTON CO.	71

HISTORY OF CLARKE COUNTY, ALABAMA

VIRGINIA,(cont)	G.G. 217,246	WELLS,	79
. WYTHE CO.	337 WARRIOR RIVER, 118	WEST POINT,	161
VONKON,F.H.	193 WASHINGTON & LEE UNIVE-	WEST VIRGINIA,	
WADDELL,EDMUND	284 ERSITY, 287 287	RUSSELL CO.	229
. ELIZABETH LEWIS	284 WASHINGTON ACADEMY, 110	WESTON,MARK B.	182
. MARTHA ARMISTEAD	284 111	WEWOCOE,	37
.	285 WASHINGTON COLLEGE, 337	WHATLEY,	202
WADE,ROBERT	184 WASHINGTON DC., 230,245	. F.B.	148
. W.S.	212 287,313,329-330	. MARTIN	213
. W.W.	218 WASHINGTON,W.F. 293	. WARREN	213
WAINRIGHT, 176,310	WATTS, 162	WHEELER,	153
. JULIA	178 THOMAS 162	WHETSTONE,ADAM C.	158
. LUCK 174,176,247	WAYNE, 32	WHISENHUNT,GEORGE	117
. PORTER	174 WEATHERFORD'S BLUFF, 76	WHITE SULPHUR WELL,	17
WAITE,JOHN F.	184 WEATHERFORD, 42,75,78-81	WHITE, 33,123,203	
WALDRUM,REBECCA	291 . 142,297,334,342	. DAVID 91,98-100,103	
WALES,	265 . BILL 341	.	106,285
WALKER'S MILL,	113 . CHARLES 37	. DOOR	60
WALKER,	176 . HANNAH 38	. I.A.	190
. CALVIN 176,178	. SEHOY MCGILLIVRAY 38	. J.B.	61
. GEORGE W.	247 . WILLIAM 37-38,340	. JAMES	189
. HODGES	203 . 343-344	. JAMES L.	185
. LAURA S.	145 WEAVER,LEMON D. 185	. JOHN	150
. LEIJURD A.	186 WEBB,JAMES S. 183	. LESLIE	183
. TANDY	63 . JOHN 183	. NELSON C.	193
. WILLIAM	203 . JOHN H. 182	WHYTE,	120
WALLACE,JOHN W.	186 WEBSTER, 223	WIGGINS,BONNER C.	181
WALLER,THURMAN C.	183 WEEKS, 235	. J.C.	150
WALTON, 104,106	STEPHEN B. 228	. JOHN COLLINS	156
. SIMEON	242 WEIBLING,	. JOHN N.	184
. WILLIAM	98 . JOSEPHINE A. -	. W.C.	185
WARD,	80 . LANKFORD 304	. WILLIAM A.	185
WILLIAM	180 . LANKFORD 304	WILCOX,	81-83
WARNER,C.L. 207-208,217	. WILLIAM M. 304	WILKINSON,	27,33
CHARLES L.	182 WELCH,HARRISON 331	. SAMUEL 127,131,141	
WARNUCH,JOSEPH	104 . RIP 153	.	241-243
WARREN,B.H.	246 . W.R. 162	WILLIAMS,	191

HISTORY OF CLARKE COUNTY, ALABAMA

WILLIAMS,(cont)	. KOSSIE 282	WOOD,	29,32
. H.H. 190	. LEROY 330	. J.H.	191
. HARRIS 186	. LEWIS 282	. L.	104,106
. ISAAC L. 186	. M.E. 178	WOODARD,CHARLES E.	138
. J.B. 212,217	. MARY SAVAGE 330	. ELIZABETH BALL	326
. J.E. 261	. MASSEY 241,245,262	. ELIZABETH H. BALL	325
. J.S. 147	. MATHEW 82	. EUGENIE H.	325
. JOE 186	. OSCEOLA 140	. FRANK W.	246
. LEE 186	. PAUL C. 181	. J.R.	246
. T.H. 215	. PEARL LEE 273	. R.J. 127-128,243,326	
. THOMAS 182	. PEARLEE 282	. RICHARD J.	325
. W.L. 195	. ROBERT 248	. S.T.	212,217,246
. WILLIAM 122	. ROSA LEE 217	. W.F.	218
WILLIAMSON,ALBERT 184	. SALLIE 263	WOODRUFF,	81
. JAMES 181	. SALLIE MARSHALL 281	WOODS,	35,161,163
. JOHN L. 184	. SALLIE WILSON 263	WOODSON,C.G.	232
WILSON, 119,282	. SHELLIE A. 182	WORLEY,C.	119
. ALBERT 262-263	. THOMAS CROSS 183	WRIGHT,	129
. ANNIE MARSHALL 282	. W.W. 141	O.H.P.	59,323
. BILLY 192	. WILLIAM 99,105	YARRINGTON,VIRGINIA	145
. BOWMAN 181	WIMBERLY,JOHN 185	YORK,	116,203
. DAVID T. 186	WIMPEE,ERNEST W. 185	. MARION	148
. E.P. 245	WINDBUSH, 213	. OSCAR	248
. ED 262	WING, 176,310-311		
. EUGENE 290	. A.M. 176,247,309		
. FANNIE MAYER 281	. 312-313		
. G.D. 140	. CORA DUBOSE 313		
. HELEN 282	. CORA R. 178		
. J.R. 128,140,243	. GLOVER 313		
. J.T. 264	. LULA 314		
. JACK R. 246,262	. NELSON C. 181		
. JACK ROPER 281	. NELSON CLAYTON 313		
. JOHN C. 183	WINN,FRANK 241		
. JOHN D. 185	WINTER,HELEN WILSON 282		
. JOHN M. 195,243,248	K.C. 282		
. 262,273,282	WIXEY,FELIX 182		
. JOHN MARSHALL 281	WOCCOCOIE, 37		

www.ingramcontent.com/pod-product-compliance
Lightning Source LLC
Chambersburg PA
CBHW020637300426
44112CB00007B/147